I0810593

IMAGES
of America

INDIANAPOLIS RHYTHM AND BLUES

On the Cover: The Presidents were formed in 1960. Their performances at the Place to Play Tavern were intensified by the electrifying voice of Baby Leon. See page 55.

IMAGES
of America

INDIANAPOLIS RHYTHM AND BLUES

David Leander Williams
Foreword by Richard Pierce

ARCADIA
PUBLISHING

ISBN 978-1-4671-2947-3

Published by Arcadia Publishing
Charleston, South Carolina

Printed in the United States of America

Library of Congress Control Number: 2018938613

For all general information, please contact Arcadia Publishing:
Telephone 843-853-2070
Fax 843-853-0044
E-mail sales@arcadiapublishing.com
For customer service and orders:
Toll-Free 1-888-313-2665

Visit us on the Internet at www.arcadiapublishing.com

In memory of Wilma Gibbs-Moore, senior archivist for African American history, Indiana Historical Society, who dedicated her life to the empowerment of her people in search of the knowledge of self.

And to my parents, relatives, and friends Lomax Mahone, Emogene Carson-Williams-Mahone, Jessie Carson, Claude Deon Williams, Betty Jean Williams, Rudd Kenneth Williams, Jessica Williams, Susie Yvonne Williams, Janice Leona Williams-Valentine, Donald Ralph Valentine, Oadie Lee Crider, Winford Cork, and Woodie Carpenter.

Contents

FOREWORD

The mid-20th century in African American neighborhoods around the country was characterized by the absence of many rights and privileges that were taken for granted by music lovers in the majority community. In Indianapolis, radio stations refused to play rhythm-and-blues music performed by African Americans and referred to this music with the pejorative label of "race music" or "coon music." It was deemed crude, unrefined, hyper-sexual, and animalistic. Radio station executives feared that this type of music would infuriate Christian, law-abiding, conservative, white Americans by demoralizing white youngsters, and adversely affect the advertisement dollars of their stations.

In the early 1950s in Indianapolis, African American music lovers and teenagers waited until midnight and listened to either Randy's Record Shop radio program from Gallatin, Tennessee, or its competitor, Ernie's Record Mart radio show from Nashville, Tennessee. Although located in the segregated South, both programs broadcast rhythm-and-blues music performed by African Americans without fear of backlash and economic repercussions fueled by racism.

Rhythm-and-blues music performed by local artists in Indianapolis was a liberating force for music lovers and specifically teenagers during this period. Perhaps it is the province of teenagers to seek solace and identity through music, but in the midcentury, the music genre of choice for white teenagers was the rhythm-and-blues music so detested—and feared—by the older members of the community. Rhythm and blues legitimized them and helped ease their marginalization.

In this book, author David Leander Williams chronicles the rise of popularity of rhythm and blues music throughout the United States and demonstrates how this genre ignited a musical revolution in Indianapolis. This revolution disregarded the dictates of the majority community and created a genre that music lovers and teenagers were proud to call their own. Williams meticulously connects these artists to Indiana Avenue entertainment venues during the days of segregation and the advent of the "Chitlin' Circuit," a network of venues where African Americans sought entertainment because of the many rigid Jim Crow laws that prohibited their entry to white establishments throughout the Midwest and South. Many youngsters who harmonized under streetlights at night formed groups and headed to the recording studios to record music that celebrated their experiences. Rhythm and blues was much more than lyrics and music notes on a composer's score; it was a force that broke the chains of mental degradation and marginalization and offered its fans and practitioners a new and positive outlook on life.

Richard Pierce, PhD
John Cardinal O'Hara, CSC, Associate Professor of History
University of Notre Dame

ACKNOWLEDGMENTS

I am greatly indebted to the late Wilma Gibbs-Moore, senior archivist for African American history, Indiana Historical Society; Dr. Stanley Warren, professor emeritus, DePauw University; Dr. Patricia A. Payne, coordinator, Crispus Attucks Racial Equity Office; Annmarie Amor Byer, education consultant, Crispus Attucks Racial Equity Office; Kisha Tandy, associate curator of social history, Indiana State Museum; Lorna Dawe, events and communication coordinator, Indiana University–Purdue University at Indianapolis; Cassandra Williams, clinical faculty, Africana Studies, Indiana University–Purdue University at Indianapolis; Patrick R. Pearsey, curator, Indianapolis Metropolitan Police Department Lichtenberger History Room; Todd Gilbert, public services librarian, Indianapolis Public Library; Gerald Hause, Lockefield historian; Julia Harris-Conner, Lockefield historian; the late John Dumas-Haamid; Rosalind Dumas-Haamid; Kenney Adams; Carole Adams; Harold Andrews; Freida Andrews; Waller Chappel; Martha Chappel, Lockefield Civic Association; Darlene Levy, Indiana State Library; Fred Robinson, Crispus Attucks High School Alumni Association; Pamela Hurley-Shultz, computer specialist; Winford Cork, jazz historian; Woodie Carpenter, jazz historian; the late Mattie Louise Ferguson-Ballow; Carole Ferguson-Finnell; Thomas Ridley; Nancy Holliman-Johnson; Frazier King; Fred Taylor; Olivia McGee-Lockhart; Dorothea Embry-Whitfield; Andrew Ramsey; Ethel Milligan-Middlebrook; Frances Glenn-Jennings; Nina Shirley-McCoy; Larry Richard Shirley; Louise Smith; Dennis Nichols; Audrey Buford-Taylor; Brenda Gibbs-King; Henry Woods; Ruth Woods; Guy Russell; Alice Keno; Ruth Keno; Ruth Bernard-Black; Godfrey Muhammad; EyasuChernet; and Howard Daniel Pipes Sr. Special thanks to Carl Black and Glenda Stevens-Black, photographers and computer specialists, and Larry Goshen, photographer and rhythm-and-blues historian. Their contributions to the success of this book are immeasurable, and I sincerely appreciate their generosity and professionalism. Unless otherwise specified, all images are from the author's personal collection.

INTRODUCTION

The Greeks, during their military conquests of the fourth century in Africa, Europe, and the Far East, had the opportunity to gaze upon sights seldom seen by the civilized world. They named these locations the Seven Wonders of the World. Sights such as the Great Pyramids of Giza, the Colossus of Rhodes, and the Great Wall of China undoubtedly fascinated them and captured their most vivid imagination. Given the opportunity to leap over the ages and journey through a time capsule to the 20th century, they might have traveled to Indianapolis and witnessed the Eighth Wonder of the World—Indiana Avenue, sometimes referred to as just "the Avenue."

If one were to imagine the magnificence and aura of Indiana Avenue during the 20th century, one might envision an astronaut peeping out the window of his spacecraft as he circles the globe and being thrilled by the million points of light sparkling below. Each light represents a focal point of enjoyment and excitement on Indiana Avenue. He recognizes the towering Walker Theatre, which stands tall like a pyramid of ancient Egypt, built by African American millionaire Madame C.J. Walker, who amassed her fortune in the beauty culture industry. Standing majestically on the corner of Indiana Avenue and West Street, the building has a gigantic neon sign shaped like a vertical arrow whose lightbulb luminosity begins at the top of the building, high above the marquee, and descends to the bottom, where it points to the name "Walker Theatre." Its interior, which features a North African Moorish décor with Egyptian sphinx sculpture, Moorish arches, spears, and African masks, gives authenticity to its grandeur.

The astronaut might also see far below the small figure of a frustrated and angry Duke Ellington, who nervously paces the red carpet of the Sunset Terrace Ballroom gritting his teeth. He has just been informed that showtime is in 15 minutes, and his drummer, Sonny Greer, has gotten so drunk that he toppled off the bandstand onto a table occupied by a bevy of beautiful ladies waiting for the show to begin, spilling food and drinks over everyone. Ellington darts outside the club and searches for an immediate replacement. He engages a young teenage drummer named Willis Kirk to mount the bandstand and occupy the chair of the inebriated Greer. Kirk does not disappoint. Ellington's jaws are so tight that one can imagine smoke emanating from his nostrils.

Another image that captures the eye of the astronaut is a young, virtually unknown guitarist, Wes Montgomery, who performs on stage with Monk Montgomery on bass, Paul Parker on drums, and Melvin Rhyne on keyboards at Jacque Durham's Missile Room jazz club as great jazz saxophonist Julian "Cannonball" Adderley strolls in one night. Cannonball has been advised to go down on Indiana Avenue and "see this Montgomery dude because he may be something special." Cannonball leisurely enters the club, sits down, and is totally mesmerized by Wes Montgomery's artistic mastery. He rushes to the telephone, calls Riverside Records producer Orrin Keepnews in New York, and tells him "You just gotta hear this Montgomery play, he's out of sight and please try to sign him up as soon as possible!"

Farther up the Avenue, which crosses Capitol Avenue, is Tuffy Mitchell's Pink Poodle. There on stage, the astronaut witnesses a bug-eyed, mismatched clothed, toothless Jackie "Moms" Mabley strut across the stage and have the audience in stitches with her jokes about loving young men. Later, a troupe of female impersonators called the Jewel Box Revue sashay across the stage in beautiful, flowing, multicolored fashion-plate gowns as the orchestra plays the burlesque tune "The Stripper" and the audience whistles and howls. Finally, a cherubic-like, African-American rhythm and blues singer hits the stage and wows the audience with her latest hit, "Rock-A-Bye Your Baby." Folks are amazed at how such a wonderful, soul-stirring voice could possibly be belted out by an 18-year-old young lady. She steals the show! Decades later, the world would recognize her greatness, first showcased at the Pink Poodle, and crown her—Aretha Franklin—the "Queen of Soul."

Down the street heading toward General Hospital, the astronaut observes two tiny objects of light. One is Jimi Hendrix, a left-handed guitarist who later received international acclaim at the historic 1969 counter-culture concert at Woodstock, New York, and his drummer/bandmate, a short, rotund Billy Cox. They return from the Brass Rail nightclub downtown after the owner discovers that they are African Americans and decides to cancel their contract for fear of upsetting some patrons. They travel to George's Bar to enter a "battle of the bands" contest and win second place to Baby Leon and the Presidents, but because of their empty pockets, they have to sleep overnight in their car in an alley behind a vacant building.

Around the corner on West Street near Sea Ferguson's bowling alley and Crispus Attucks High School, the light illuminates a dapper Count Basie who picks up his clothes from Wickliff's cleaners and returns to Indiana Avenue to perform at the Sunset Terrace Ballroom. He drops by Pat's barbershop near the canal to get his processed hair tightened up and his shoes shined. Pedestrians gawk and crane their necks to see this royal, internationally known jazz great in their midst.

The astronaut hears a crash, a thud, and a scream that escapes from Ida Geller's Tavern adjacent to Rag Alley, the notorious spot where many of the most dangerous venues are located. With the police en route and a body on the floor, there stands a massive, angry Anna Redd with a chair in her hand and fire in her eyes. She has just pummeled a man and beat him mercilessly with the chair because of his refusal to repay her loan. Anna Redd is a legendary Indiana Avenue toughie who beats up men or women for the slightest infraction. Later, she appears in court for her latest offense, and the judge peers down from his bench and exasperatingly asks, "Anna Redd, why did you beat that man so savagely with that chair?" Anna lifts her head, looks the judge in the eye, and innocently replies, "Judge, your honor, I couldn't lift that heavy table to save my life."

The seeds of *Indianapolis Rhythm and Blues* were sown decades ago on the courtyards and playgrounds of the Lockefield Gardens public housing project in Indianapolis. They unfortunately germinated and produced young shoots on the deathbed of Indiana Avenue in the 1970s, when the sun refused to shine. The beautiful flower of entertainment bowed its head in agony, wept, and withered on the vine due to the arrival of three major causes that dictated its ultimate demise. First, the onset of integration on the social scene gave many Indiana Avenue patrons the green light to abandon their favorite entertainment venues and seek new social experiences in downtown nightclubs, hotels, or theaters. Many of these venues had previously prohibited African American patronage; nevertheless, blacks deserted Indiana Avenue in droves with their almighty dollar in hand and love and dedication to Indiana Avenue culture in their wake. As the thrill-seekers left, Indiana Avenue experienced a decrease in entertainment attractions in many of the venues and sparse pedestrian traffic; consequently, the cash registers fell silent.

Second, the federal highway system of the mid-1960s cut a path through midtown Indianapolis, demolished homes, uprooted churches, and caused total calamity. Indiana Avenue was left in tatters. Nightclubs closed, "for sale" signs popped up, and housing deterioration and neglect of city services took its toll. Third, the encroachment and ultimate expansion of Indiana University–Purdue University of Indianapolis were the final nails in the coffin. Neighborhoods were torn asunder, and tenants and homeowners were jettisoned like unworthy human cargo to the outer city limits as their homes were expropriated by eminent domain. Many owned homes, worked their entire lives, and joyfully anticipated retirement, but they were forced to secure rental accommodations during this calamity. A pall hung over Indiana Avenue. Things would never be the same.

During the 1950s and 1960s, walking down Indiana Avenue was a delightful adventure. Patrons passed various entertainment venues and were serenaded by musical notes and lyrics that seemingly only Indiana Avenue artists could produce. The Sunset Terrace Ballroom, Cotton Club, George's Bar and Orchid Room, the P&P Club, the Red Keg, and Henri's produced entertainment that rivaled any productions that the Ed Sullivan *Toast of the Town* television program or the theater district of the "Great White Way" of Broadway in New York had to offer.

In addition to the jazz notes produced by Wes Montgomery, J.J. Johnson, Freddie Hubbard, Carl Perkins, Leroy Vinnegar, Jimmy Coe, or David Baker, there were other sounds that filled the airways and added to the artistic mystique of Indiana Avenue. Those notes came from the bandstands of the rhythm-and-blues clubs that lined Indiana Avenue. Stars like Johnny Ace, Little Richard, Fats Domino, the Orioles, the Penguins, the Wrens, Larry Darnell, the Five Dots, the Four Sounds, and the Counts added to the spirit and soul of the virtual soundtrack of Indiana Avenue. The vision of people walking and talking in cadence with the lyrics and notes that escaped these venues and the wonderful aroma of barbecue chicken and fine pastries that floated in the air from the doors of Forrest and Mary Jones's Bar B-Q Heaven was surreal. Young children entered and exited the MacArthur's Conservatory of Music on sunny Saturday mornings for music and dance lessons, which thrilled many and spoke volumes of the future of Indiana Avenue entertainment. The raucous laughter and smiles of bootleg cab drivers parked on Indiana Avenue and Blake Street waiting to take residents with limited financial resources to the Monument Circle in order to pay a bill were heard. Excited youngsters lined the street on a hot summer day as members of the Persian Temple Shrine Band and the Prince Hall Masons paraded down the Avenue. Sporting red fezzes adorned by a sequined star and crescent and tassel, balloon-legged pants, white blouses, and curved, single blade sabers swinging at their sides, they played marching music, and spectators enjoyed the merriment of this festive event. These factors were some of the ingredients that created the ambiance in which rhythm and blues developed and gained prominence on Indiana Avenue.

The entertainment scene on Indiana Avenue was much more than glitzy nightclubs, smartly dressed patrons, and jazz and rhythm-and-blues music. It did not develop in a vacuum devoid of external societal forces such as fast-talking baseball ticket men, astute politicians, enterprising businessmen, and ladies of the evening. Its concoction contained folkloric legends like Anna Redd, respected policewoman Evelyn Ridley (the only person who could control Anna Redd), and other heroes and "sheroes" who gave Indiana Avenue a unique entertainment appeal that accentuated the excitement.

The astronaut smiles and waves from his spacecraft high above in the heavens as he completes another orbit. He has been transfixed by the sights, sounds, and events of the Eighth Wonder of the World—Indiana Avenue.

One

Early Rhythm and Blues Pioneers

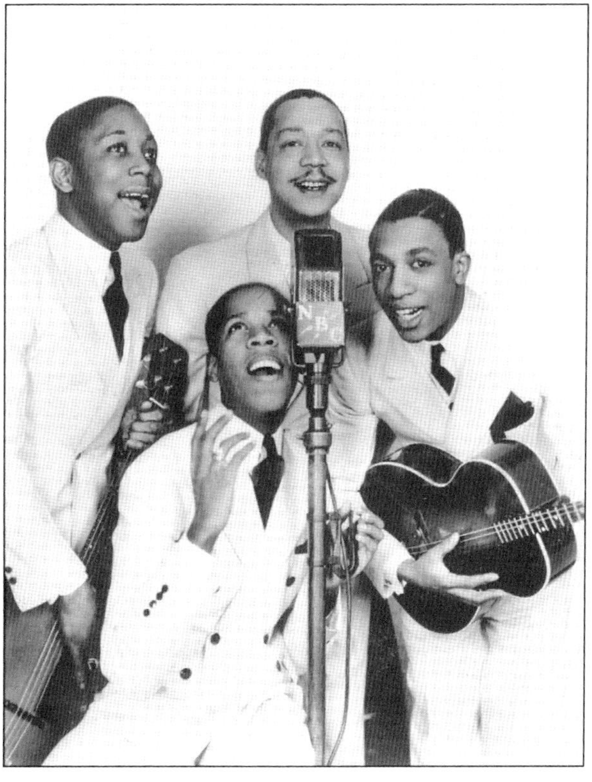

Before they could get booked into the clubs, some performers displayed their talents on the street, and the recently opened Walker Theatre was a great place to attract attention. On a warm spring day in 1928, three young dancing singers performed on Indiana Avenue in front of the Walker Theatre to the delight of pedestrians who deposited coins into their coffers. The youngsters were Leonard Reed, James "Mif" Campbell, and Orville "Hoppy" Jones. After gaining a little popularity with their sidewalk performances, they sought work in more permanent venues and named themselves the Peanut Boys. Many years later, after several personnel changes and the new name the Ink Spots, they acquired Baltimore native Bill Kenny and recorded their first million-selling record, "If I Didn't Care." The song, which was their biggest hit, sold a whopping 19 million copies. (Indiana Historical Society.)

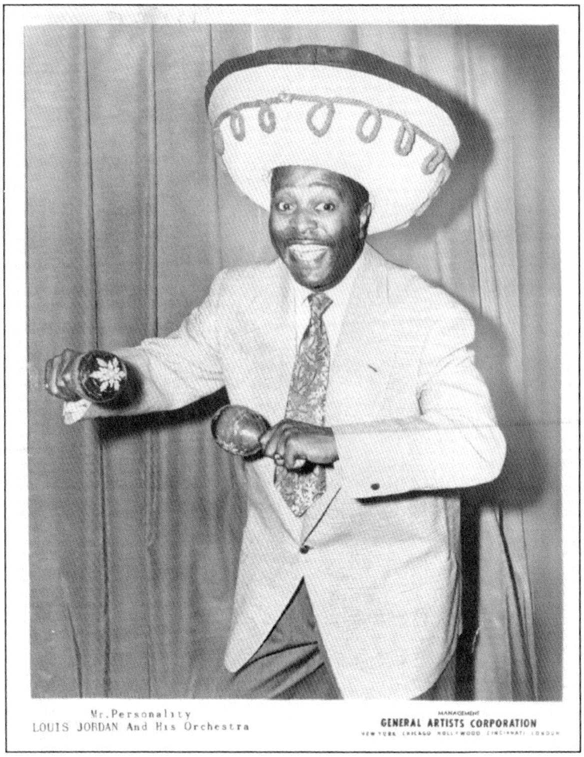

The mere mention of the names Louis Jordan and the Tympany Five sent seismic shockwaves that reverberated among revelers when he came to town. Lines formed hours before showtime and stretched blocks down Indiana Avenue. Jordan, one of the most popular African American musicians of the 20th century with his genre of boogie-woogie/jump blues, was given the zany appellation "King of the Jukebox." Jordan's tunes topped *Billboard* magazine's rhythm-and-blues charts during the 1940s and 1950s. One of his most popular tunes, "Caldonia," was the musical soundtrack for many comedic routines performed on stage in clubs during this era.

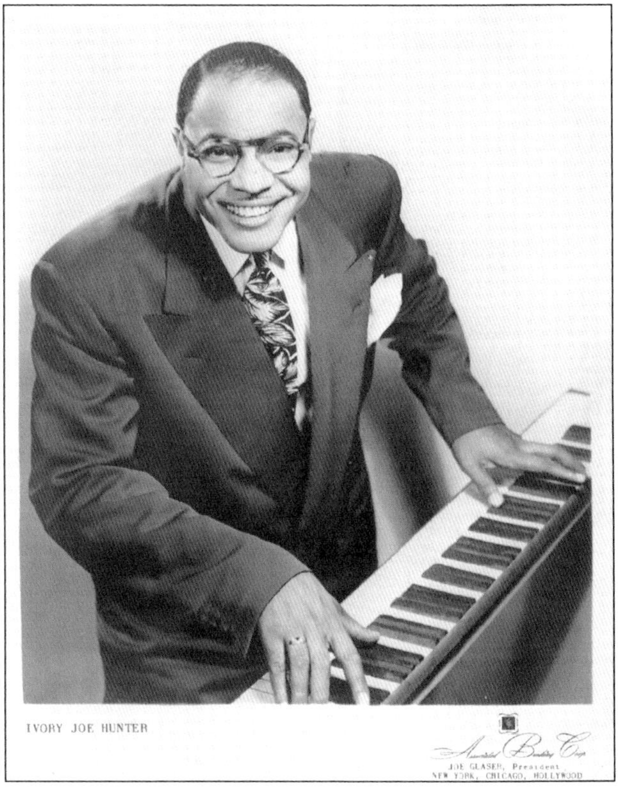

Ivory Joe Hunter was a mainstay at the Sunset Terrace Ballroom and the Walker Theatre during the early 1950s. This six-and-a-half-foot, bespectacled, burly Texas-born entertainer was one of the original "honkers and shouters" who defined this period. His early tunes were "I Almost Lost My Mind" and "Since I Met You Baby." He was called the "Baron of Boogie" and the "Happiest Man Alive" due to his warm smile and pleasant demeanor. Elvis Presley covered his tunes "I Will Be True" and "It's Still There." Pat Boone covered his mega-hit "Since I Met You Baby," which climbed to the top of the charts. On Sunday, September 17, 1950, Hunter appeared at the Sunset Terrace Ballroom and sang his hit song "I Need You So."

Lyrics from the rhythm-and-blues hit and dance-craze "The Huckle-Buck" boomed from loudspeakers up and down Indiana Avenue during the late 1940s. Written by saxophonist Paul "Huckle-Buck" Williams, this jump tune sent lively dancers to the fourth-floor casino of the Walker Theatre, where they jitter-bugged all evening long. White rhythm-and-blues singer Georgia Gibbs covered the song, but Williams's version remained the most popular. Later, Williams took jazz pianist great Carl Perkins with his orchestra to Los Angeles, where Perkins joined the orchestra of song stylist Diana Washington.

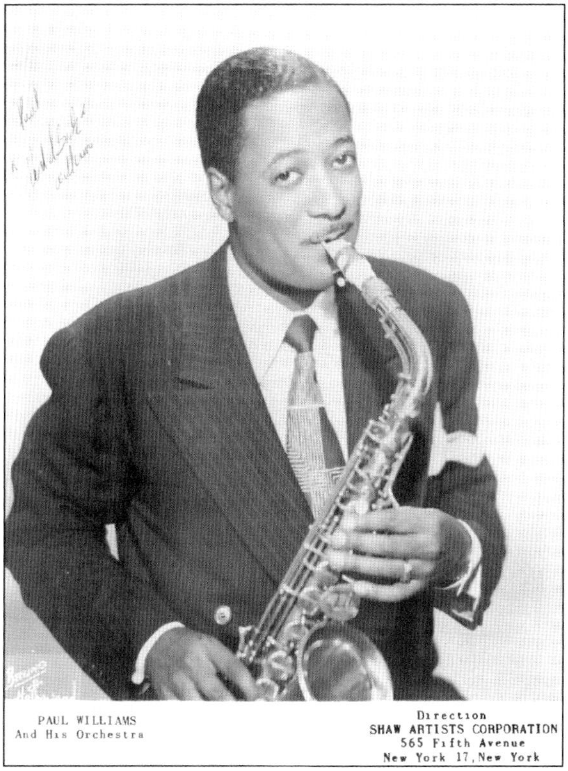

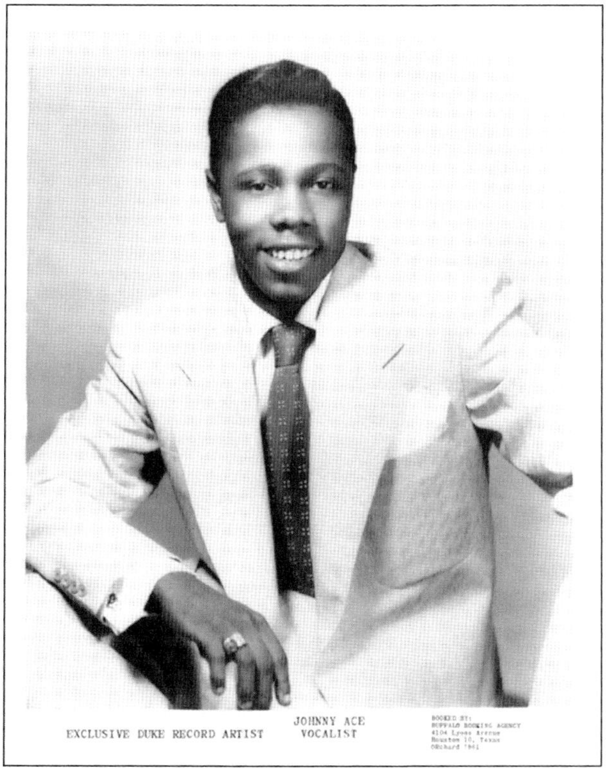

John Marshall Alexander Jr., known as Johnny Ace, was at the summit of the rhythm-and-blues world with his hits "Saving My Love For You," "Cross My Heart," and "The Clock" and toured the country to packed arenas. Rhythm-and-blues lovers were lined up on Indiana Avenue desperately waiting to see their star. On Sunday night, February 21, 1954, he appeared with "Big Mama" Thornton at the Sunset Terrace Ballroom. The world of rhythm and blues was turned upside down on Christmas Day 1954 in the City Auditorium of Houston, Texas, when Johnny Ace was allegedly killed by a self-inflicted gunshot wound to his head.

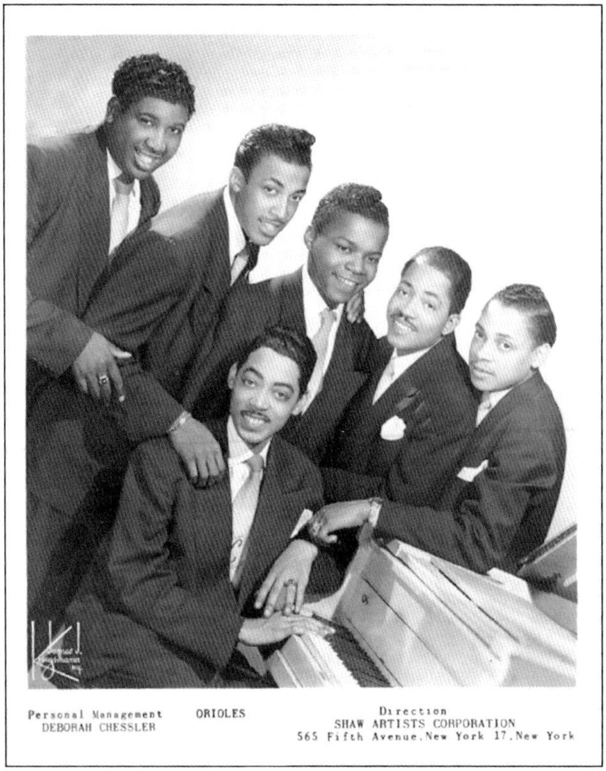

One of the first rhythm-and-blues groups on television, the Orioles appeared on NBC's musical variety program *The Eddie Condon Floor Show* in March 1949. Their greatest hit, "Crying in the Chapel," was released in 1953. Their success led other groups to adopt ornithological monikers. There were the Cardinals, Crows, Flamingos, Larks, Penguins, Ravens, and Wrens.

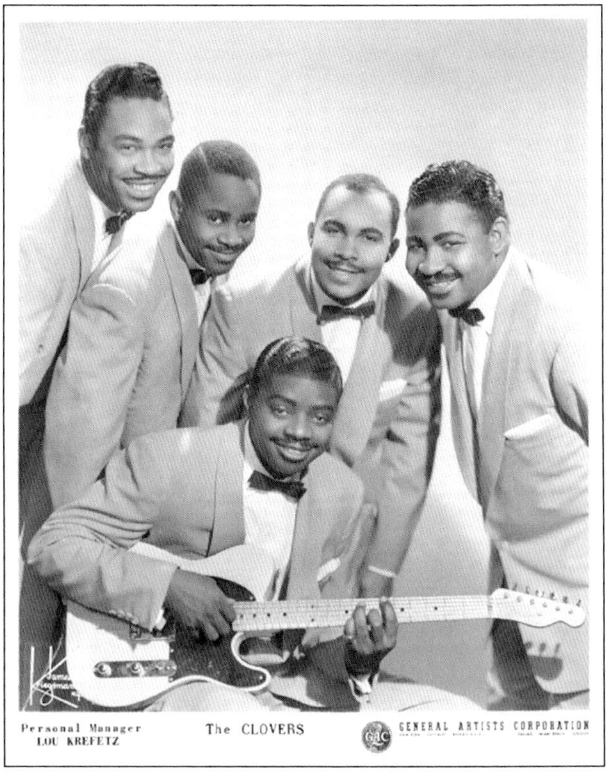

Among the earliest of the rhythm-and-blues groups, the Clovers appeared at the Sunset Terrace Ballroom.

"There Goes My Baby," sung by the Drifters, was the first rhythm-and-blues song backed by strings. The string arrangement was the work of Belford Hendricks of Evansville, Indiana. The Drifters appeared at the C.I.O. Century Hall in Muncie, Indiana, on Saturday, October 27, 1956.

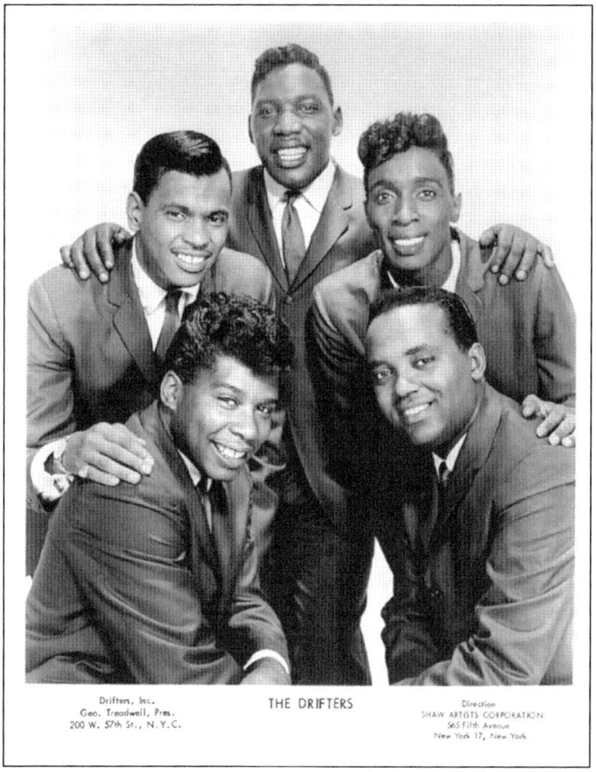

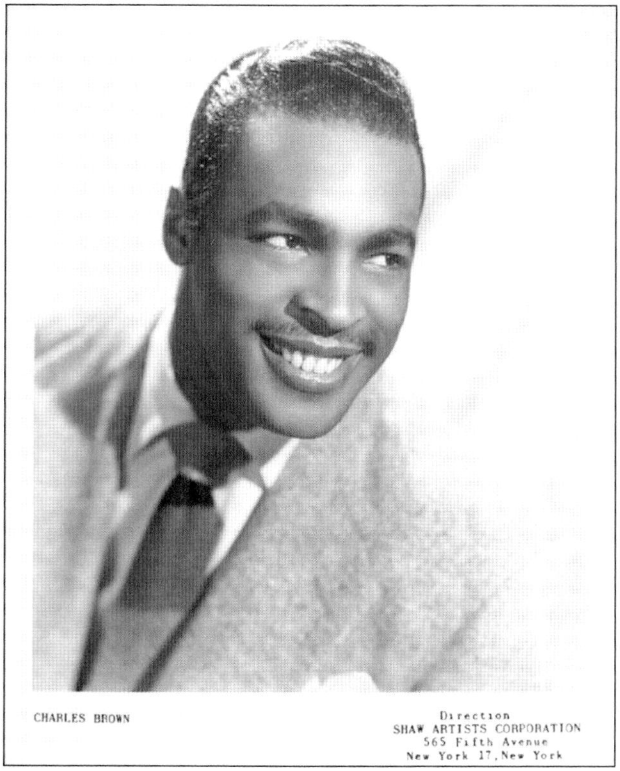

"Please Come Home for Christmas" was a major hit for Charles Brown and charted at No. 76 on the rhythm-and-blues charts in 1960. Brown appeared at the Sunset Terrace Ballroom on Sunday, September 10, 1960.

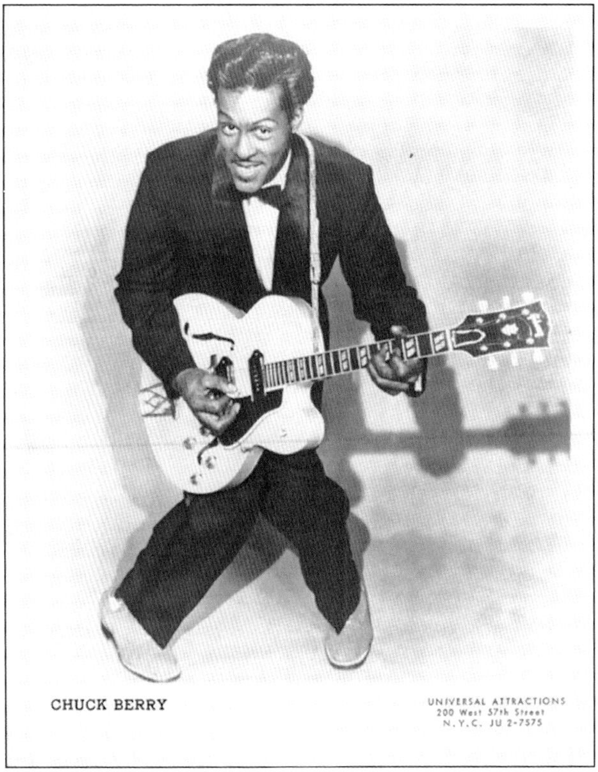

Although Hollywood crowned Elvis Presley as the "King of Rock and Roll" in the 1950s, many in the African American community were incensed. They opined that the origins of rock and roll began with the introduction of Chuck Berry on the American entertainment stage. Berry electrified the music lovers with his mega-hits "Maybellene" in 1955, "Roll Over Beethoven" in 1956, "Rock and Roll Music" in 1957, and "Johnnie B. Goode" in 1958. He was a member of the inaugural class of inductees in the Rock and Roll Hall of Fame in 1986.

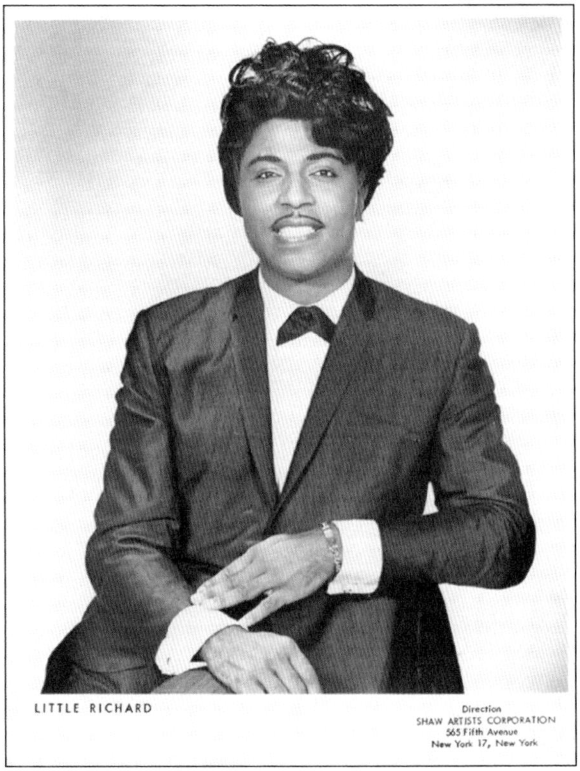

Richard Wayne Penniman, later known as "Little Richard," was another pioneer in the birth and development of early rock and roll. He received national attention with his soaring falsetto rendition of "Tutti Frutti," which climbed to No. 17 on the *Billboard* Hot 100 in 1955. Other subsequent hits like "Good Golly, Miss Molly" and "Long Tall Sally" further established him as one of rock and roll's early great performers.

The Flamingos, Jacob and Ezekial Carey, bass and second tenor, respectively, with cousins Paul Wilson, baritone, and Johnny Carter, first tenor, met at a Hebrew Israelite temple in Chicago. After numerous personnel changes, in 1959, they released their mega-hit "I Only Have Eyes for You," which was an instant million-selling record.

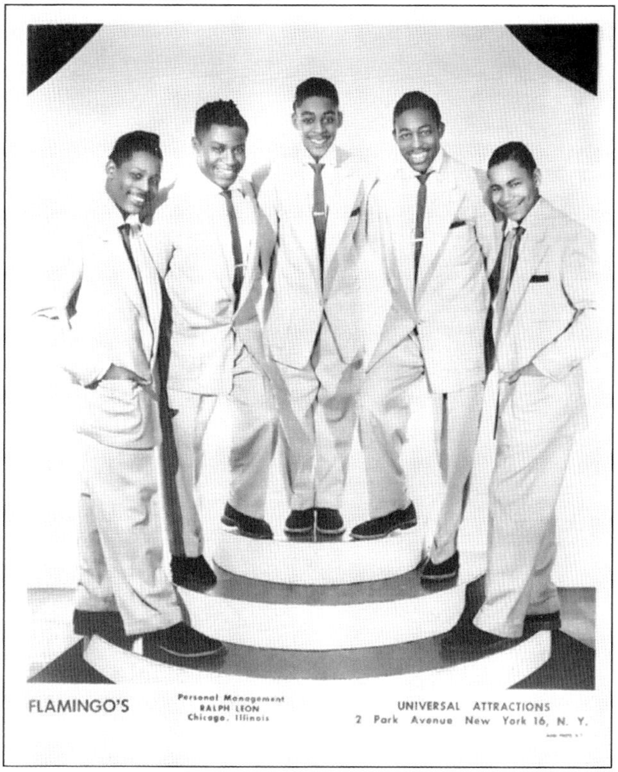

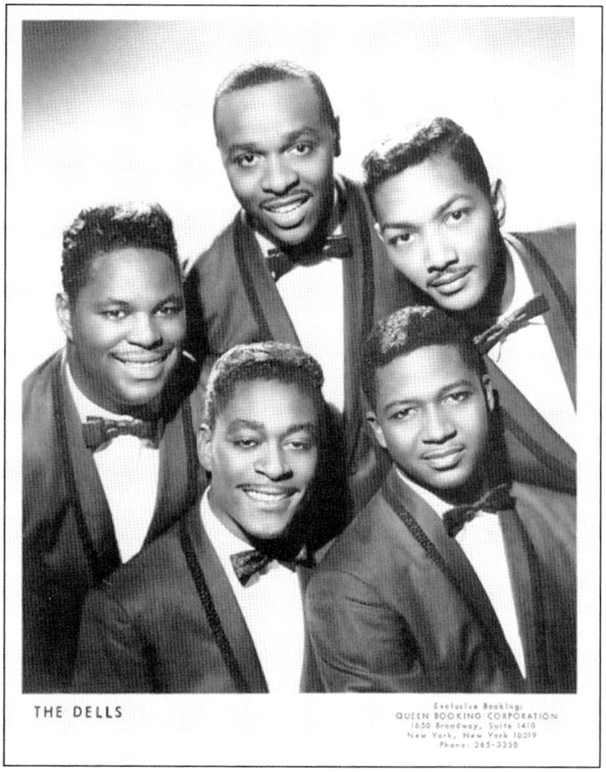

The Dells—Marvin Junior, Verne Allison, Johnny Funches, Chuck Barksdale, and Mickey and Lucious McGill—formed while attending Thornton High School near Chicago. In 1956, they released their chart-topping hit "Oh What a Night," which sold millions of units. Johnny Carter, whose soaring falsetto popularized many of their hits, was one of a few individuals to be voted into the Rock and Roll Hall of Fame twice. He entered as a member of the Flamingos and the Dells.

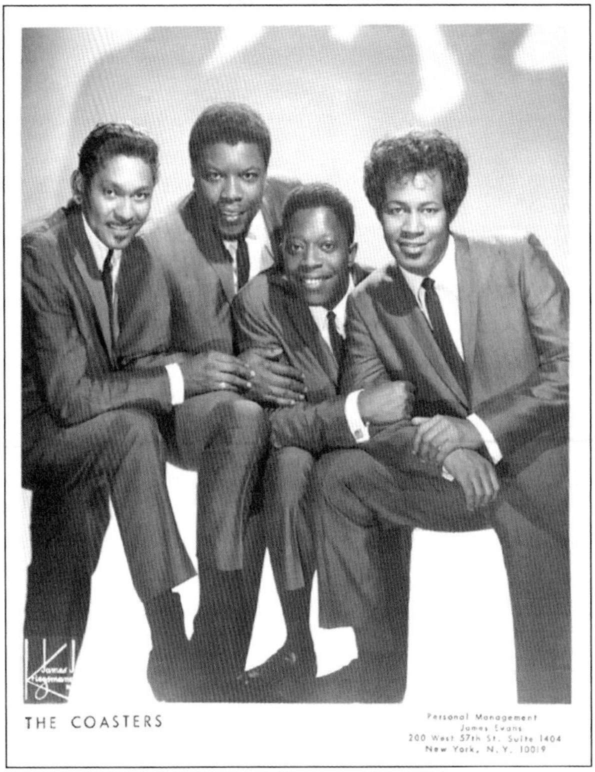

During the 1950s, the Coasters produced a number of hits that introduced comedic lyrics to rock and roll and gained worldwide popularity. The original members were Carl Gardner, Bobby Nunn, Billy Guy, Leon Hughes, and guitarist Adolph Jacobs. Their hits "Yakety Yak," "Charlie Brown," "Poison Ivy," and "Along Came Jones" provided interesting storylines with a comedic slant. In 1987, the Coasters became the first vocal group inducted into the Rock and Roll Hall of Fame and, in 1999, were inducted into the Vocal Group Hall of Fame.

The Platters formed in Los Angeles in 1952, and the original members were Alex Hodge, Cornell Gunther, David Lynch, Joe Jefferson, Gaynel Hodge, and Herb Reed. They had a sophisticated, silky-smooth delivery that appealed to all segments of America. Many radio stations that refused to play African American rhythm and blues were forced by telephone calls and telegrams from their listening audiences to play music by the Platters. Their signature hits were "Smoke Gets in Your Eyes," "Only You," and "The Great Pretender." On August 7, 1995, they performed at the Beef & Boards entertainment restaurant.

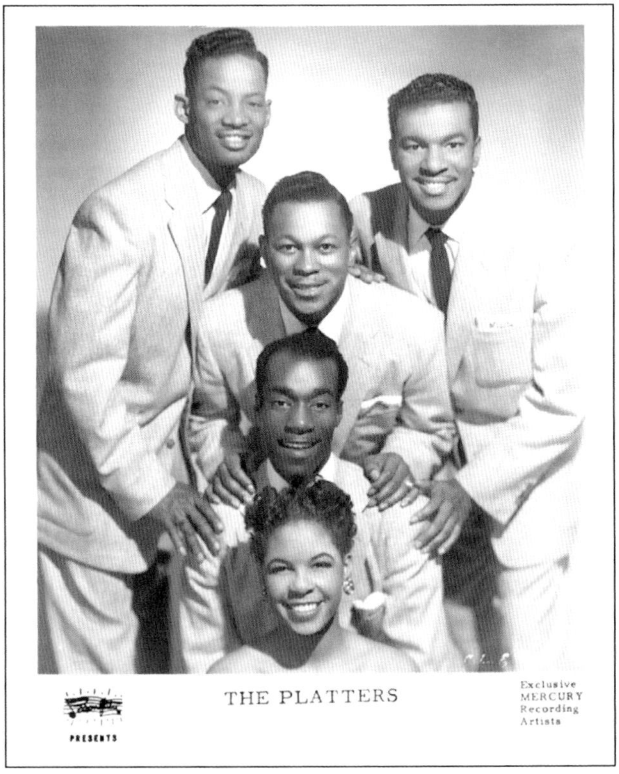

If one were to search for rhythm and blues and rock and roll in the dictionary, one might discover a photograph of a smiling, bespectacled Bo Diddley. Born Ellas Otha Bates in Mississippi, Diddley appeared on the popular Ed Sullivan television program and reintroduced rhythm and blues and rock and roll to America. He was one of the earliest African American artists to appeal to both black and white audiences. His signature song "I'm a Man," recorded in 1955, topped the *Billboard* chart. On Friday, April 10, 1970, Diddley headlined a rock-and-roll show with Chuck Berry, Bill Haley & His Comets, the Coasters, and the Shirelles at the Indiana Roof.

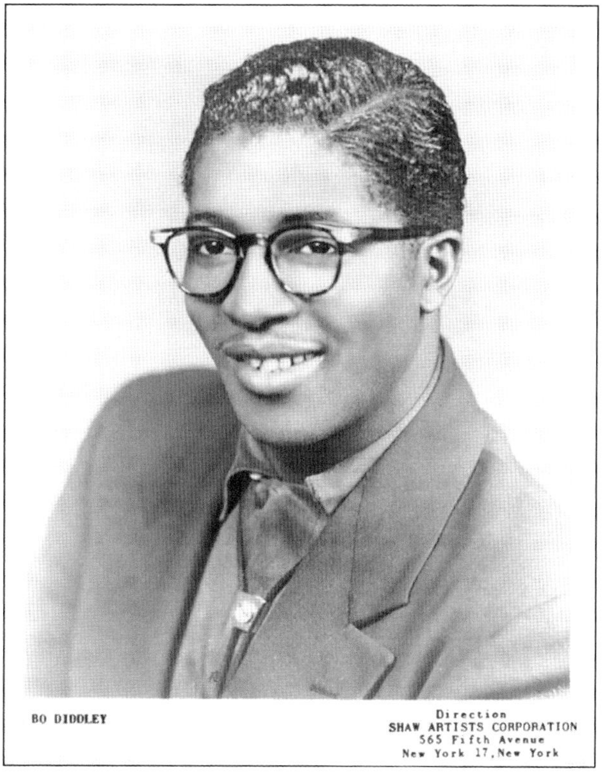

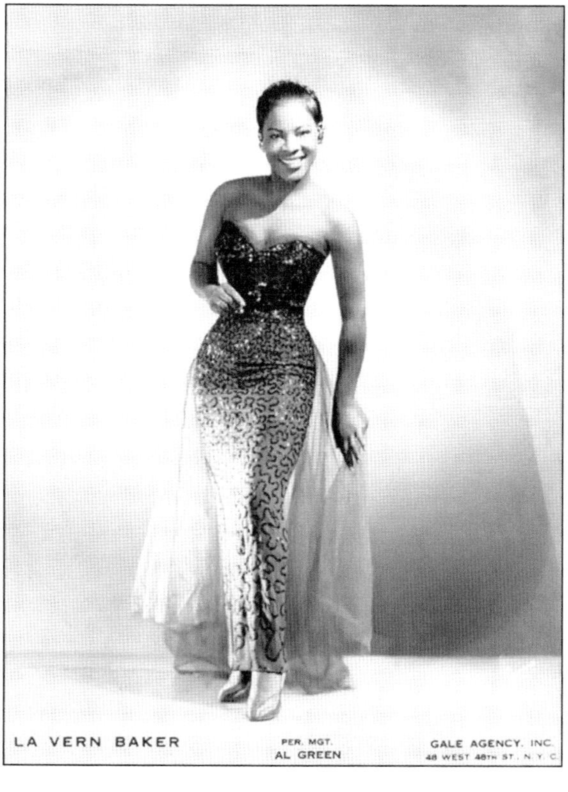

Although early rhythm and blues was dominated by male individuals or groups, in the early 1950s, LaVern Baker arrived on the scene and charted a new course. Baker dominated the music charts with a series of hits that cemented her name in the annals of rhythm-and-blues history. Her first hit, "Tweedle Dee," recorded in 1955, was a snazzy, up-tempo song that charted No. 4 on the *Billboard* Hot 100 and No. 17 on the popular music chart. Later hits were "Jim Dandy," which climbed to No. 1 on the *Billboard* chart and No. 17 on the popular music chart. "I Cried a Tear," "I Waited Too Long," and "See See Rider" were subsequent hits that topped the charts. On May 1, 1958, Baker appeared at the Indiana Theater with Sam Cooke, Clyde McPhatter, Paul Anka, and George Hamilton IV.

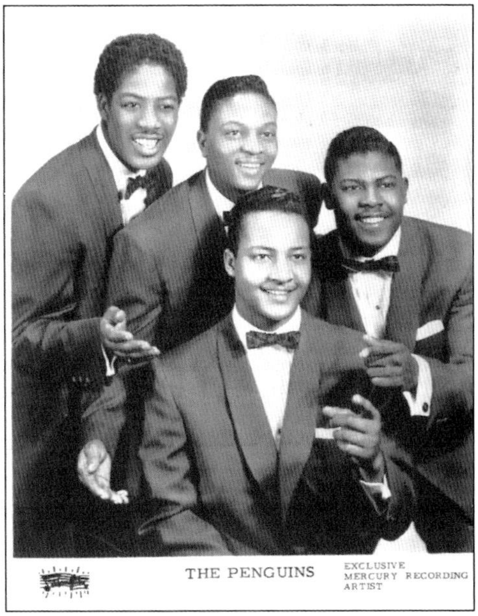

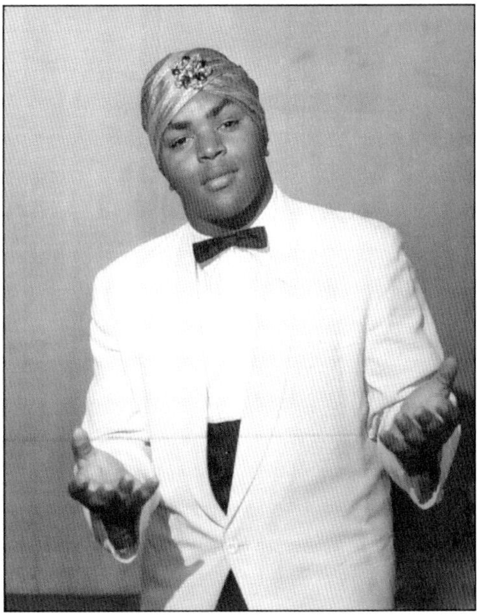

The Penguins (left) defined rhythm and blues in the early 1950s, and their classic song "Earth Angel" was the anthem for the burgeoning rhythm-and-blues nation. The original members were Cleveland Duncan, Curtis Williams, Dexter Tisby, and Bruce Tate. The choice of the name "Penguins" was very interesting. One of the members smoked Kool cigarettes, which had as its trademark "Willie the Penguin;" they considered all members of the group to be cool, hence the name. The A side of this record was "Hey Senorita," but when the radio audience heard "Earth Angel," they flooded the switchboards demanding to hear the B side. The B side made rhythm and blues history. The Turbans, a Philadelphia quartet formed in 1953, consisted of Al Banks, lead tenor; Matthew Platt, second tenor (pictured at right); Charlie Williams, baritone; and Andrew "Chet" Jones, bass. Their hit songs were "When You Dance" and "Sister Sookey."

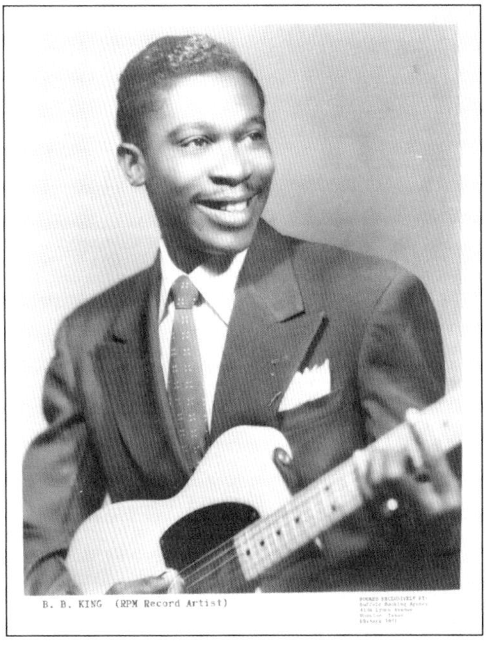

B.B. King *was* the blues. Indiana Avenue blues lovers flocked into the Sunset Terrace Ballroom to hear this blues mega-star. Clutching his beloved guitar "Lucille," he belted out blues tunes that nobody in the universe could duplicate. On many evenings, his bus with the name "B.B. King Ork" cruised down Indiana Avenue.

Robert Calvin Bland, internationally known as Bobby "Blue" Bland, was one of the early blues pioneers who defined the genre and took it to another level. Often referred to as the "Lion of the Blues," Bland cut his teeth with Memphis-based blues stars like B.B. King, Rosco Gordon, Junior Parker, and Johnny Ace, and recorded with numerous record companies. His introductory hit was "Farther Up the Road," which topped the rhythm-and-blues charts and scored the No. 43 spot on the *Billboard* Hot 100. He performed with B.B. King at the Indianapolis Convention Center's Battle of the Blues Concert on November 15, 1976.

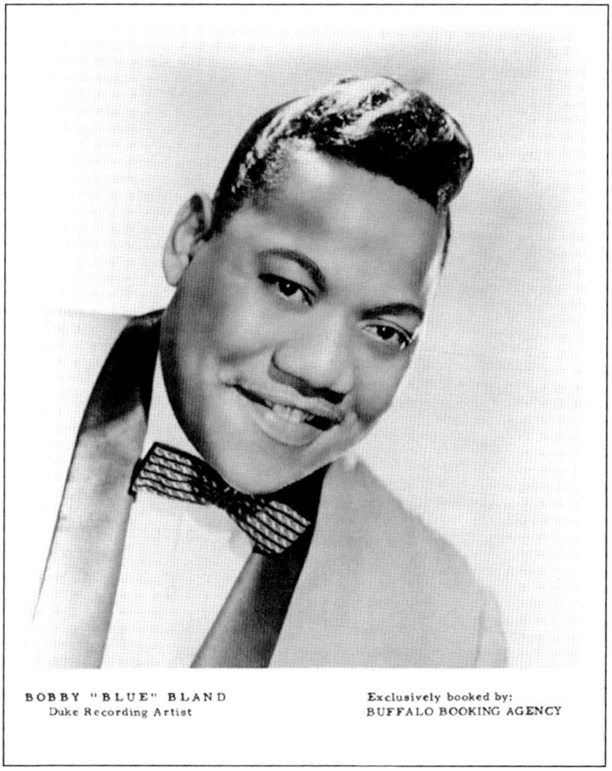

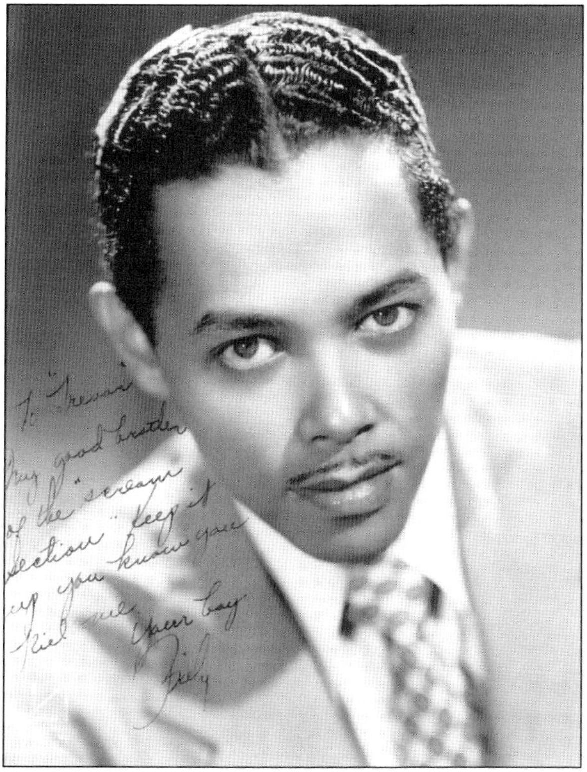

Billy Eckstein, better known as the "Fantabulous Mr. B.," was a frequent performer in many of the high-class establishments on Indiana Avenue. Women screamed wildly when the curtain rose and he appeared on stage. Legend has it that many husbands and boyfriends did not permit their spouses or girlfriends to go to his concerts alone for fear that they might not remember how to return home. This handsome troubadour electrified the Avenue in every venue in which he performed. As the old saying goes, "imitation is the most sincere form of flattery," and Eckstein's trademark on stage was a white shirt with a distinctively curved collar, which was given the name "Mr. B." Indiana Avenue men flocked to the clothing stores to buy the Mr. B. to honor their "songsational" hero Billy Eckstein. (Beverly Johnson.)

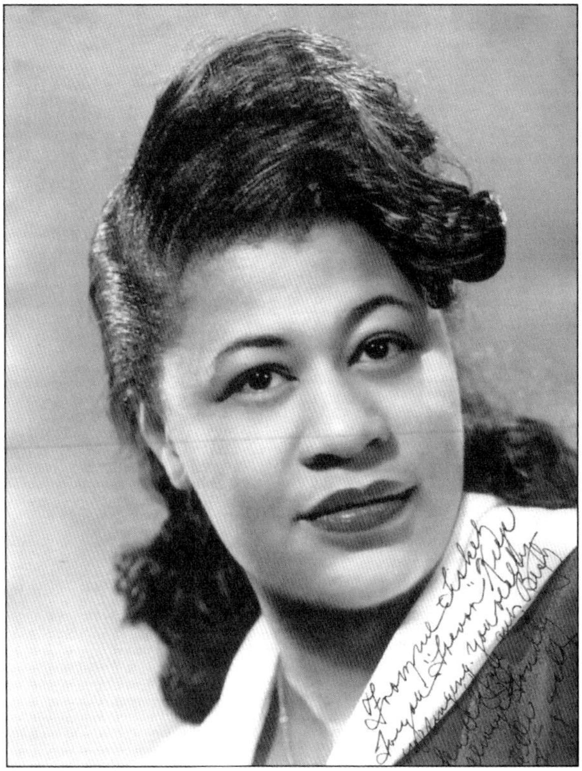

"Enchantress of Swing," "a Sunny Storm in Song," and "the Mellow Lady"—these and other superlatives splashed across the pages of the *Indianapolis Recorder* announcing the May 17, 1941, appearance of Ella Fitzgerald at the Sunset Terrace Ballroom. Only three years earlier, she graced the music world with her recording of "A Tisket, a Tasket," which dominated the popular charts. Indiana Avenue was blocked off at both ends to accommodate the heavy traffic en route to the Sunset Terrace Ballroom. (Beverly Johnson.)

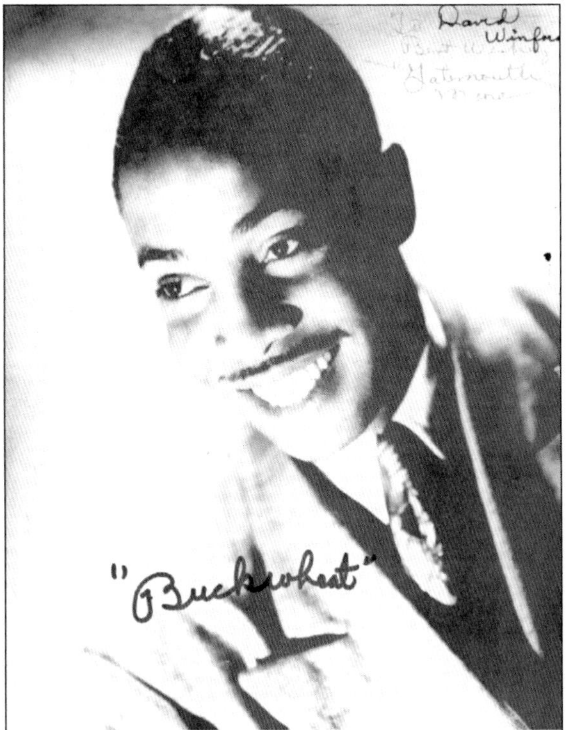

ARNOLD D. (GATEMOUTH) MOORE

In 1947, Dwight "Gatemouth" Moore mounted the stage at the Club De Lisa to sing his signature song," Somebody's Got to Go" and paused with a confused look on his face and sang a Christian song as patrons looked on in disbelief. Moore, who had thrilled blues lovers on Indiana Avenue, had an on-stage epiphany and walked away from the blues and headed toward the pulpit. In the early 21st century, Moore returned to Indianapolis and preached lively sermons at the Bethel African Methodist Episcopal Church. He always included his transition from the blues to the pulpit in his sermons.

Many Sunset Terrace Ballroom patrons fondly remember Nat King Cole casually standing on the corner of Blake Street and Indiana Avenue, talking to the many fans who attended his performances. One such patron, Kenney Adams Sr., related, "Nat King Cole was a regular gentleman, no false pretenses and a very nice fellow. I remember standing at the bar, shoulder to shoulder with him in the Sunset . . . he treated everyone as if they were old friends he'd just met . . . a beautiful brother . . . we were so proud of him because he was a great Hollywood star who made us feel special."

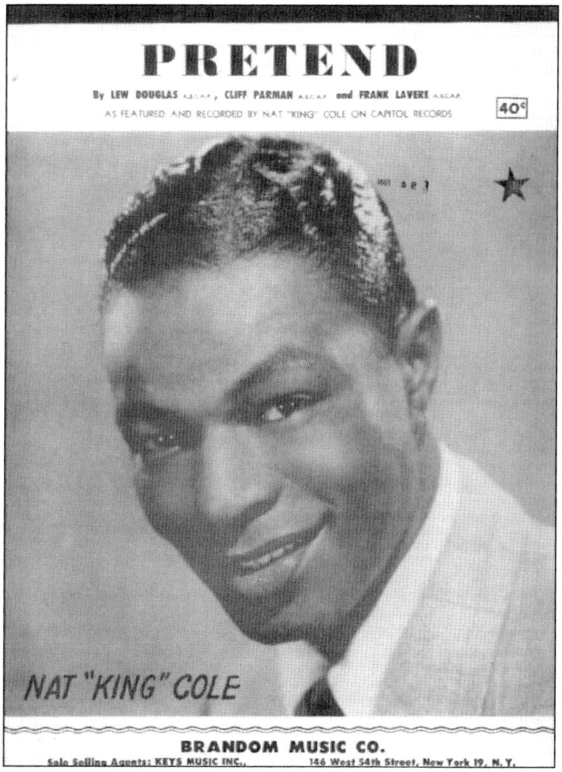

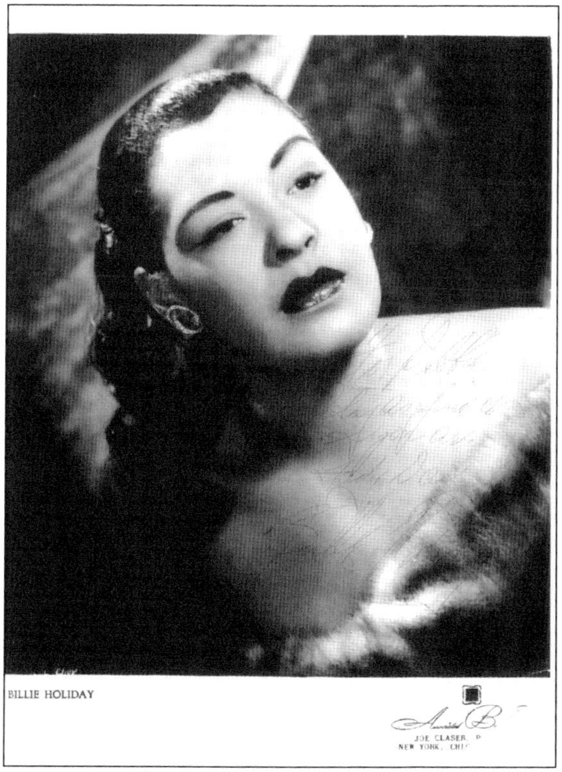

Walking down Indiana Avenue in the early 1950s, the music of Billie Holiday emanated from many of the record shops and nightclubs over large loudspeakers mounted on tall poles outside. Many of the female vocalists honored Holiday and incorporated her phrasing and vocal clarity into their songs. A September 1956 issue of the *Indianapolis Recorder* advertised a book based on the life of Holiday titled *The Lady Sings the Blues*. (Beverly Johnson.)

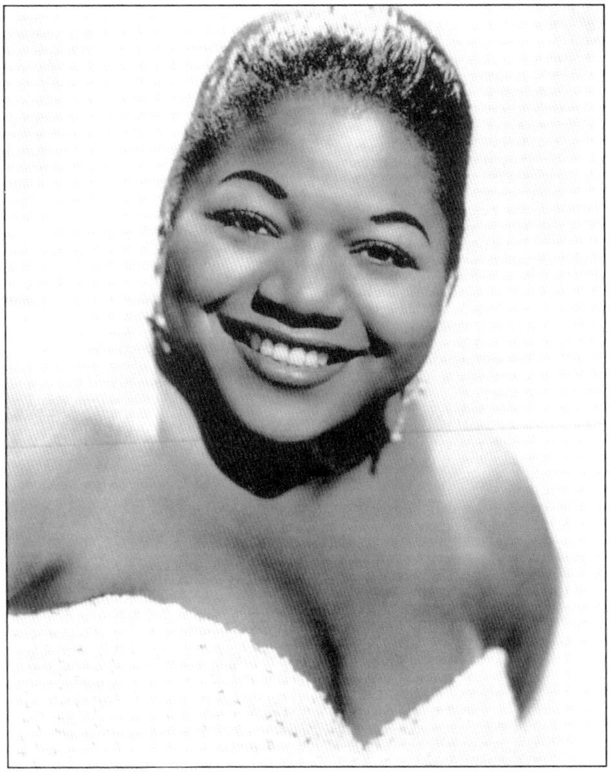

Big Maybelle was the queen of the blues on Indiana Avenue. Her signature song "Candy" received the Grammy Hall of Fame Award in 1999. The February 11, 1961, edition of the *Indianapolis Recorder* reported, "Big Maybelle Heads Show at the Walker Casino."

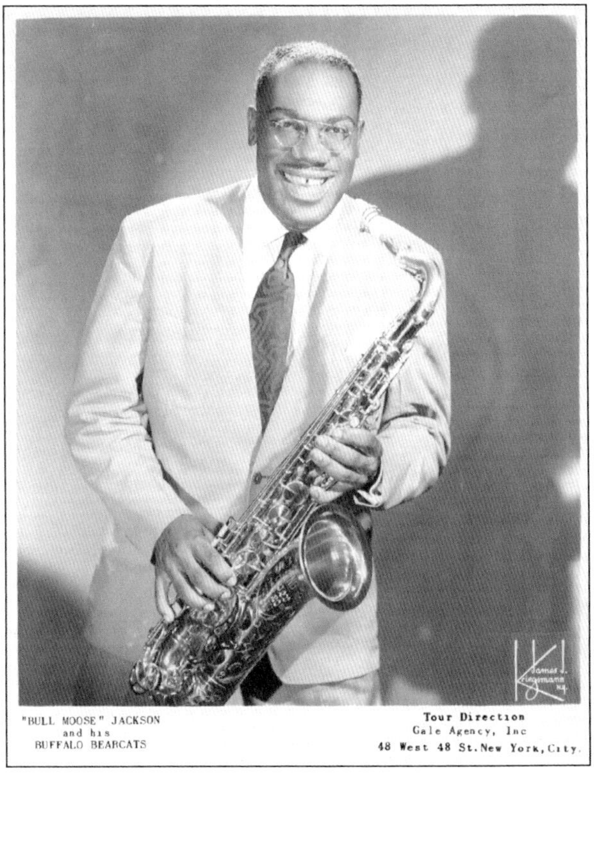

Benjamin Clarence "Bull Moose" Jackson was a frequent blues and rhythm-and-blues entertainer in many venues in the 1950s and 1960s. He was given his nickname for his long chin, floppy ears, and wide, bovine-like eyes. According to blues fan the late Howard Daniel Pipes, "Ladies would come into the club waiting to see this handsome, debonair Billy Eckstein-like crooner and out comes Bull Moose. He looked like a bull moose, but boy could he sing." On November 8, 1947, Bull Moose appeared at the Sunset Terrace Ballroom as the featured singer with the Lucky Millinder Orchestra.

The Roy Milton Trio featured the lovely Camille Howard as their main vocalist, who thrilled blues aficionados on the ivories as well. Her signature tunes were "You Don't Love Me," "Fiesta in Old Mexico," and "Money Blues." She appeared with Roy Milton at the Sunset Terrace on October 3, 1948.

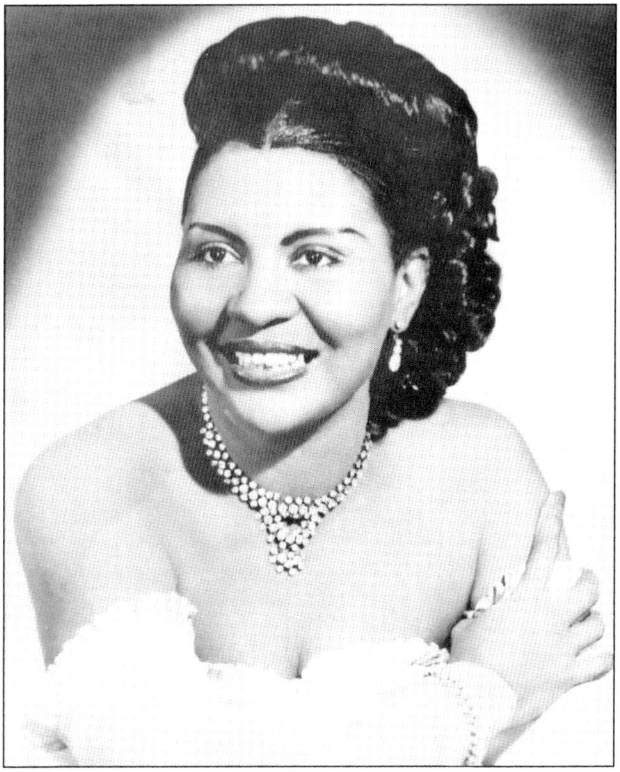

Of all the many orchestras that appeared on Indiana Avenue, Lucky Millinder's aggregation was one of the very best. Millinder (left) did not read music or play an instrument, but he sure could entertain. He would bounce around on the stage with his baton in one hand and his feet slipping and sliding in time with the beat. The crowds went wild whenever Millinder mounted the stage because they knew they were in for a spectacular show.

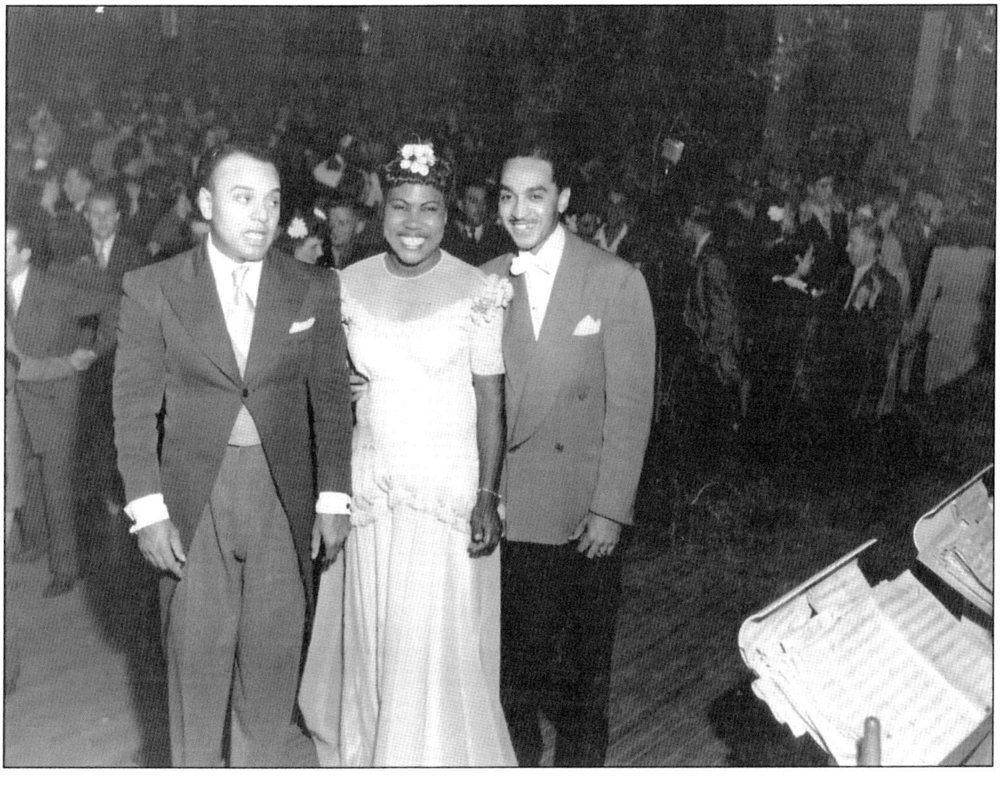

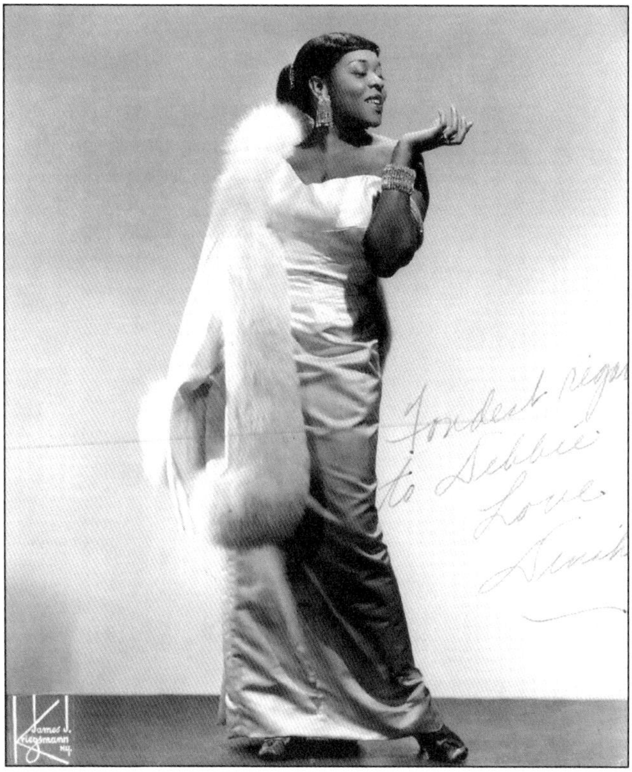

"What a difference a day made, twenty-four little hours"—these were the sultry and soothing words that flowed from the bandstand of Dinah Washington. This was her first song to crack the top-10 list of the popular chart. Washington performed at many of the Indiana Avenue nightspots and was known to be a very engaging personality who lovingly related to her fans.

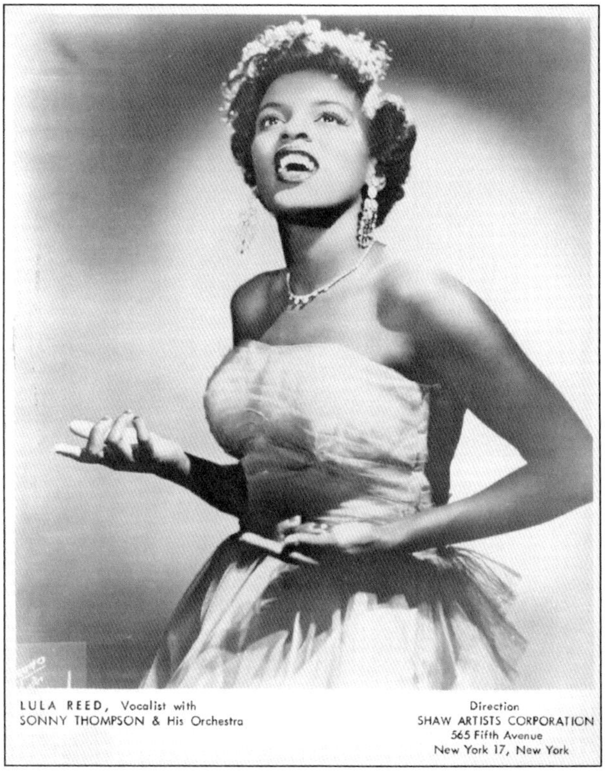

On Christmas Eve 1966, backed by the Johnny Lytell orchestra, Lula Reed appeared at the Walker Casino. Still capitalizing from her earlier song "I'll Drown in My Tears," which reached the No. 5 position on the *Billboard* rhythm-and-blues chart, Reed was backed by the Sonny Thompson Orchestra.

In July 1956, the songstress Della Reese appeared with Illinois Jacquet's Rockin' Rhythm Band at the Circle Theater. During her early teens, she sang with gospel great Mahalia Jackson. In 1959, she recorded her blockbuster signature song "Don't You Know," which climbed to the No. 2 spot on the *Billboard* Hot 100. Later, she appeared on television as Tess on the award-winning program *Touched by an Angel.*

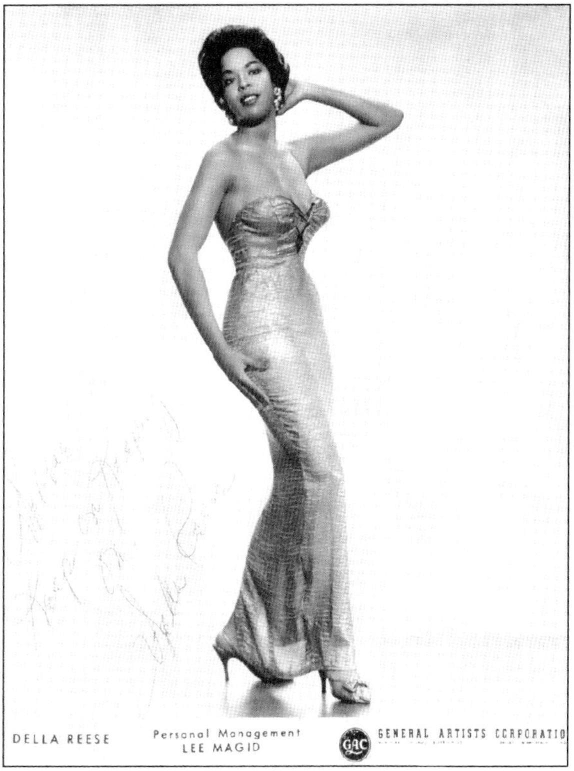

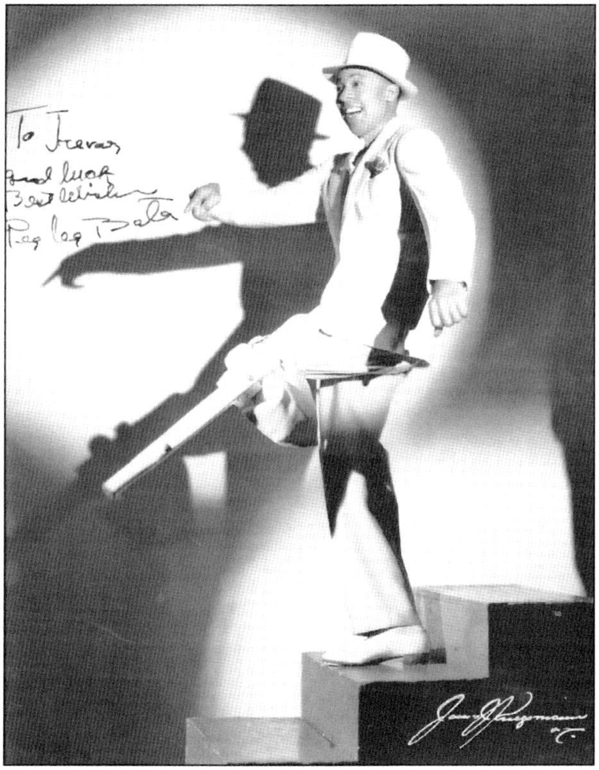

Indiana Avenue residents were thrilled on many Sunday nights as Clayton "Peg Leg" Bates gingerly danced across the stage on one leg during the Ed Sullivan *Toast of the Town* television entertainment hour. Bates lost his leg at the tender age of 12 as the result of an accident wherein his leg was mangled and severed by a cotton gin in South Carolina. In Europe, he held command performances for the King and Queen of England in 1936. On June 5, 1943, he headlined a show with the Ink Spots, Lucky Millinder, Trevor Bacon, and Sister Rosetta Tharpe at the Sunset Terrace Ballroom. (Trevor Bacon Jr.)

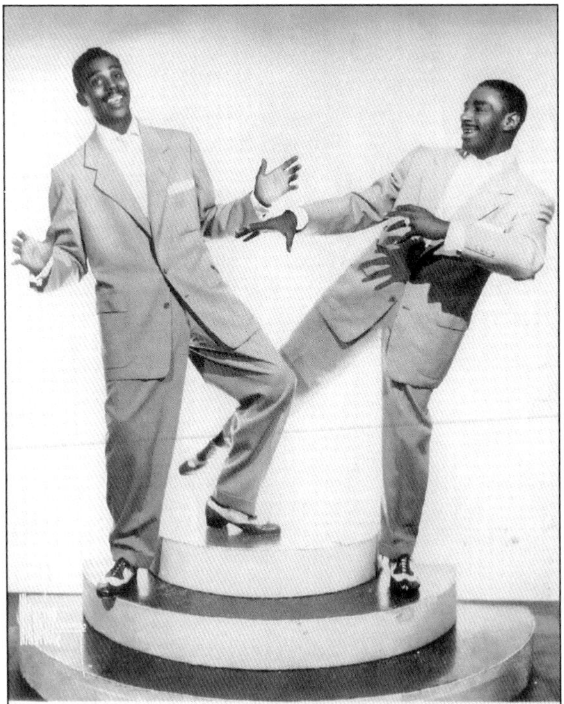

TWO GENTLEMEN OF TAP
LEONARD and LEONARD

Leonard and Leonard, Leonard Chester Thomas and Paul Leonard Harrell, comprised a duo of Indiana Avenue hoofers who electrified their audiences with their fancy footwork and comedic dialogue. Thomas was a well-respected resident of the Lockefield Gardens public housing development, and both men practiced their craft daily in the backyard of the Pipes family, who lived nearby. In July 1955, Indiana Avenue history was made when they appeared at the Palladium Theatre in Sydney, Australia. On October 12, 1958, they appeared on Ed Sullivan's *Toast of the Town* and received rave reviews in New York newspapers.

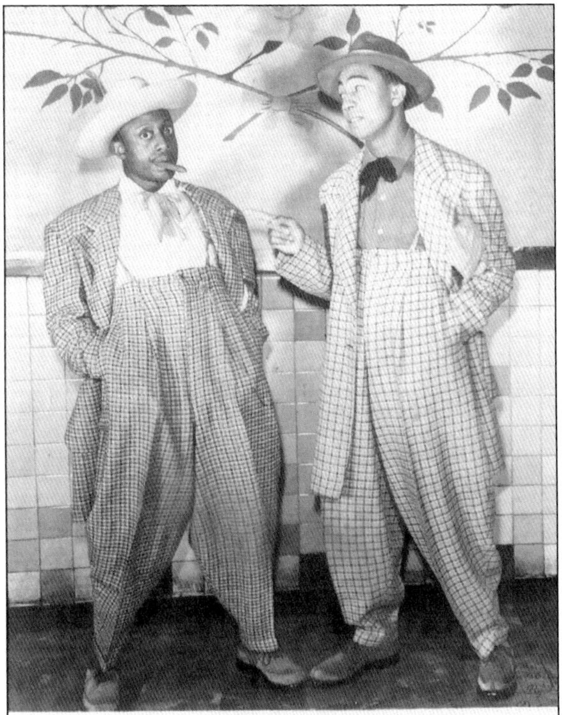

SCRATCH and PATCH
Comedy Dance Team

Scratch and Patch were an out-of-town dancing duo whose routine was very similar to the most popular dancing team in town, Leonard and Leonard.

Ophelia Hoy appeared nightly at the segregated Brass Rail nightclub on Ohio Street in the 1950s. Regrettably, she was required by the management to create a persona of an antebellum, Aunt Jemima–esque character, to the delight of many of the howling and screaming folks in the audience. Although her performances were very well appreciated, deep down inside, she was a proud African American woman who had to perform in this manner in order to survive. According to longtime Indiana Avenue patron Howard Daniel Pipes, "She smiled on the outside but behind that smile, I saw a lot of sadness."

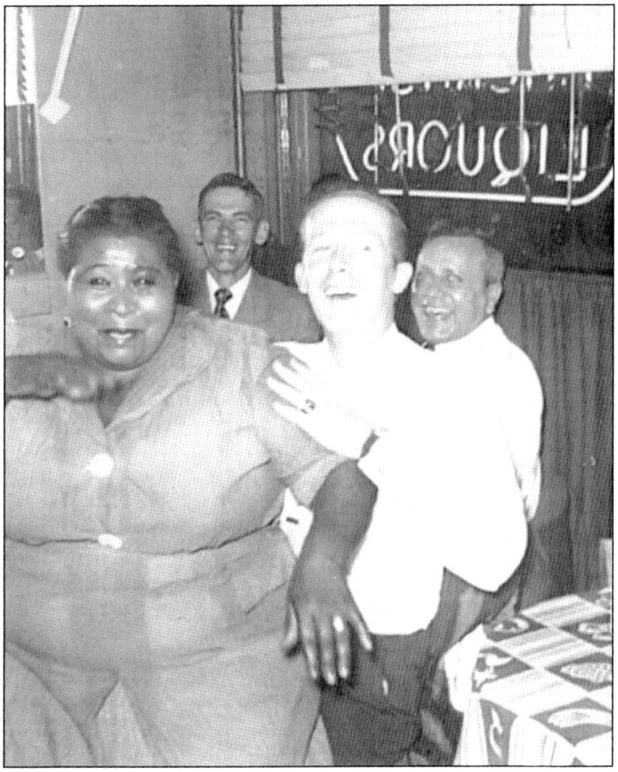

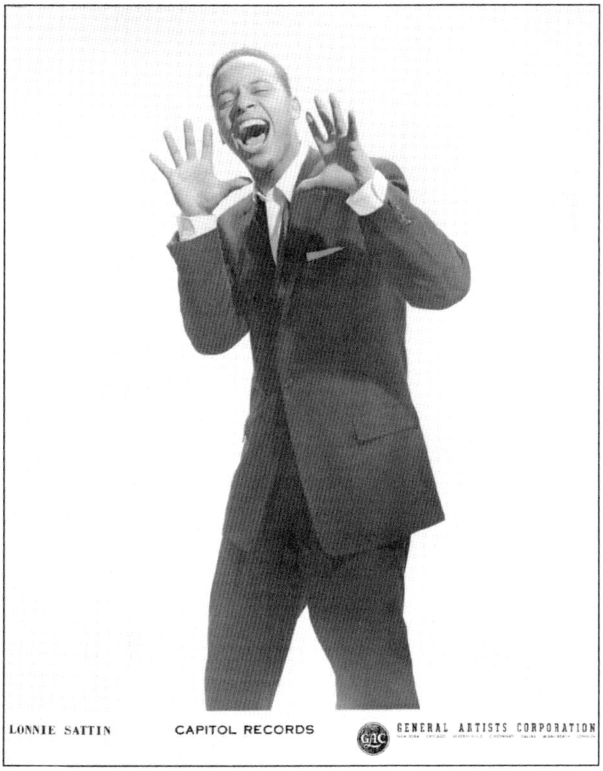

The December 12, 1953, edition of the *Indianapolis Recorder* spoke volumes in reference to the popularity of Lonnie Satin: "Chicagoans are raving over the brilliant performance of baritone Lonnie Satin who's rocking the new club De Lisa. A songwriter of high repute, Satin has been rated by well-known theatrical writers and booking agents and will soon be seen in a network television show. Satin sells a batch of familiar tunes today." Satin appeared at the Pink Poodle in April 1963.

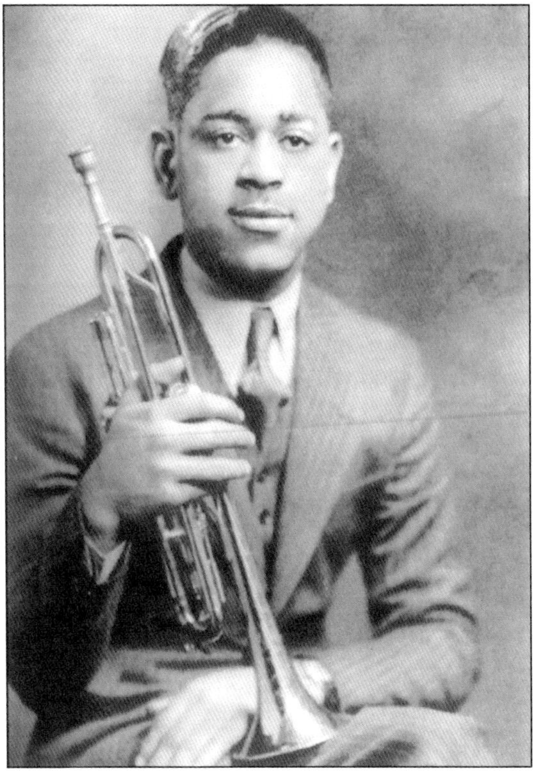

John Burks Gillespie, also known as "Dizzy," thrilled the audience with his trumpet playing and scat singing at Denver Ferguson's Sunset Terrace Ballroom on July 6, 1946. The editors of the *Indianapolis Recorder* opined, "He's called Dizzy because of his constant grin, his school-boyish voice, his dreamy look, his utter lack of concern for anything else except his trumpet and last but not least, for his mad, whimsical sense of humor."

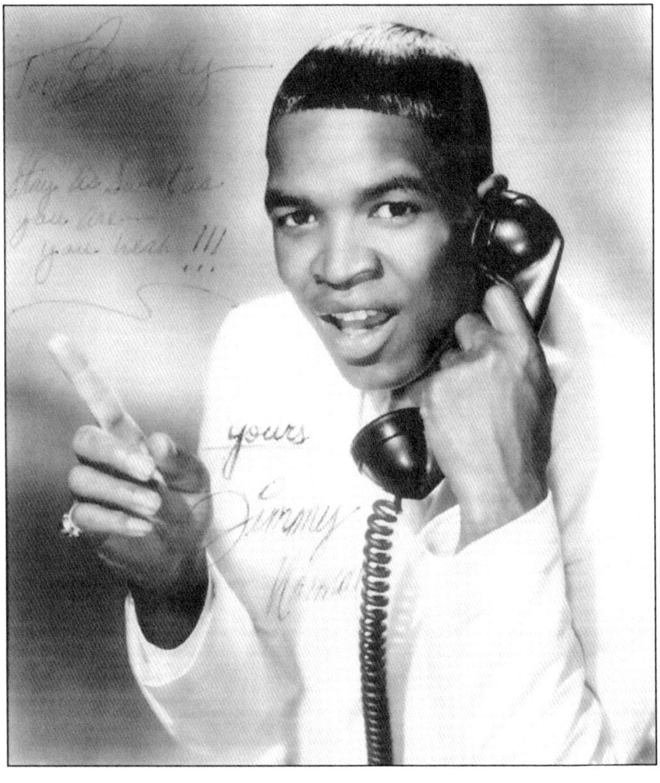

Songwriter and rhythm-and-blues musician Jimmy Norman was an integral part of the development of rhythm and blues songs His signature song was "I Don't Love You No More."

New Orleans–born and popular Indiana Avenue bluesman "Champion Jack" DuPree sponsored "The Midnite Rambles" at the Douglas Theatre, which was an after-midnight talent show that gave local singers, dancers, comedians, and musicians the opportunity to showcase their talent. Many of the Indiana Avenue entertainers were graduates of this show. Two greats, Ophelia Hoy and Flo Garvin, got their start at the Douglas.

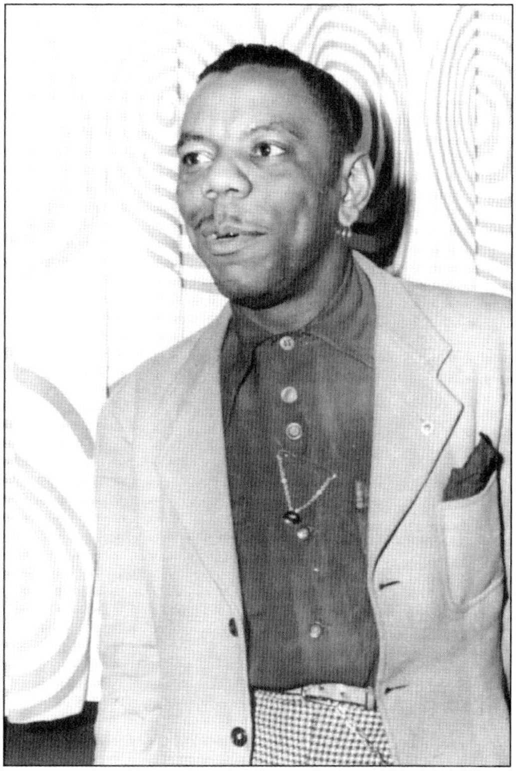

The bicycle shop at 613 North West Street, near Indiana Avenue, drew many of the neighborhood youngsters who repaired their bicycles there. This photograph was taken in 1917. (Indiana Historical Society.)

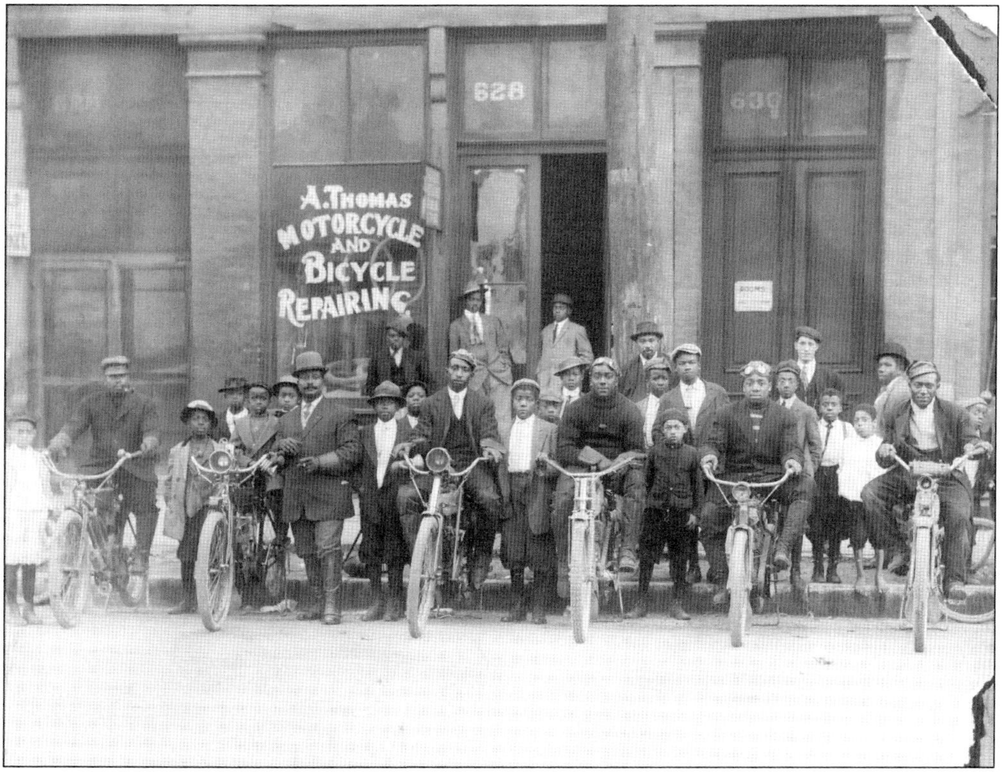

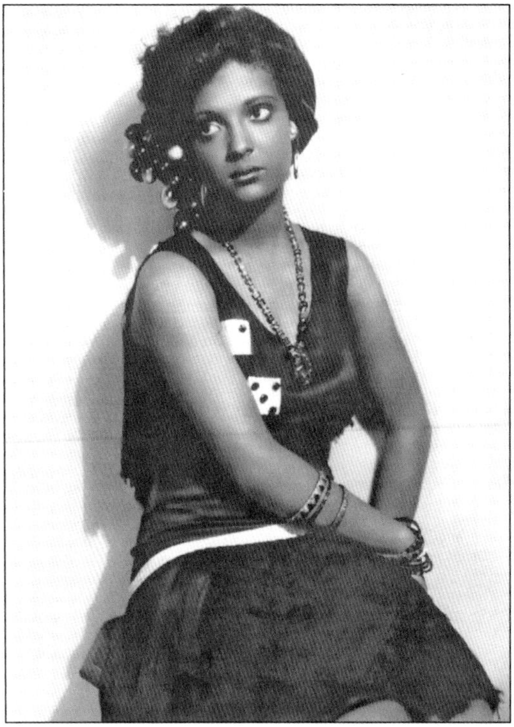

The silver screens of the Walker Theatre presented African Americans with the best that Hollywood had to offer. In 1929, actress Nina Mae McKinney graced the screen in her portrayal of a troubled southern beauty caught up in a problematic relationship with a jealous suitor. This King Vidor film was one of the first African American films produced by a major Hollywood studio.

The airways in Indianapolis crackled with the laughter of the *Amos 'n' Andy* radio program. The stars, Freeman Gosden and Charles Corell, were two white men who created a situation comedy that many felt made buffoonish caricatures of the African American community. When both made public appearances in character, they blackened their faces, bugged their eyes, and spoke in an inarticulate, supposed "Negro dialect." Many African Americans were highly offended and demanded that the show be removed from radio.

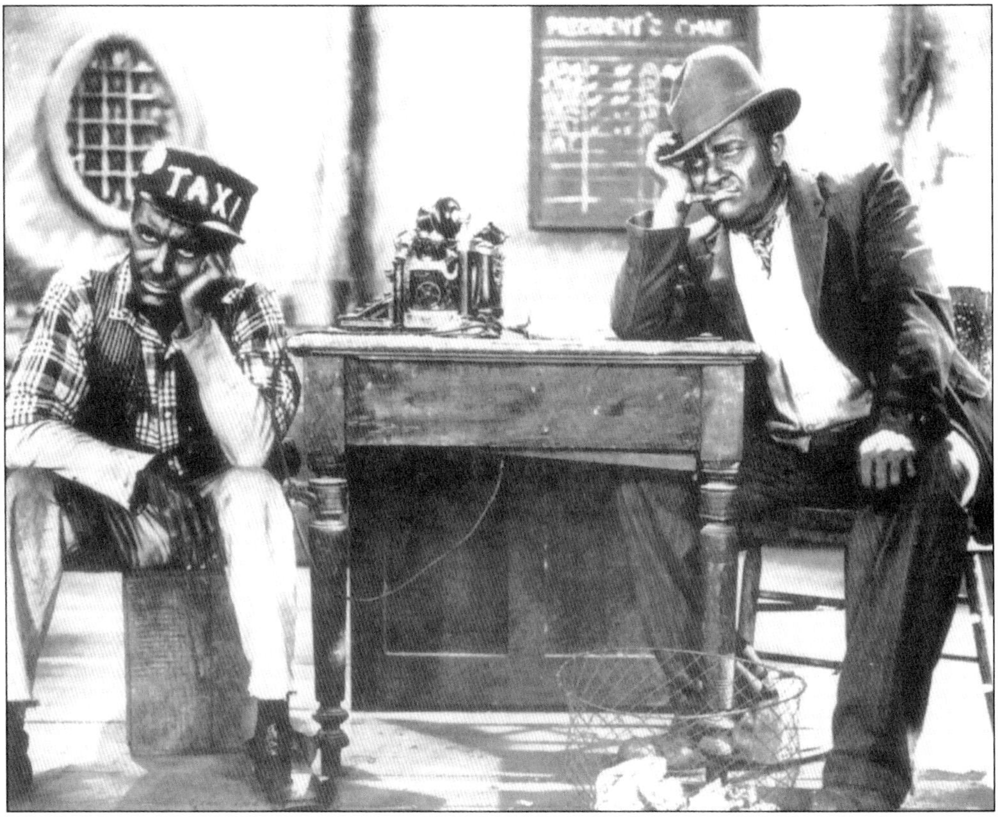

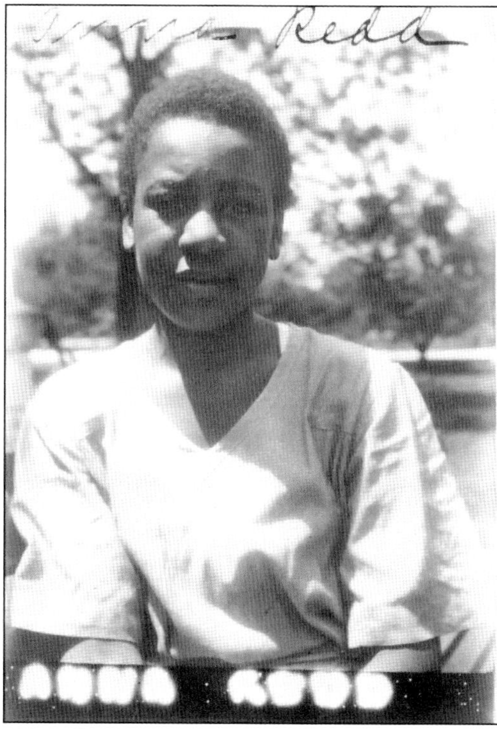

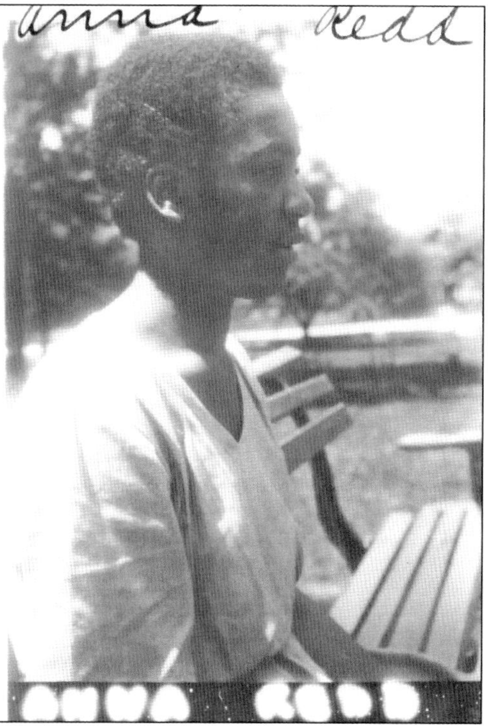

Ida Geller's Tavern, located at 541 Indiana Avenue, was a favorite spot for Anna Redd (above). Although from a well-to-do family that owned two businesses near Indiana Avenue, Redd was a pugilistic ruffian who was known to knock out men or women who got in her way. The patrolwoman Evelyn Ridley (right) was the only person who could control her. In spite of her roughness, she had a very gentle heart and was known to take in and care for homeless dogs and cats that were found outside in the cold. (Right, Tom Ridley.)

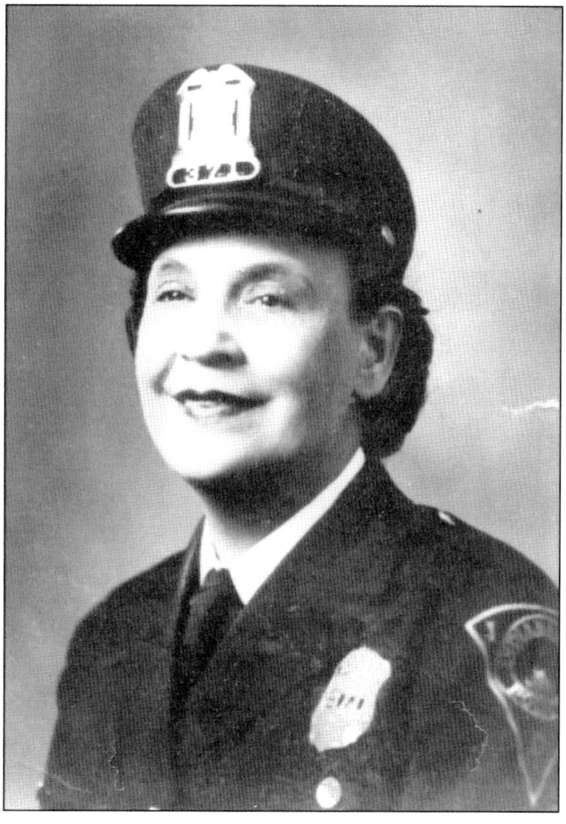

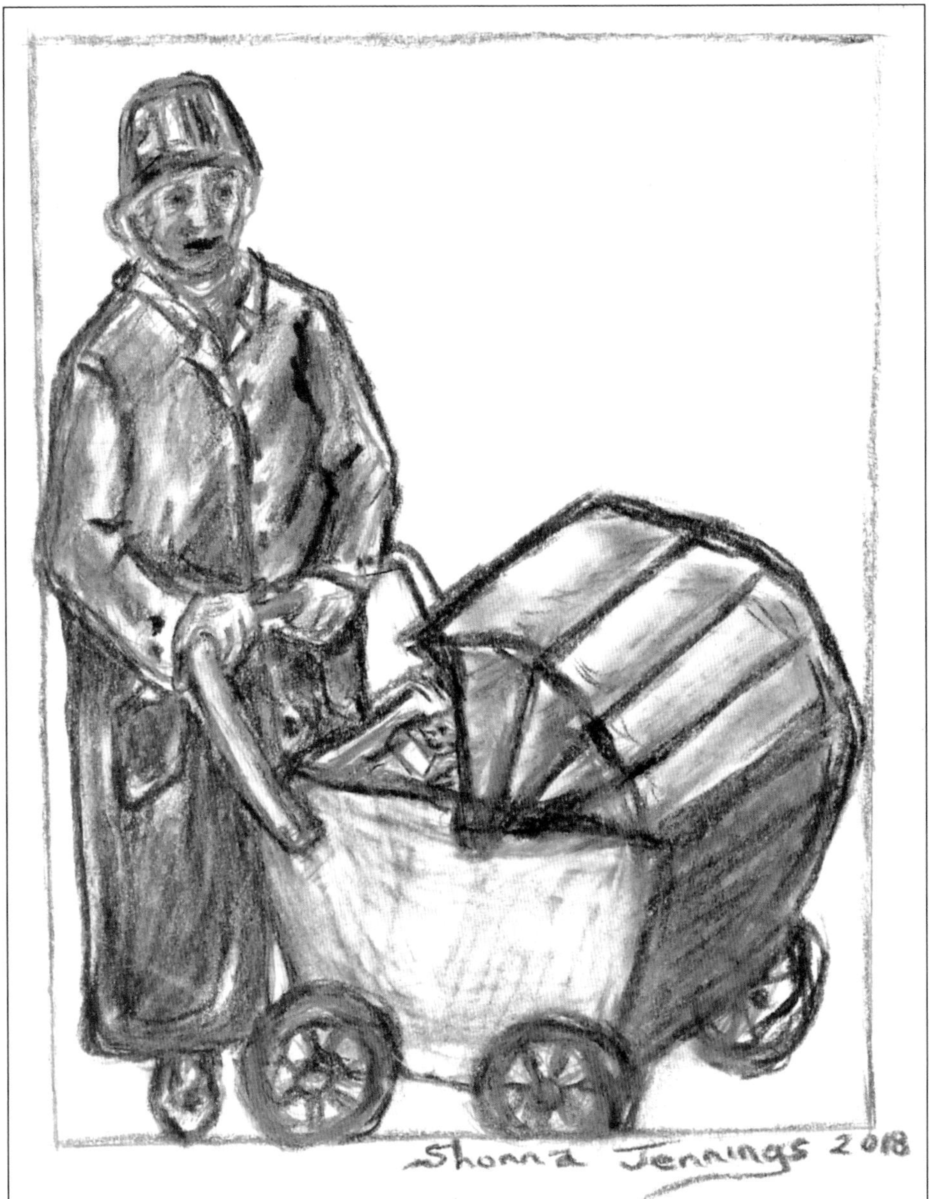

There are many sad stories that seemingly came from a Charles Dickens novel, and the story of "Minnie the Moocher" is one of the most sorrowful. Born Minnie Preston Gayton in Louisville, Kentucky, in 1868, Minnie was destined to achieve great things in life. Trained in classical music, Minnie was the pianist/organist at the leading African American churches. The birth of a child out of wedlock, her congregation's scathing rebuke of her character, and the removal of her position in the church caused Minnie a great deal of emotional distress, which she was not able to cope with. She began a strange nomadic existence on Indiana Avenue with a baby carriage and an imaginary baby inside. She wore many layers of clothes in 100-degree weather, shouted, and cursed people who teased her and threw bricks from her baby buggy at the slightest provocation. Sadly, Minnie died frozen to the sidewalk in front of the home of Mary Coleman, at 753 Indiana Avenue, on November 6, 1951. (Shonna Jennings.)

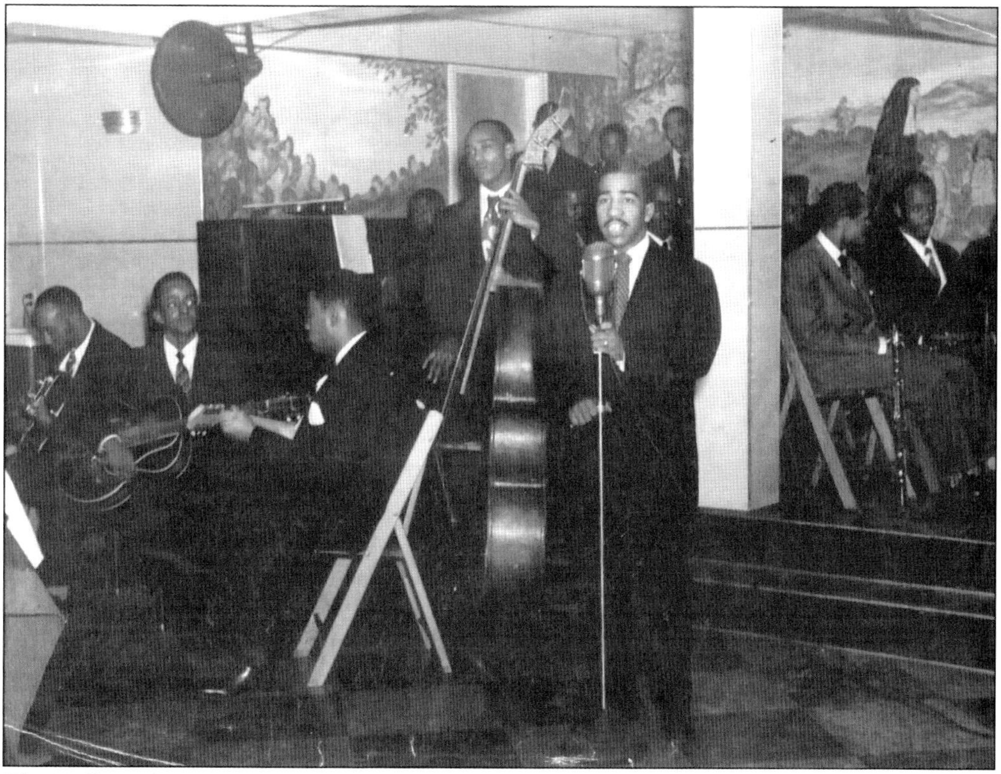

The Walker Christmas show showcased several entertainers who were residents of the Lockefield Gardens public housing development. One such person was Ray Foster, who appeared in many of the venues on Indiana Avenue, then later relocated to New York and sang with internationally renowned crooner Al Hibbler. His signature song was Hoagy Carmichael's "Skylark." (Indiana Historical Society.)

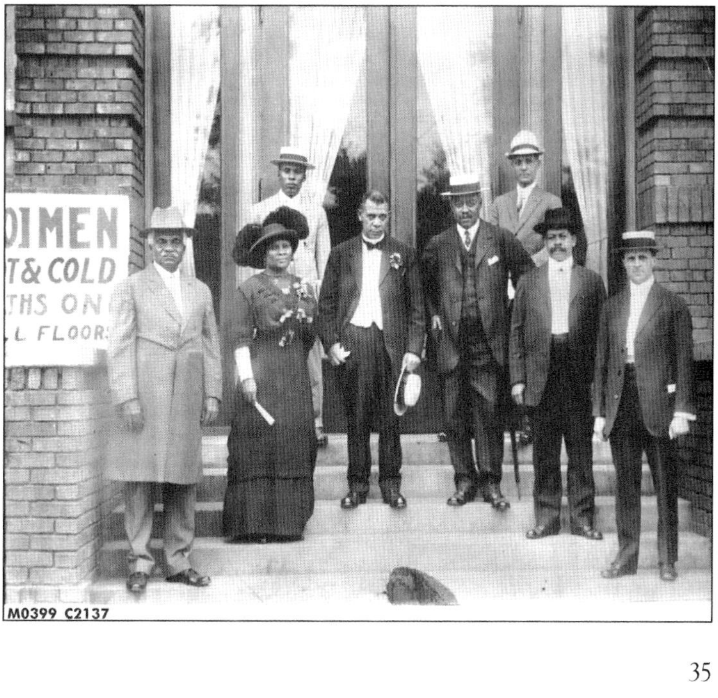

The Senate Avenue YMCA was established in the early 20th century and was dedicated to the uplift of the African American community. (Indiana Avenue Historical Society.)

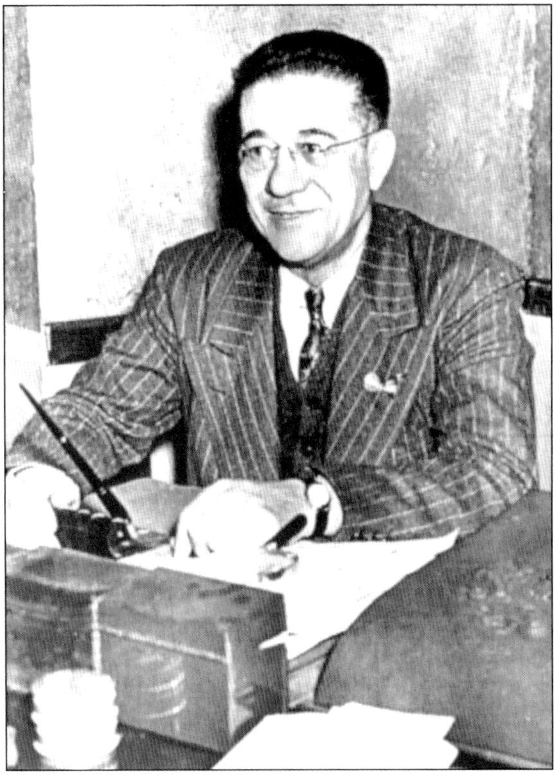

In 1913, Faburn DeFrantz relocated to Indianapolis from Topeka, Kansas, and took the position as physical director of the Senate Avenue YMCA. Three years later, he was appointed the branch executive secretary and served in this position for 36 years. DeFrantz was a trail blazer in the arena of civil rights and spent many years combating all forms of racial discrimination in Indianapolis. In October 1924, David Curtis Stephenson, the grand dragon of the Indiana Ku Klux Klan, planned a parade down Indiana Avenue in full regalia. According to David DeFrantz, Faburn's grandson, "Granddad approached Stephenson at his headquarters to emphatically demand that the Klan must not march down Indiana Avenue with their hoods. Before DeFrantz could reach Stephenson, a klan bodyguard intervened to block him. He picked up the bodyguard and moved him out of the way."

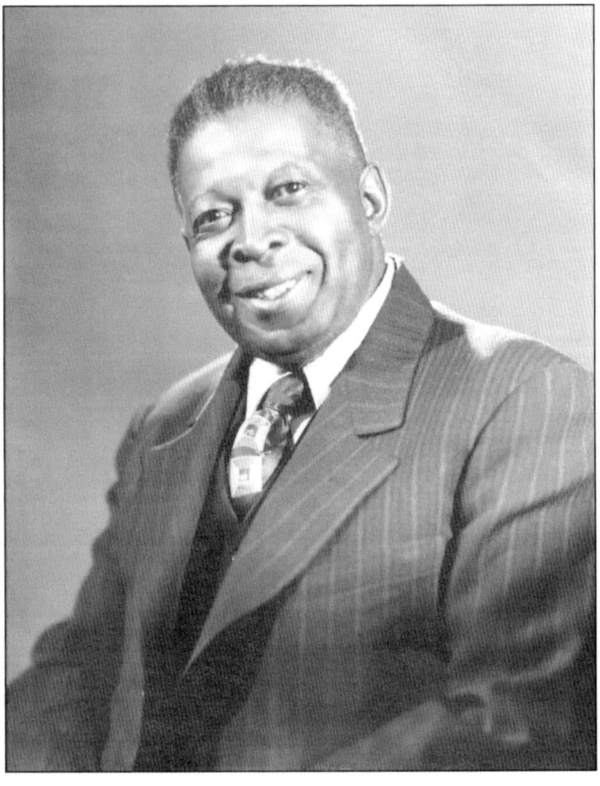

The Harris Brother Photography Studio, a brown stucco brick structure at 631 North West Street, was founded by Charles Kingsley Harris and his wife, Johnnie M. Harris, in 1917. Johnnie managed the business for five years before the death of her husband in 1952. Charles (pictured) was a very prominent civic leader and member of the NAACP. (Indiana Historical Society.)

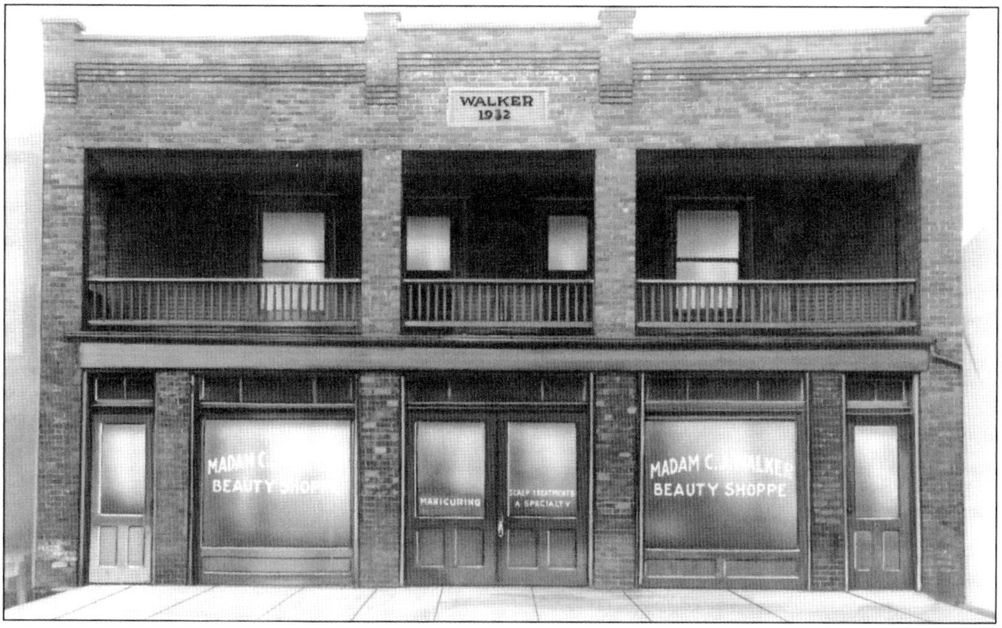

Located directly across West Street from the Phyliss Wheatley YWCA sat the building that housed the Madame C.J. Walker Manufacturing Company. Shipments of beauty-culture products were prepared, packaged, and shipped from this site. Throughout the day and late into the evening, small trucks exited the back alley and headed to the Union Station downtown to deliver shipments to be sent around the country. (Indiana Historical Society.)

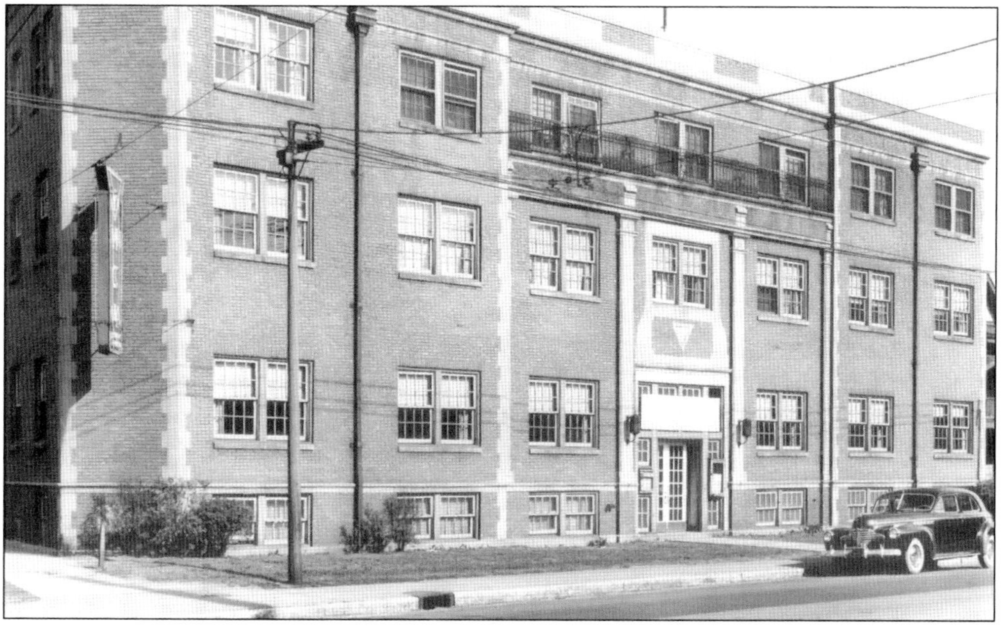

On January 1, 1923, a group of African American women established the Phyllis Wheatley YWCA at 640 North West Street, directly across the street from the residence of Madame C. J. Walker. Named in honor of the 18th-century African American poet, its goal was to empower black women by providing educational, cultural, occupational, and recreational programs to equip them to successfully compete in the employment market. (Indiana Historical Society.)

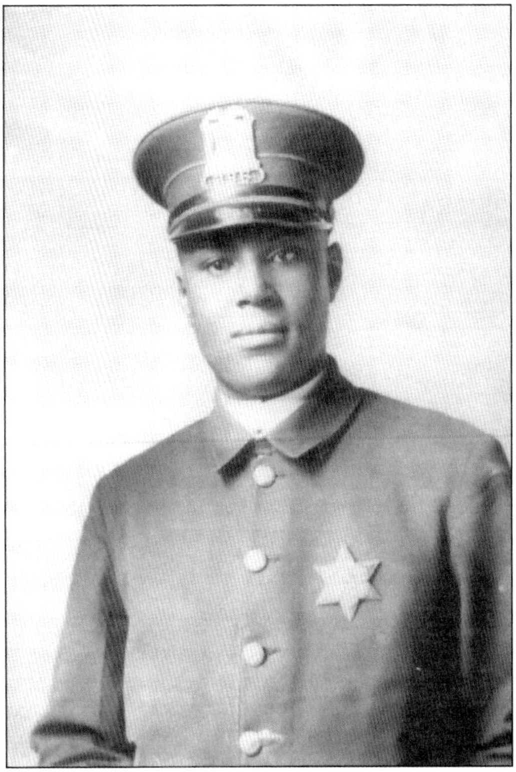

Indianapolis old-timers always had a grin on their face and twinkle in their eyes when they reminisced about the days of patrolman Jesse "Jack" Hadley on Indiana Avenue. According to Indianapolis historian Patrick R. Pearsey, "Hadley's first assignment was 'Old District 35,' an area between 9th and 16th Streets and Capitol Avenue. On one occasion Hadley arrested over twelve hardened gamblers, confiscated their money and dice and loaded them in the paddy wagon for transport to jail single-handedly." Legend has it that Hadley entered the room of the gambling joint and stood in the doorway and was so big and fat that none of the 12 gamblers could pass him. As they approached the door, he knocked them down. Jack Hadley was an Indiana Avenue personality feared by all on the wrong side of the law. (Indianapolis Metro Police Department, Lichtenberger History Room.)

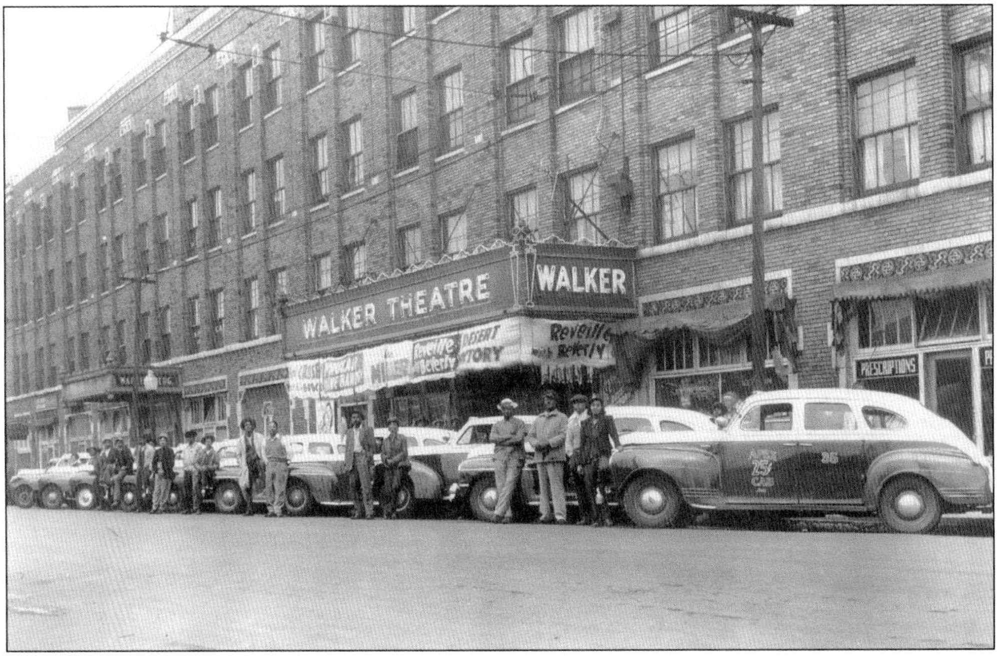

The matinee performances at the Walker Theatre were a special treat for many on Indiana Avenue. After the performances, many of the social elite ladies gathered on the bottom floor in an area called the Coffee Pot. Pictured here are taxi drivers awaiting customers in the late 1940s. (Tony Stuart.)

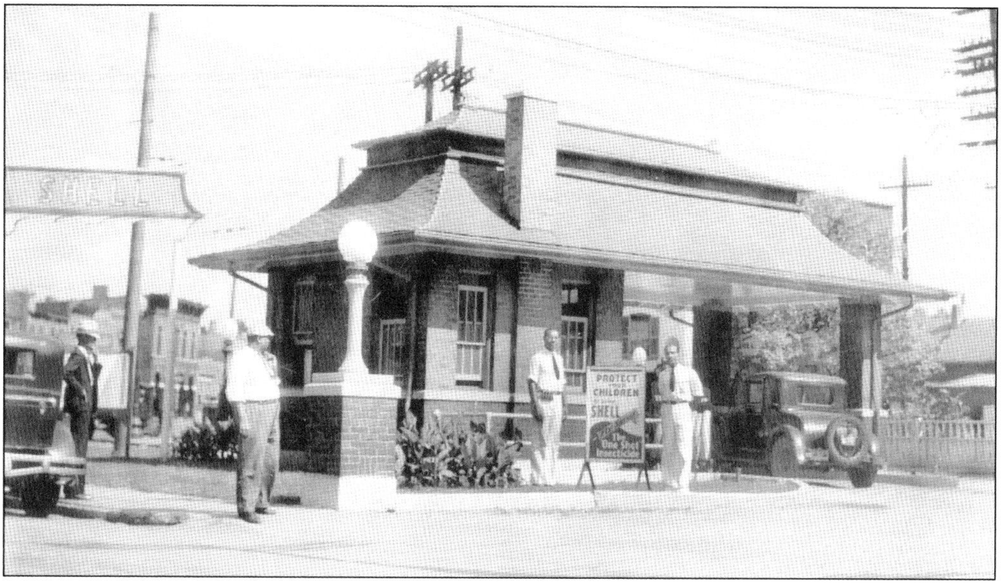

The Shell gas station was located across the street from the Walker Theatre. (Tom Ridley.)

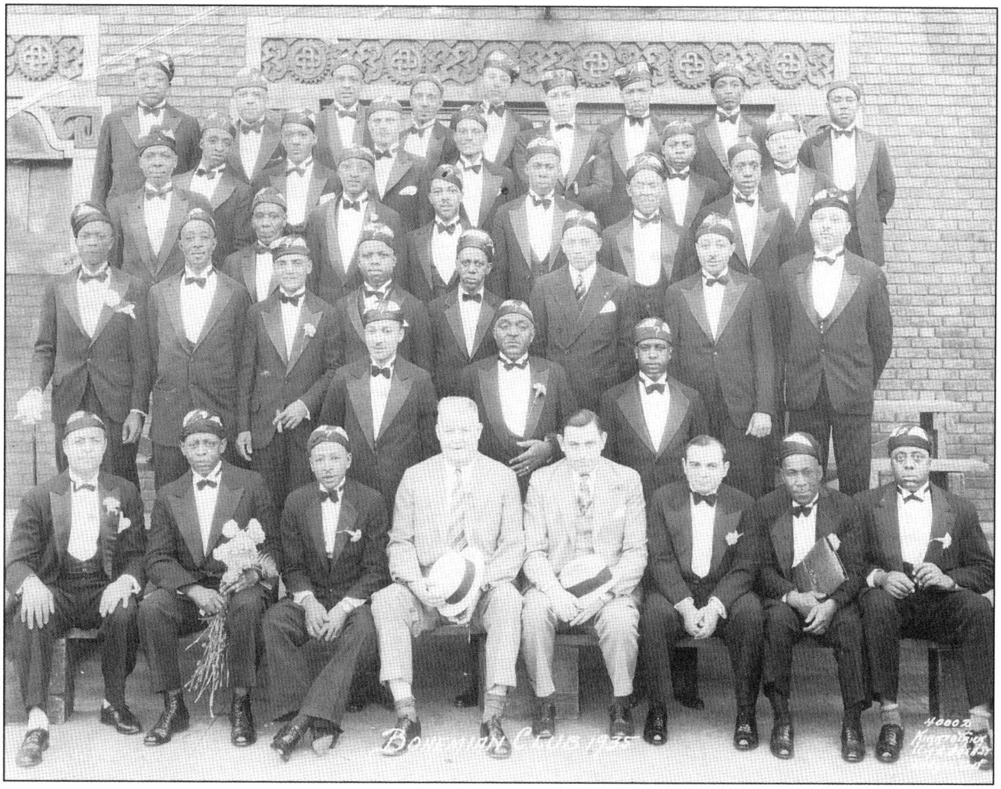

The Bohemian Club was organized in the late 1920s and was comprised of many religious and civic leaders who were dedicated to improving living conditions in the African American community by networking with various churches and civic organizations. This photograph was taken in the early 1930s in front of the Walker Theatre; businessman Joe Mitchell is third from the right in the first row.

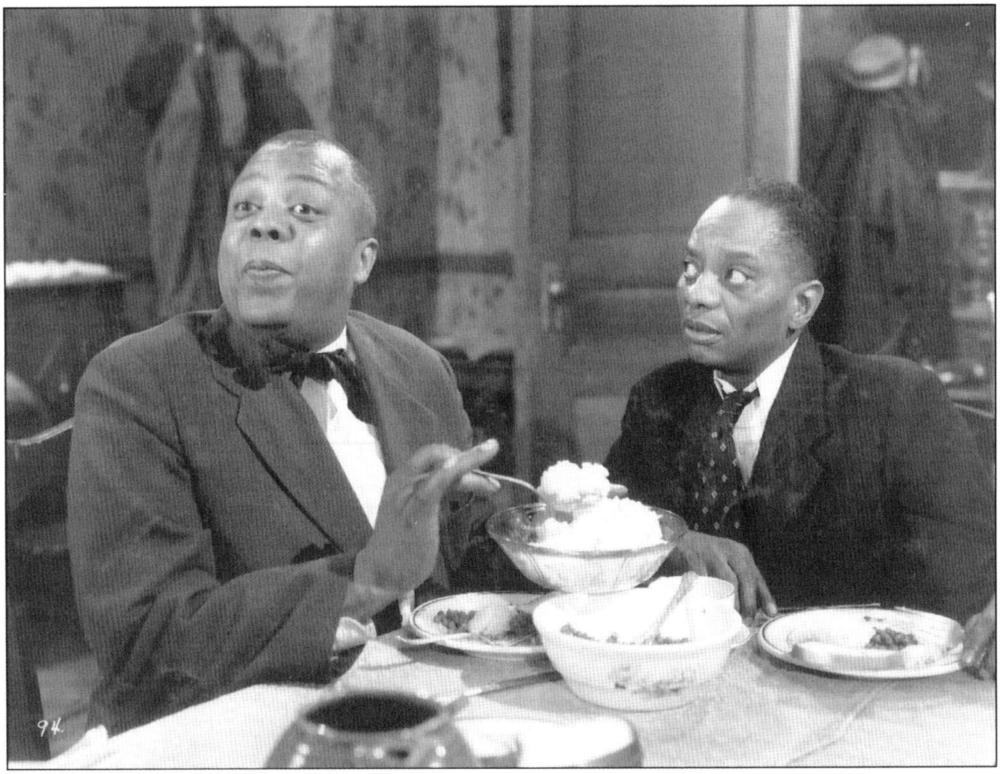

Pictured here are two comedians in a scene from a motion picture that played at the Walker Theatre around 1945. (Trevor Bacon Jr.)

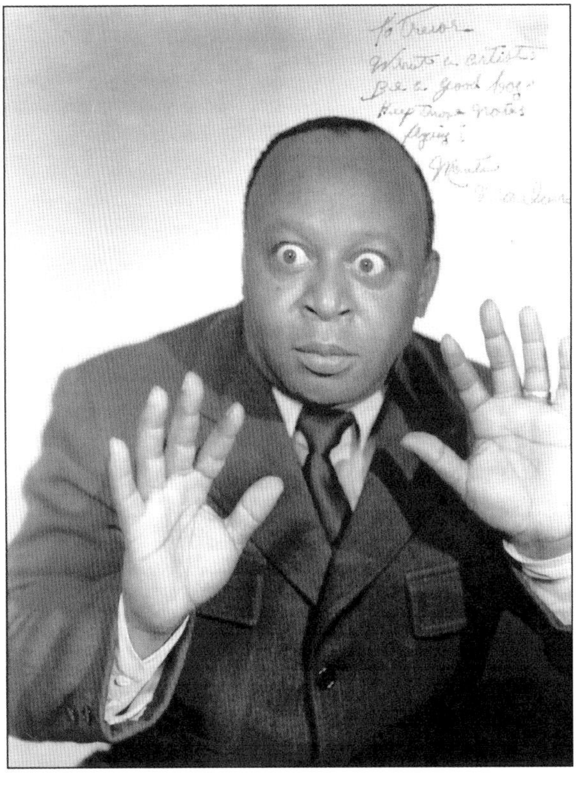

Walker Theatre patrons laughed their heads off at the hilarious routines of Mantan Moreland on the silver screen. With his bug-eyed, terrified persona, many folks considered these screen images quite amusing. Other, more socially conscious moviegoers regarded Moreland's Teppin' Fetchit' and Willie Best as racist, stereotypical caricatures of the African American male. These caricatures proved to be very lucrative to some Hollywood studios. Moreland appeared with Ray Charles at the Sunset Terrace Ballroom in June 1954.

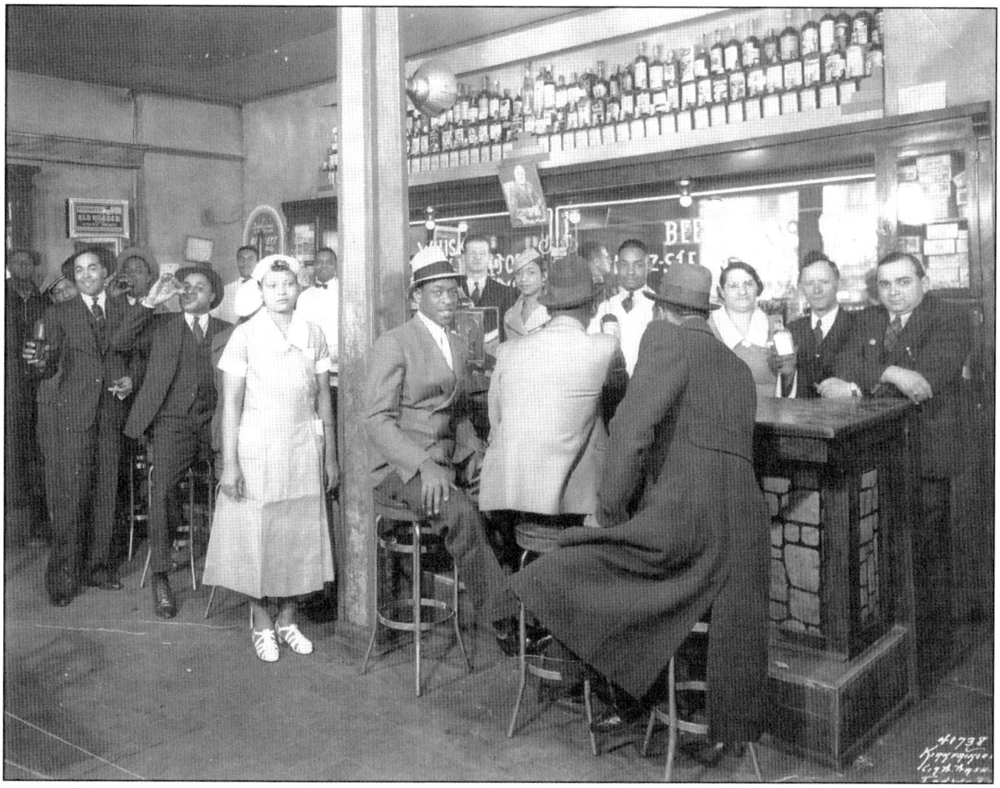

Joe Mitchell's Mitchellyne Tavern was owned and operated by Mitchell, a Russian Jew whose family escaped their homeland in the early 20th century and relocated to Indiana Avenue. He was loved by the patrons of Indiana Avenue for his kindness and willingness to help those in need. His brother Isaac "Tuffy" Mitchell (right), an Indiana Avenue businessman and entertainment promoter, owned several nightclubs, including the Pink Poodle, which was wildly popular and brought Hollywood-style entertainment to Indiana Avenue. (Both, Joe Mitchell.)

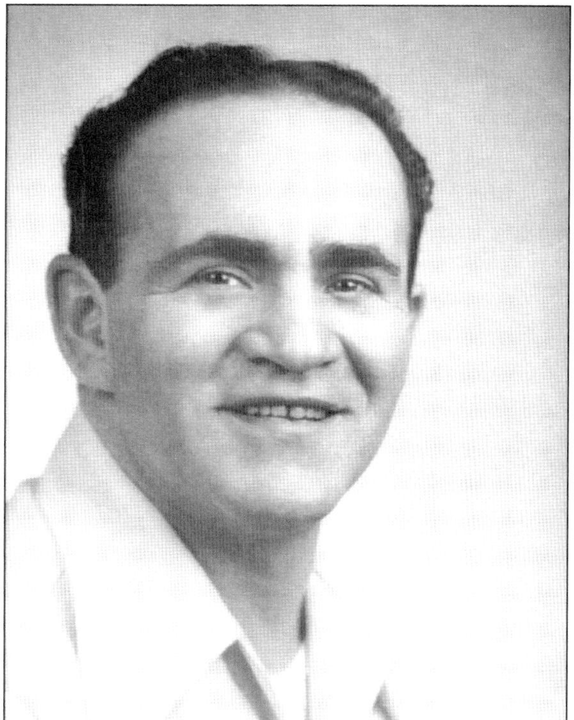

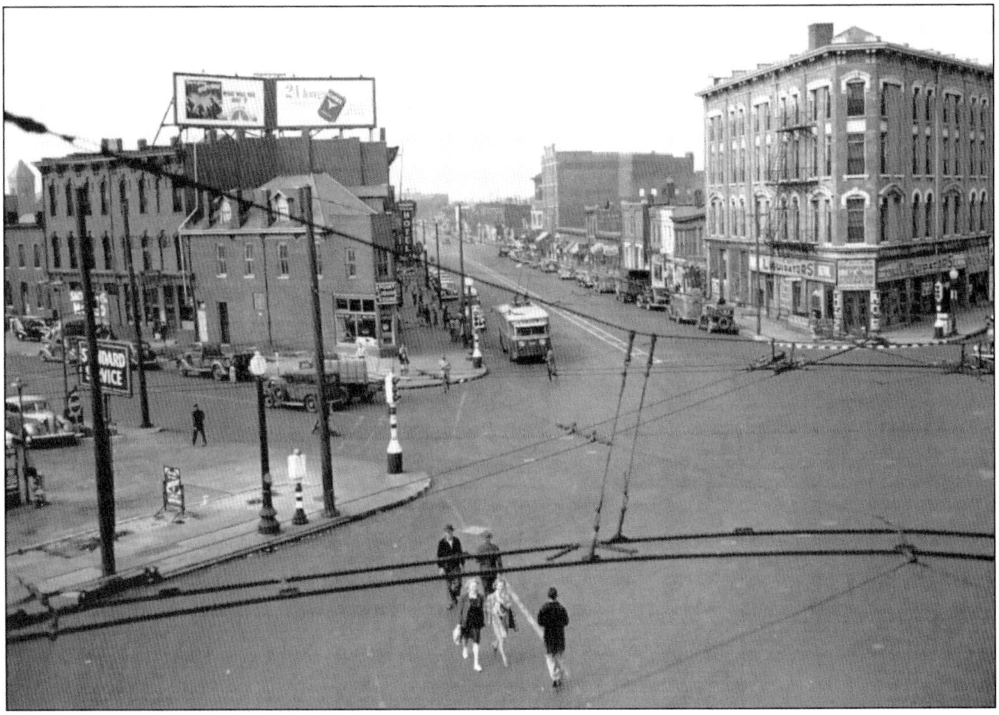

These two photographs of Indiana Avenue are from the late 1940s. Pictured above is the intersection of Indiana Avenue and Ohio and Illinois Streets. Below is the intersection of Indiana Avenue and Capitol and Illinois Streets. Known as the "Point," many of the businesses here were owned by people of eastern European descent, and the customers were racially, religiously, and culturally diverse. As one walked down the Avenue, within one block, they often heard 10 to 20 different languages spoken. One *Indiana Recorder* reporter referred to Indiana Avenue as the "Tower of Babel." (Both, Indiana Historical Society.)

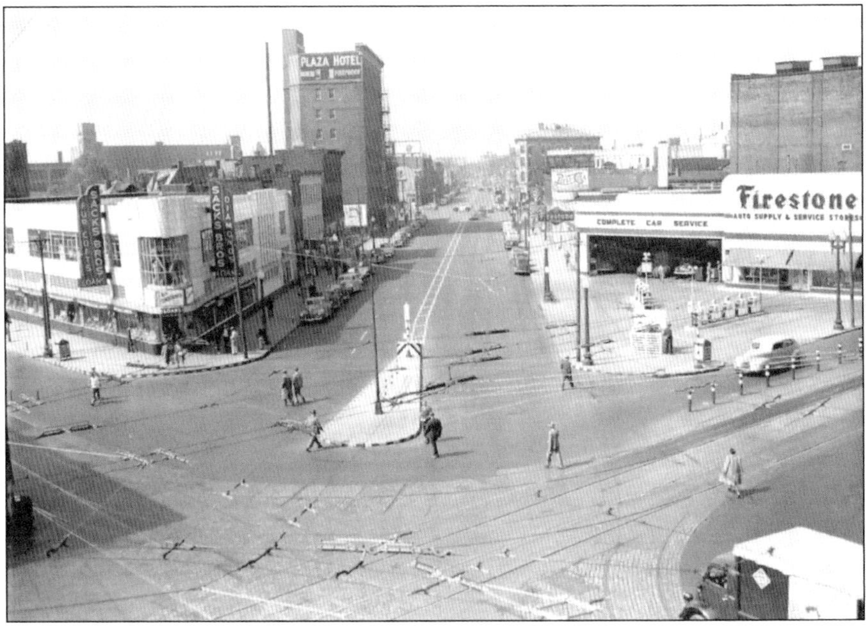

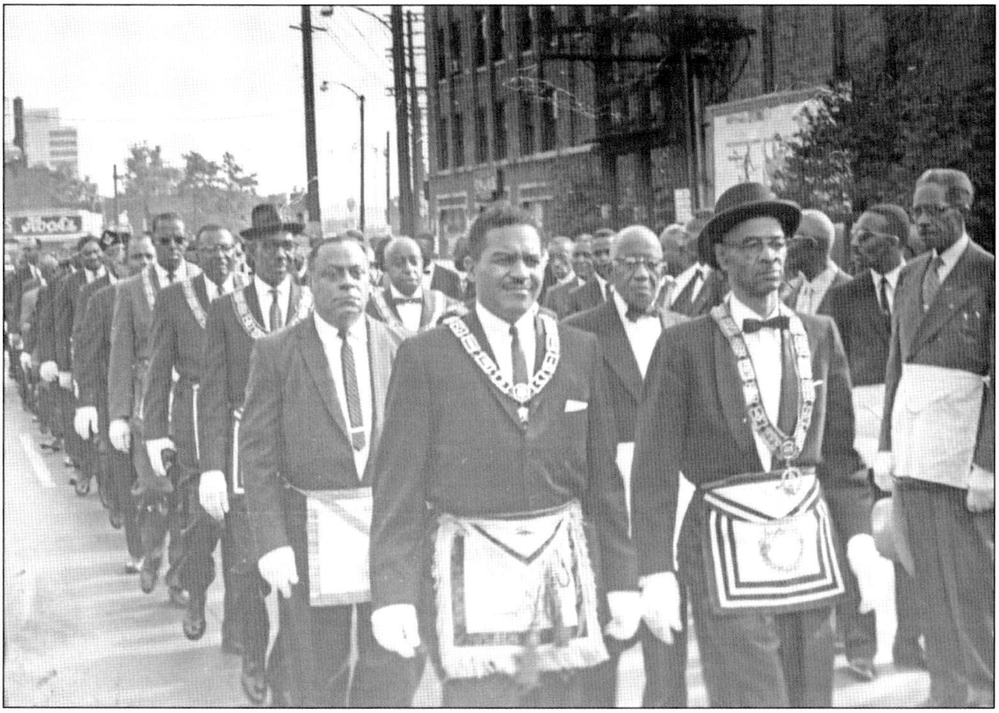

During the 1960s, the end of summer was marked by a wonderful parade. Many of the fraternal, civic, and business organizations marched with pride down Indiana Avenue to a cheering and appreciative crowd. The Prince Hall Masons and the Persian Shriner's Band were the centerpieces of this festive occasion. (Both, Indiana Historical Society.)

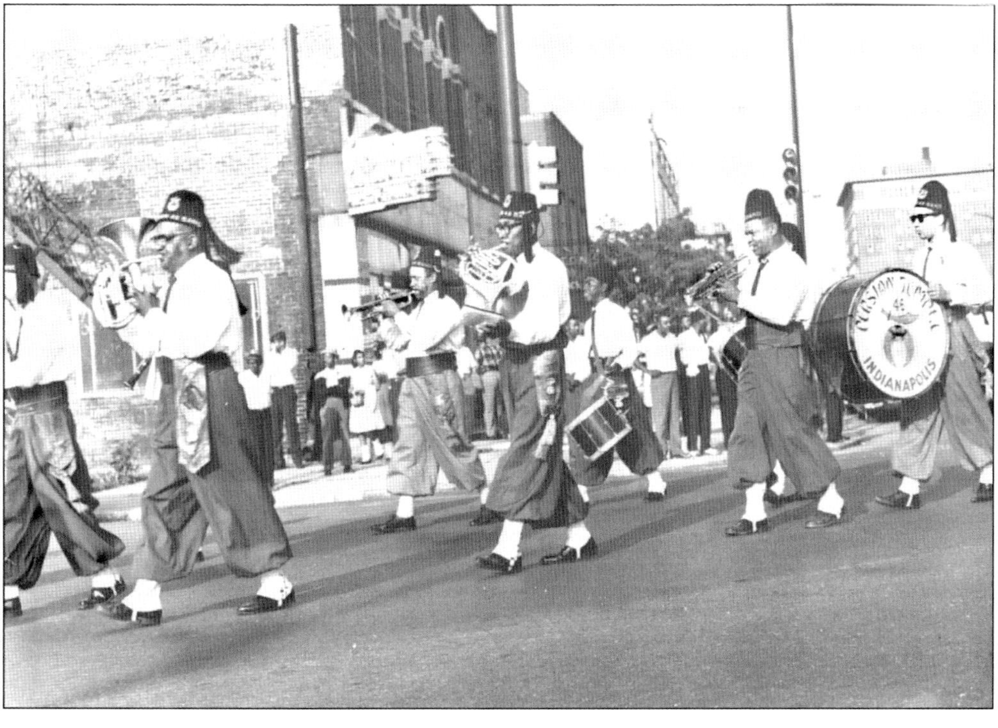

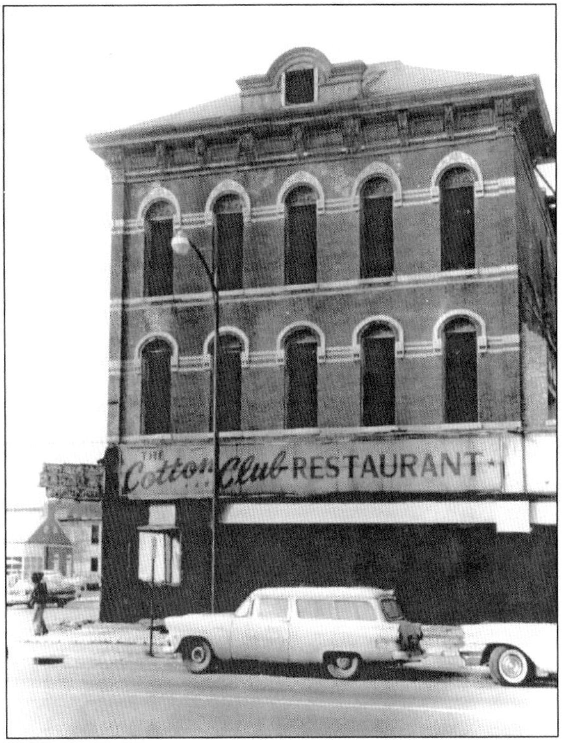

The *Indianapolis Recorder* of March 15, 1941, announced the grand opening of the Cotton Club: "Enjoy rhythmic dance, music during dinner. . . . Enjoy your Favorite Tune from a swing band, see a Big Time Floor Show." Located on the corner of Vermont and Senate Streets, there were actually two clubs in one. The top floor was the Trianon Ballroom, and the bottom floor was the Cotton Club. Both clubs advertised "electrically prepared meals and dancing." The grand opening featured the bands of Buddy Bryant and Clarence Love. (Larry Goshen.)

From the 1930s to the 1950s, the Mon-Tee Grill was a favorite gathering spot for Indiana Avenue patrons who enjoyed cigars, liquor, and fine food. Pictured here is the establishment around the mid-1950s. Many rhythm-and-blues aficionados went there after dances at the Walker Casino.

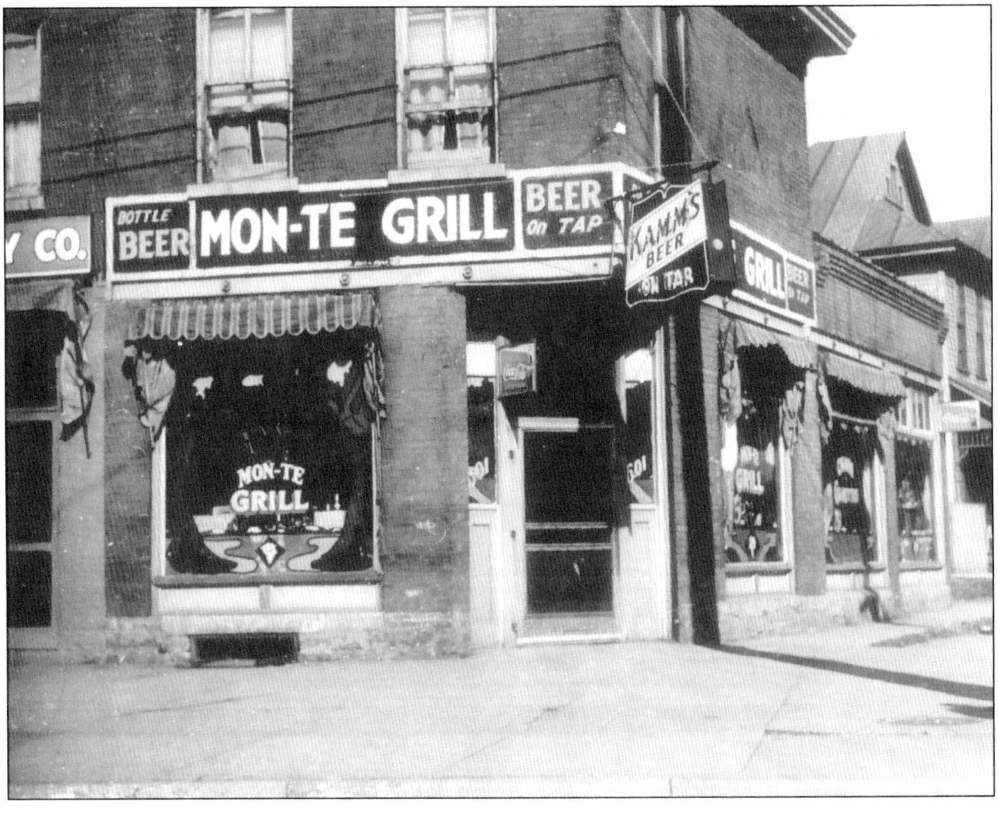

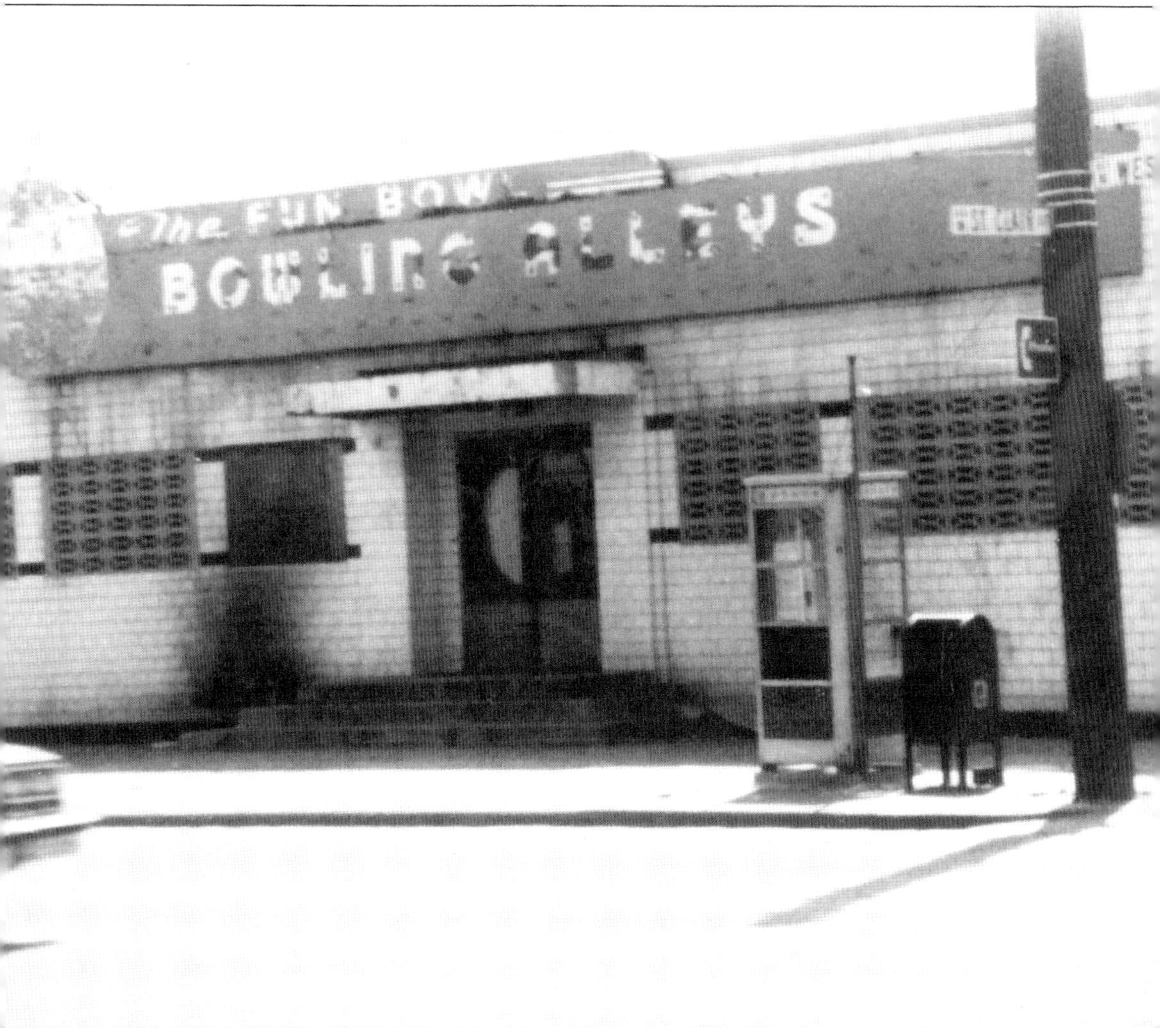

On March 21, 1942, the *Indianapolis Recorder* announced the grand opening of Sea Ferguson's Fun Bowl at 740 North West Street.

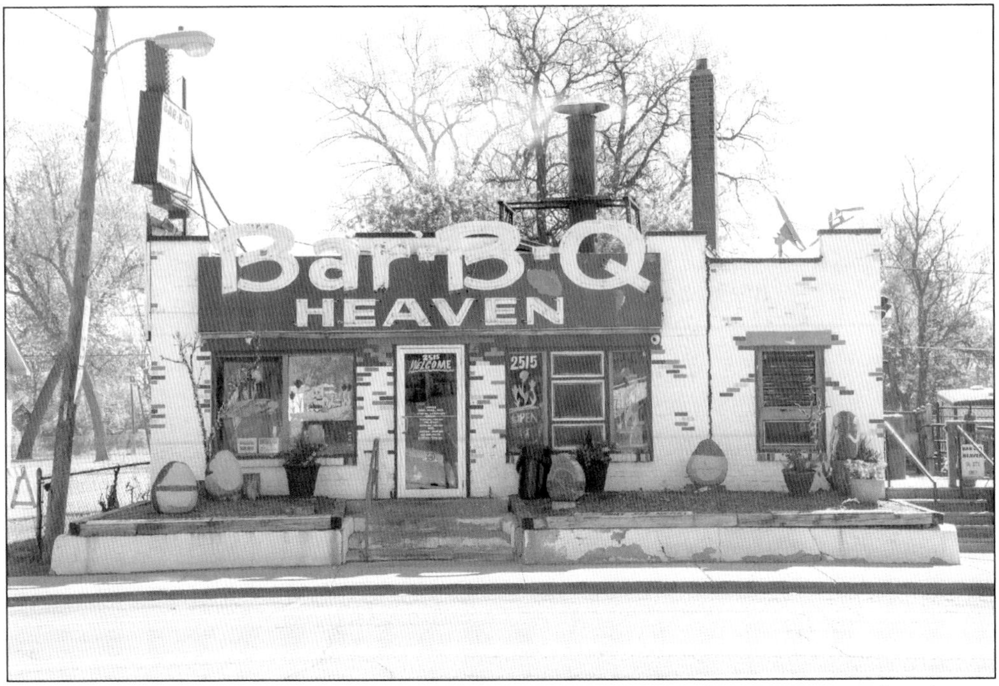

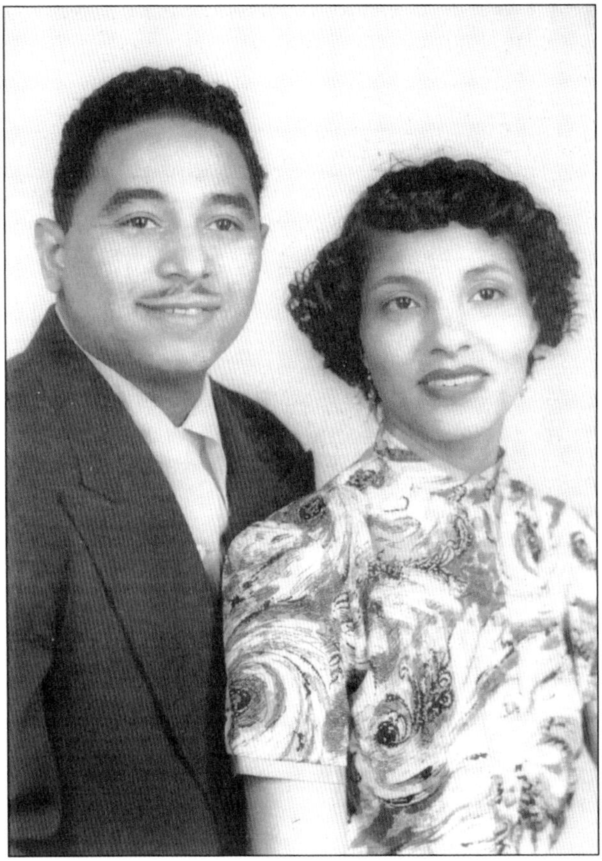

Bar B-Q Heaven opened its doors in 1952 and was originally located in a small, white cinder-block building owned by Mary Rapier next door to the Sportsmen's Bar, at 836 Indiana Avenue. It was one of Indiana Avenue's most successful businesses, and Avenue residents were proud of the fact that it provided high-quality food in a very congenial atmosphere where everyone smiled. Folks lined up sidewalk deep at the door to taste the delicious mouth-watering barbecue, chili, pastries, and other dishes. Ronald Jones, son of the owners, Forrest and Mary Jones (left) fondly remembered that many Hollywood stars dropped by their business during their stints in Indianapolis and thoroughly enjoyed the food. Among the stars were blues vocalist Big Maybelle and comedians Jackie "Moms" Mabley and Redd Foxx. (Both, Ronald Jones.)

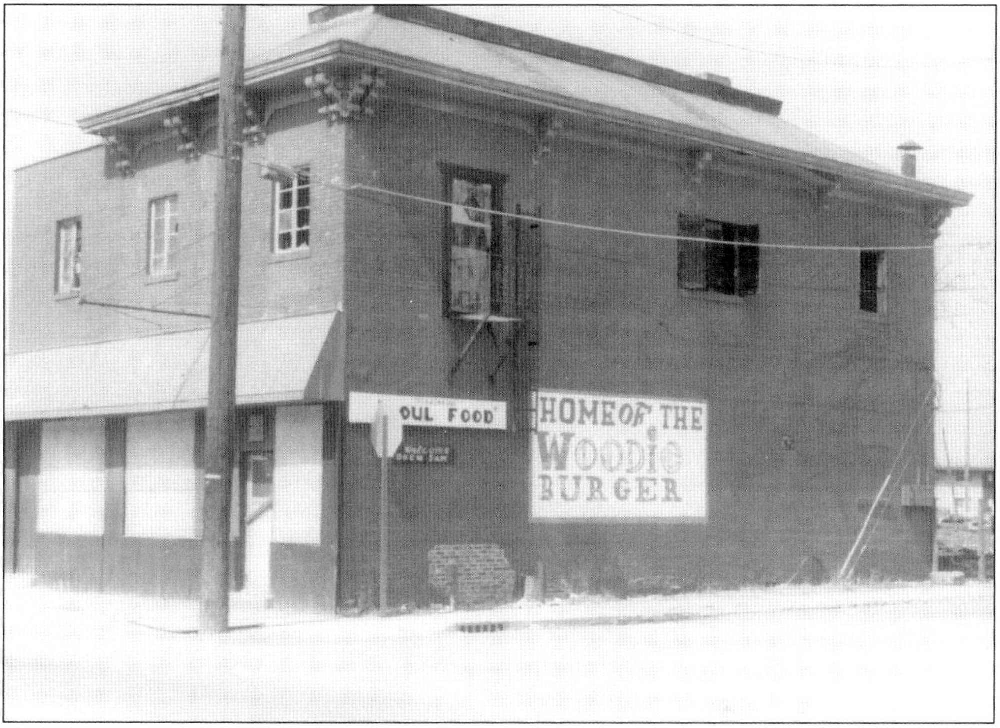

The Sunset Pool Room occupied the corner of Blake Street and Indiana Avenue in the 1950s and 1960s. Later, the establishment became Woodie's, known for its tasty hamburgers.

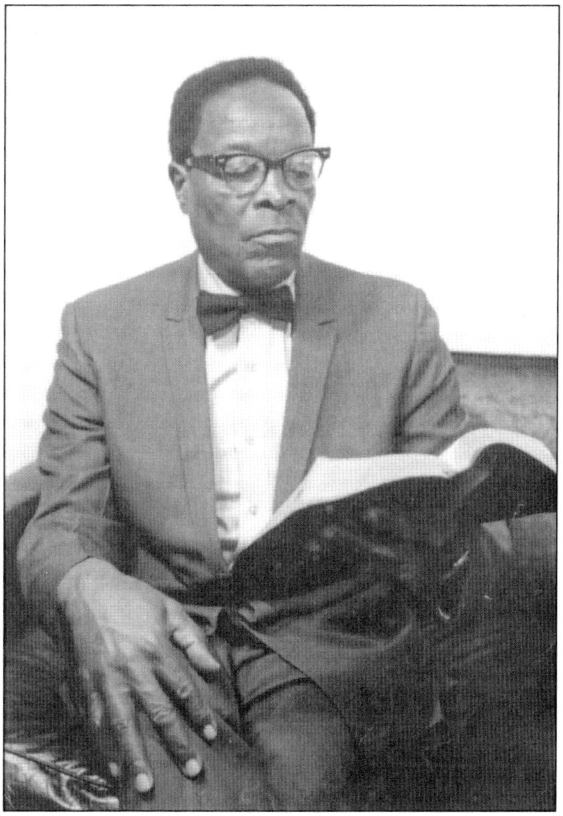

Amidst the screaming siren of an ambulance racing up and down Indiana Avenue to all corners of the city and the clamor of bootleg cab drivers arguing over a fare at their makeshift stand across the street from the Chew 'n' Chat restaurant, one heard a voice over a crackling public address system: Rev. Tanner Robert Murff. For many years, he held summer tent revivals on the corner of Indiana Avenue and Bright Street. He was a powerful preacher and had the ability to pull people from other churches, to the chagrin of many well-established men of God. In the pulpit, Elder Murff's dramatic theatrics and fire-and-brimstone preaching had a spellbinding effect on members of the audience, and many joined his church on the spot. (Indiana Historical Society.)

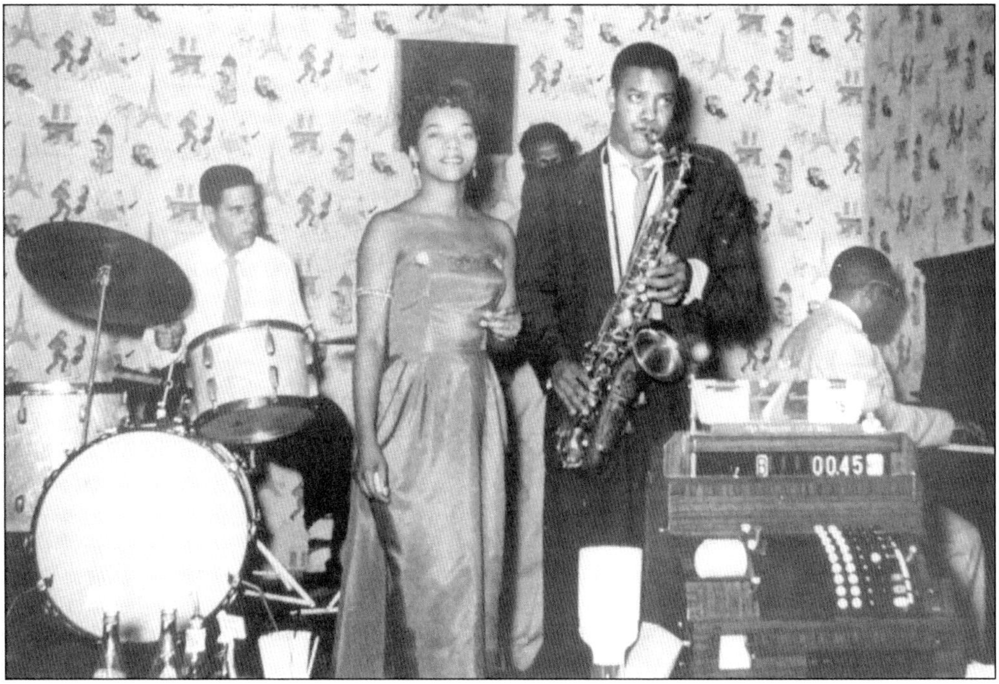

Lola Barbee was a petite, sweet, and sultry vocalist who came to town from Darby, Pennsylvania, and thrilled Indiana Avenue. She appeared in many venues on and off the Avenue, and her signature songs were "Wishing Well," "Mama," and "Don't Do It." In the *Indianapolis Recorder* musicians poll of 1953, which rated the top entertainers of Indiana Avenue, she was voted the top female vocalist. On many gigs, she was backed by the Buddy Parker Combo or the Count Fisher Combo. Unfortunately, Barbee died as the result of a domestic dispute in February 1955.

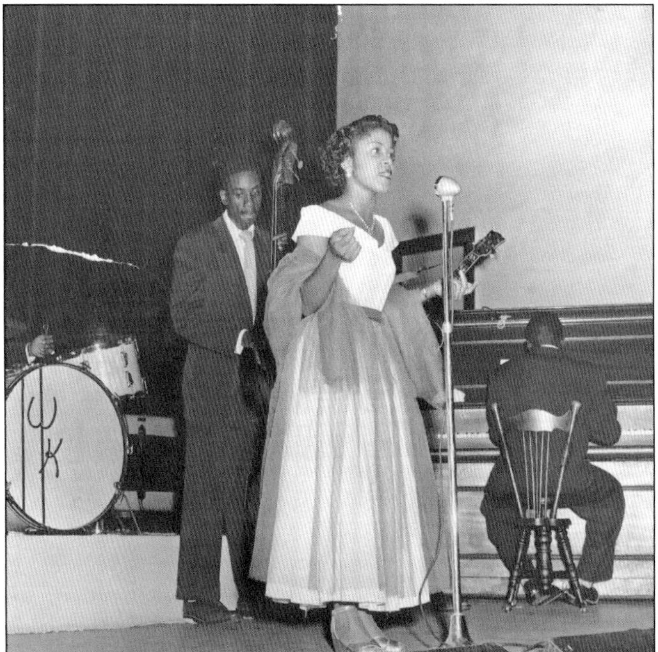

Great entertainers come in small packages, some might say. Beatrice Byers was a small package. This attractive, diminutive vocalist who stood barely over five feet was a graduate of Crispus Attucks High School and West Virginia State College, where she majored in music. She later joined the Women's Army Corp and graduated from basic training in February 1955. Byers was one of the top vocalists on Indiana Avenue and active in many musical programs sponsored by the Prince Hall Masons and Persian Shriners.

Two

Rhythm and Blues Meets Indiana Avenue

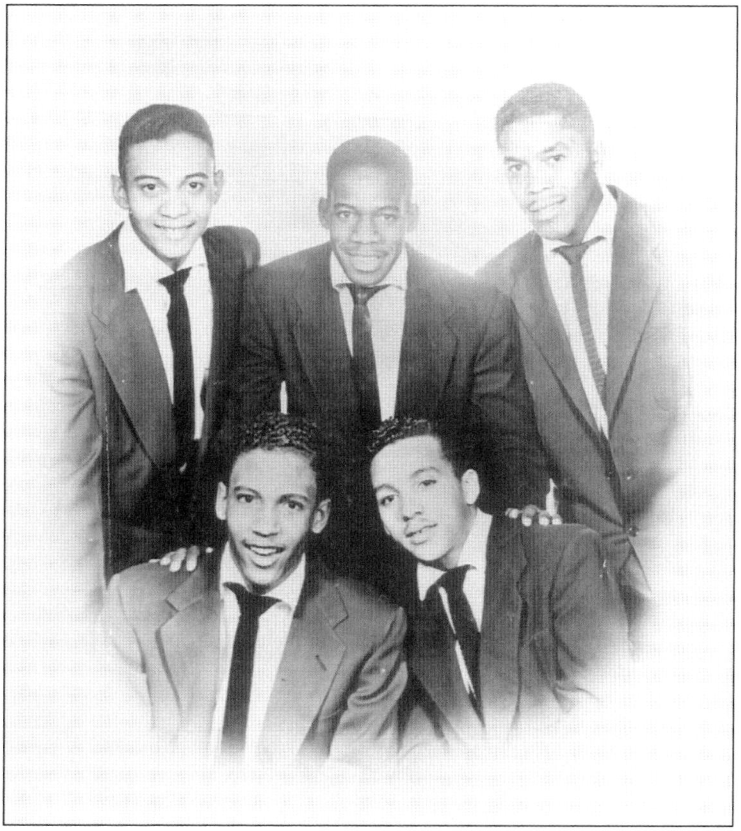

The Counts organized in 1953 and consisted of Chester Brown, Bobby Young, Robert Wesley, Bobby Penick, and James Lee. Originally called the Five Diamonds, the group quickly chose another moniker since a popular Canadian rhythm-and-blues group had already recorded and performed with that name. Their signature song "Darling Dear" was released in 1954 and began a meteoric climb up the national music charts; in two months, it reached the No. 6 spot on the *Billboard* Hot 100.

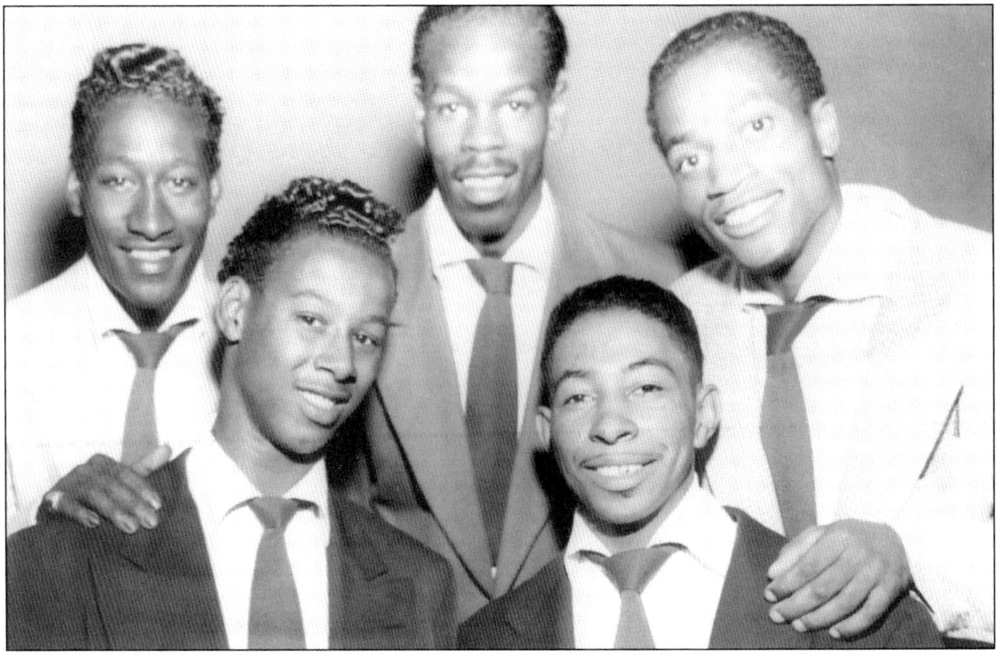

The success and celebrity of the Counts encouraged other Indiana Avenue vocal groups to test the waters of show business and try to gain recognition on the local music scene. One such group was the Five Dots, organized by Thurston Harris, a promising rhythm-and-blues singer. The Five Dots consisted of, from left to right, (first row) Harry Blackwell and DeWayne Harris; (second row) Bernard Harris, Jimmy Pierson, and Jimmy Scruggs. They performed in many of the clubs on Indiana Avenue including the annual Indianapolis Recorder Christmas Benefit Show, Walker Casino, and the Military Park Summer Music Extravaganza. Their performances were well-received, and this led to the signing of a contract with Mel Herman of Note Records. The Five Dots recorded six songs on this label with "Each Night and Every Night" being the most memorable.

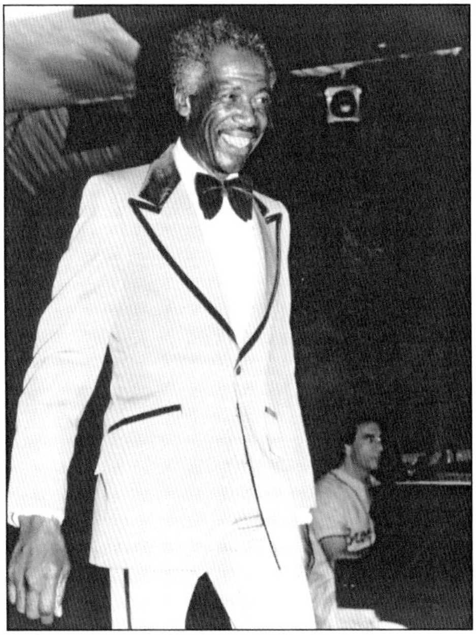

Thurston Harris was an Indiana Avenue rhythm-and-blues singer who performed with many of the early 1950s groups who were influenced by Louie Jordan, Little Richard, the Platters, and the Flamingos. However, in 1957, he became an overnight sensation with the release of the Bobby Day classic "Little Bitty Pretty One." It charted at the No. 2 position on the national rhythm-and-blues poll and No. 6 on the *Billboard* Hot 100. In 1972, it was covered by Gary, Indiana, natives the Jackson Five.

Appearing in the Apollo and Paramount Theaters in New York and the Uptown Theater in Philadelphia was much more than a stone's throw from Indiana Avenue. The Four Sounds—from left to right, William Harris, Jimmy Scruggs, Jimmy Guilford, and Kenny Moore—were the toast of the town in the rhythm-and-blues circles in Indianapolis. They recorded signature tunes such as "The Ring," "Peter Gunn," and "Fool that I Am." They also appeared locally in the Pink Poodle, whose owner, Isaac "Tuffy" Mitchell, was their manager. (Jimmy Guilford.)

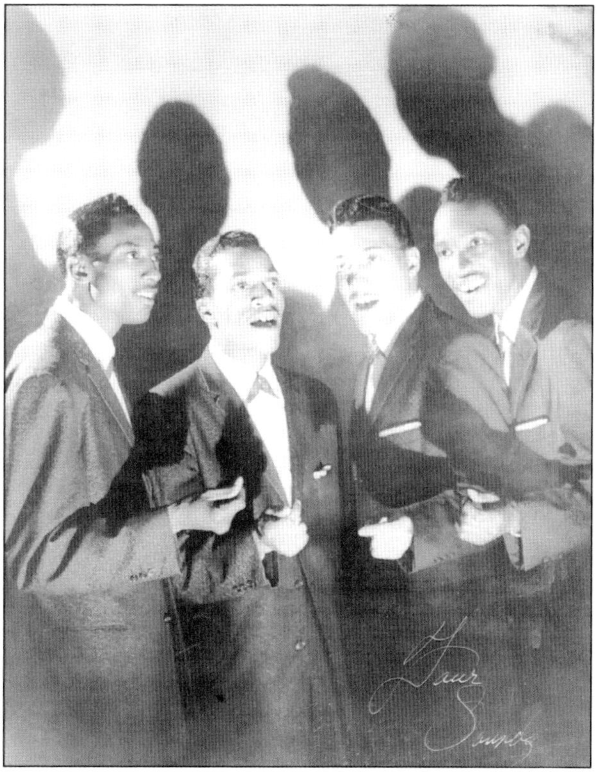

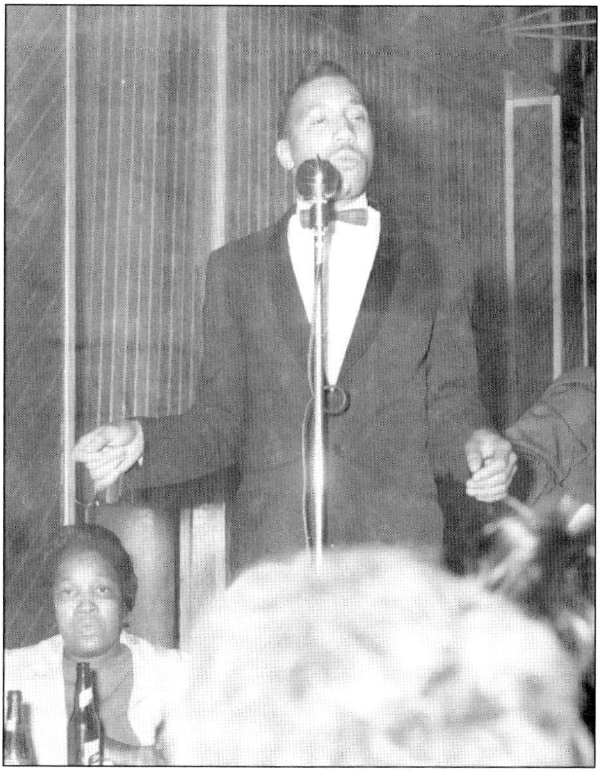

A young east-side teenager who came to Indiana Avenue daily to practice as a Copper Glove contestant in the Senate Avenue YMCA boxing program, Jimmy Guilford was bitten by the entertainment bug. He passed by the clubs on his daily jaunt to the YMCA and was captivated by the great music that escaped those venues. Years later, he performed with the world-renowned Ink Spots, Billy Ward and his Dominoes, Thurston Harris, the Lamplighters, and the Four Sounds. He was a regular headliner at the annual Recorder Christmas Show. (Jimmy Guilford.)

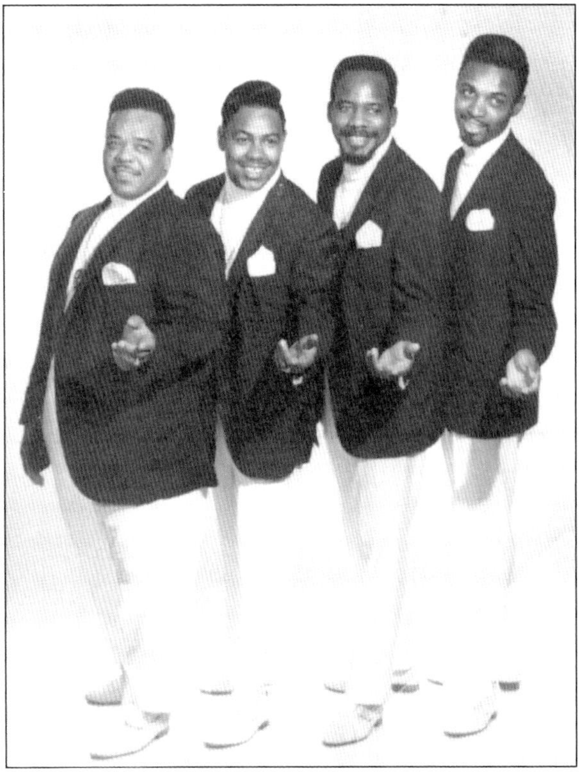

The entertainment bug did not necessarily stay around Indiana Avenue. Occasionally, it flew to the east side to Arsenal Technical High School and took up residence. The Monograms, a rhythm-and-blues group in the mid-1950s, was extremely popular with teenage music lovers. The original members were Clarence Dorsey, lead/tenor; Bobby Bernard, first tenor; Hilton Hudson and Tony Goodrich, baritones; and Herman Lewis, bass. In 1956, they recorded a song titled "Coca-Cola" that parodied the soft-drink corporate giant. Later, after several personnel changes, the Monograms were, from left to right, Charlie Anderson, Bobby Bernard, Bobby Penick, and Warren Hurley. (Warren Hurley.)

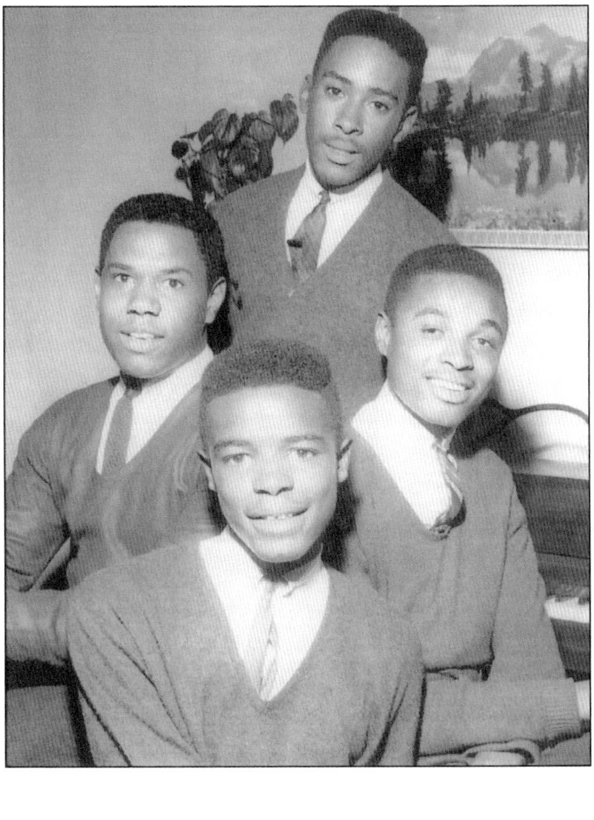

Organized in 1960 by baritone Warren Hurley, the Precisions were, clockwise from top, Ernest Jack Haley, second tenor; Warren Hurley; Robert Hurd, second tenor; and Charles "Moose" Amos, first tenor. They made their debut performance at George's Bar and subsequently left Indiana Avenue to perform at house parties and venues such as the Bar Music, located in the downtown bus terminal, the Circus and Tic Toc Clubs, and the Dan T. Supper Club. (Warren Hurley.)

Warren and Vonnie were Warren Hurley and Yvonne Davis; they both sang in the choirs of Crispus Attucks High School and Mount Olive Baptist Church. They were forerunners of the Marvin Gaye/Tammi Terrell–style of male/female singing duos and were known to put on electrifying performances. (Warren Hurley.)

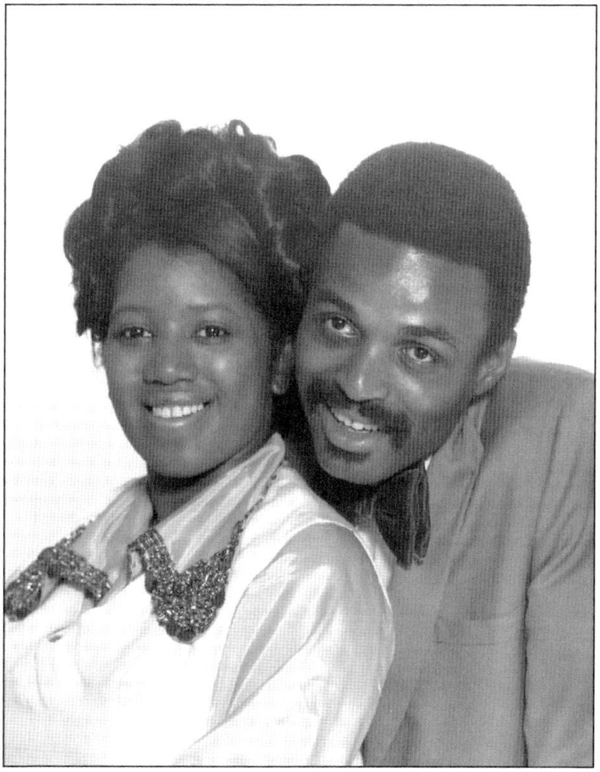

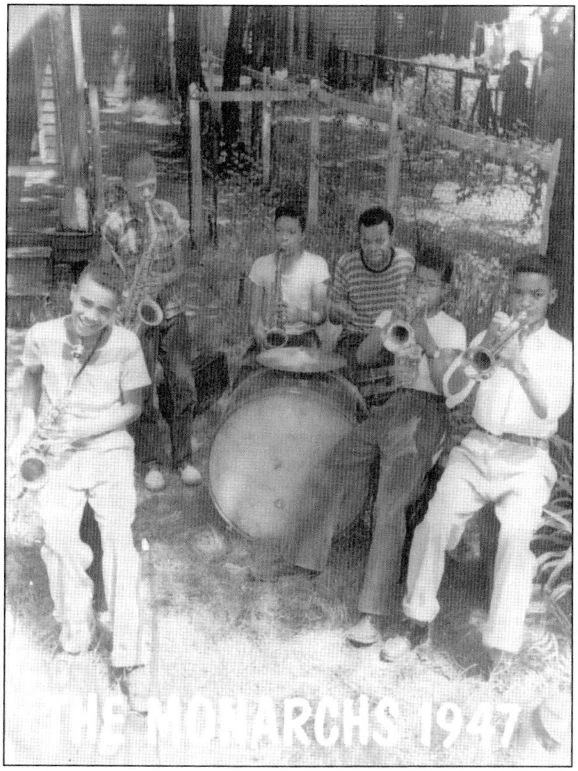

A group of young Indianapolis Public Schools music students gathered in the 1950s to explore the world of rhythm and blues. The Monarchs played at many of the shows at the Walker Theatre Casino and generated a hefty fan base. Years later, many of these youngsters transitioned to jazz and became some of Indiana Avenue's top jazz performers. From left to right are James Spaulding, Al Walton, Eugene Manning, Allen Moore, Virgil Jones, and David Hardiman. (Indiana Historical Society.)

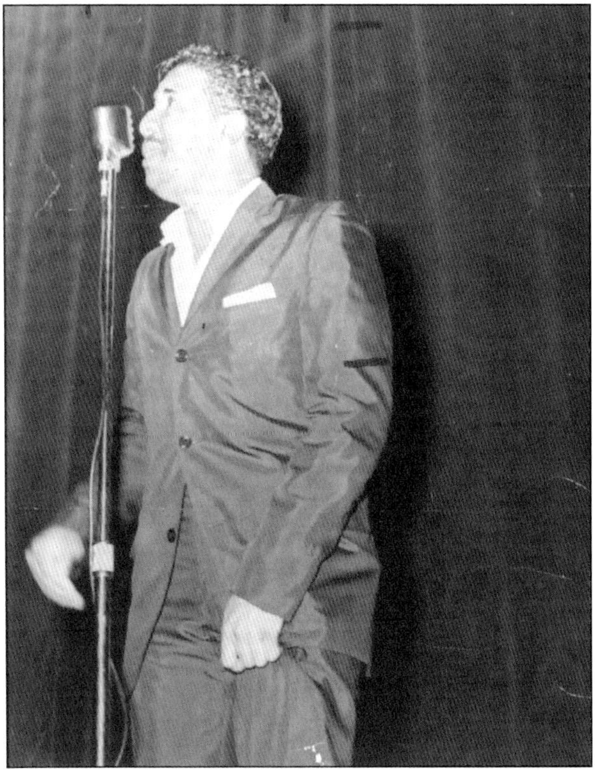

In the mid-1950s, each summer on the playground adjacent to William D. McCoy School No. 24, there was an amateur concert that featured many local singers, dancers, and aggregations of the rhythm-and-blues genre. One such group was Melvin Bell and the Bee Boppers. The group's members were Melvin Bell, Cecil Hunt, Calvin "Cool Daddy" Hall, James "Smitty" Smith, and Donald "Duck" Battles. Pictured here is lead vocalist Bell on stage. (Indiana Historical Society)

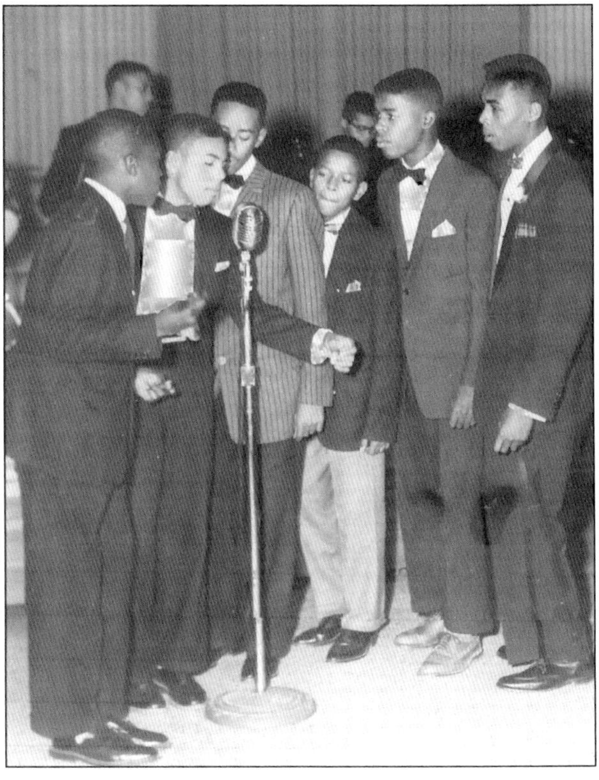

The Thrills, a group of Crispus Attucks High School youngsters with some being members of Norman Merrifield's Boy's Octet, performed rhythm-and-blues songs at school assemblies and concerts. The members were, from left to right, Reginald Gammon, Marcus Hampton, Ernest Jack Haley, Richard Pierson, Robert Hurd, and Warren Hurley. The group performed on stage in front of screaming students at a school assembly in the mid-1950s.

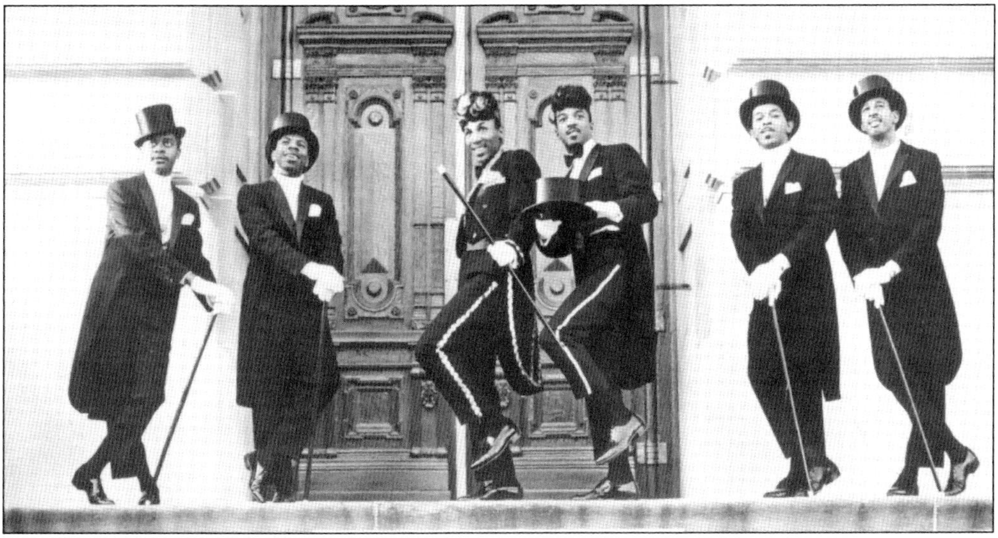

Organized in 1960, the Presidents consisted of Jonas Jarrett, tenor saxophone; William Bass, alto saxophone; vocalist William "Roach" Cochrum, lead guitar; Harry Dickerson, second guitar; Chester Slaughter, bass; Herbie Gibbs, drums; Ernest Traynor, bass and vocalist; and later, Gregory "Mousey" Scott, trumpet. The excitement of their performances at the Place to Play Tavern was intensified by the electrifying voice of a resplendently attired Baby Leon and the comedic introductions provided by the master of ceremonies, Mr. Tee.

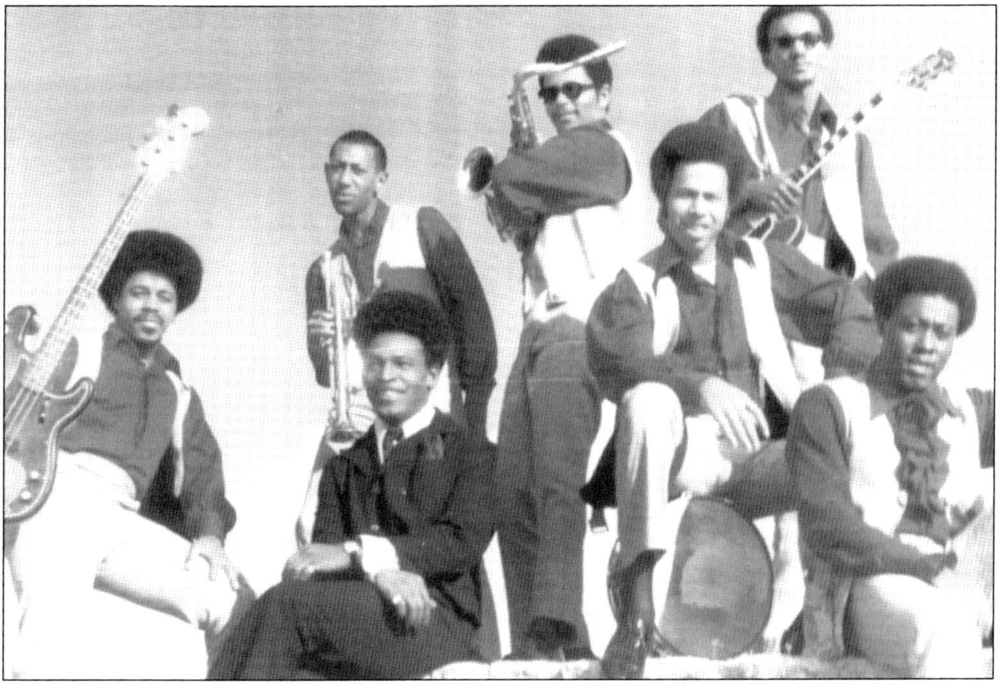

In 1963, after a successful touring engagement throughout the country with Solomon Burke, the Moonlighters relocated to Indianapolis. Their rhythm-and-blues music filled a void on Indiana Avenue that had almost exclusively consisted of jazz and a smattering of the blues. The original members were William "Roach" Cochrum, lead guitar; Chester Slaughter, fender bassist; Herbie Gibbs, drummer; Gene Kelly, vocalist; and later, Gregory "Mousey" Scott, trumpet.

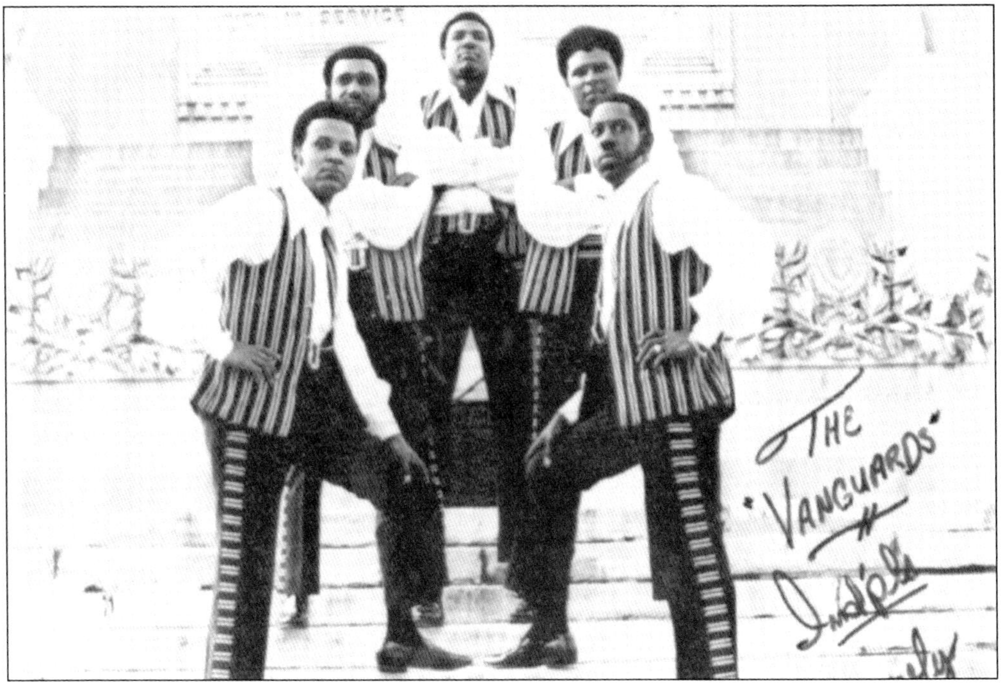

In 1968, the Vanguards organized when former gospel singers James Davis and Paul Irvin decided to make the transition from religious to secular music, which gained momentum on the popular radio stations and music charts. The group members were Davis, lead/first tenor; Irvin, first tenor/guitarist; William Gude, second tenor/baritone; Dick Pierson, second tenor; Wilbur Winston, second tenor/baritone; and Vonzell Wheeler, bass. All except Davis and Winston were former members of Norman Merrifield's Boy's Octet at Crispus Attucks High School. Their signature songs were "It's Too Late for Love" and "Somebody Please."

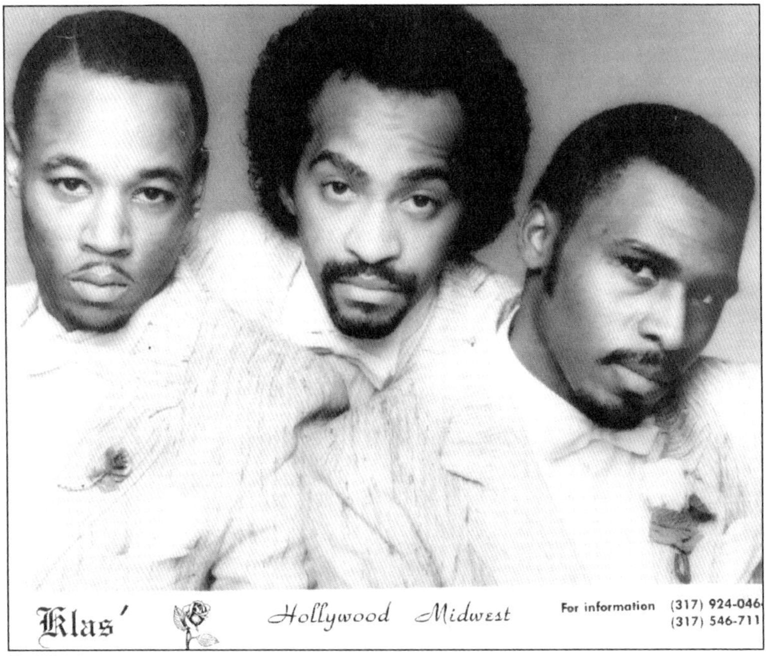

Klas was a smooth aggregation of singers who appeared in many venues around the city. Their rotating lineup included Rick Gaddis, Tony Bingham, Freddie Poston, Larry Jackson, Kim McCrackin, Warren Burris, and Michelle Burris. (Larry Jackson.)

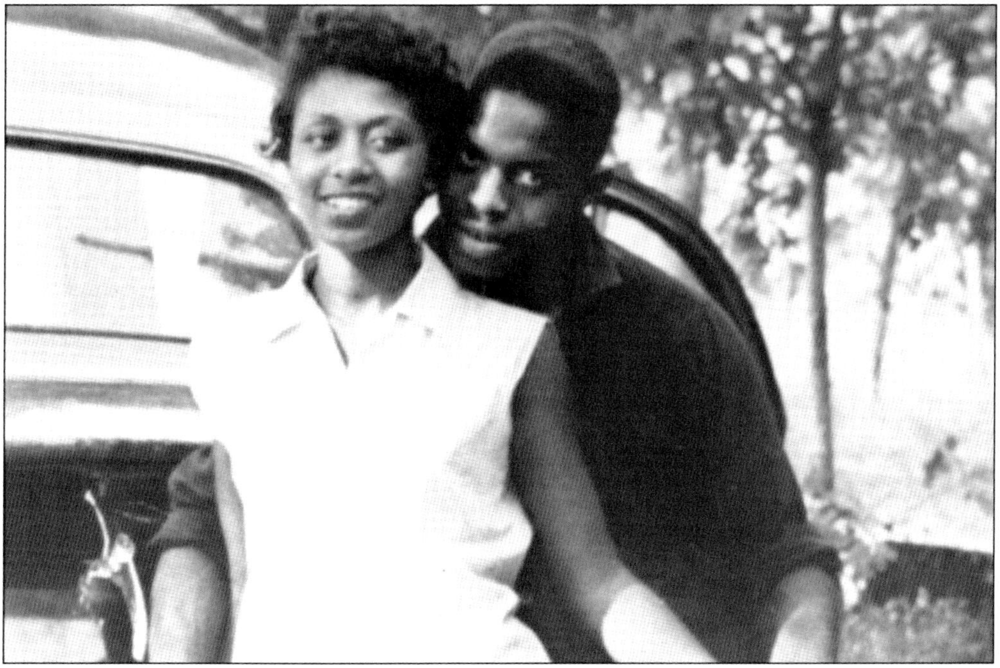

One of the most popular rhythm-and-blues tunes to rock Indiana Avenue was Percy Williams's rendition of "Have Mercy, Mr. Percy." Williams, the blues shouting sensation, emceed and entertained the folks at the Clown's Playhouse and annually appeared at the Walker Theatre Christmas benefit show. The *Indianapolis Recorder* wrote, "Mr. Percy emcees the show and keeps it rolling with a feelin'. His blues singing has endeared him to local entertainment lovers over the years." Many youngsters walked down the Avenue popping their fingers and singing "Have Mercy, Mr. Percy."

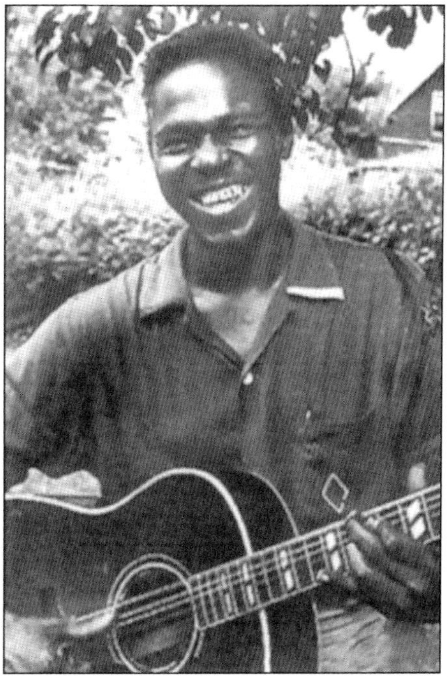

The blues is the godfather of rhythm and blues, and Edward Lamont "Guitar Pete" Franklin was a favorite son. His parents, both Tennessee natives, played the piano and sang songs of wildly popular down-home blues honkers and shouters like Robert Johnson, Son House, Lightnin' Hopkins, and Charlie Patton. On many nights, the sounds of raucous laughter and great music reverberated throughout the house and figuratively shook the structure off its foundation. In 1945, Franklin joined the US Army Air Force and played guitar and sang the blues as an entertainer in the Special Service Unit. His first recording was on the RCA/Victor label and was titled "Casey Brown Blues," with blues harmonist Jazz Gillum, guitarists John Brim and Tampa Red, and pianist Sunny Land Slim.

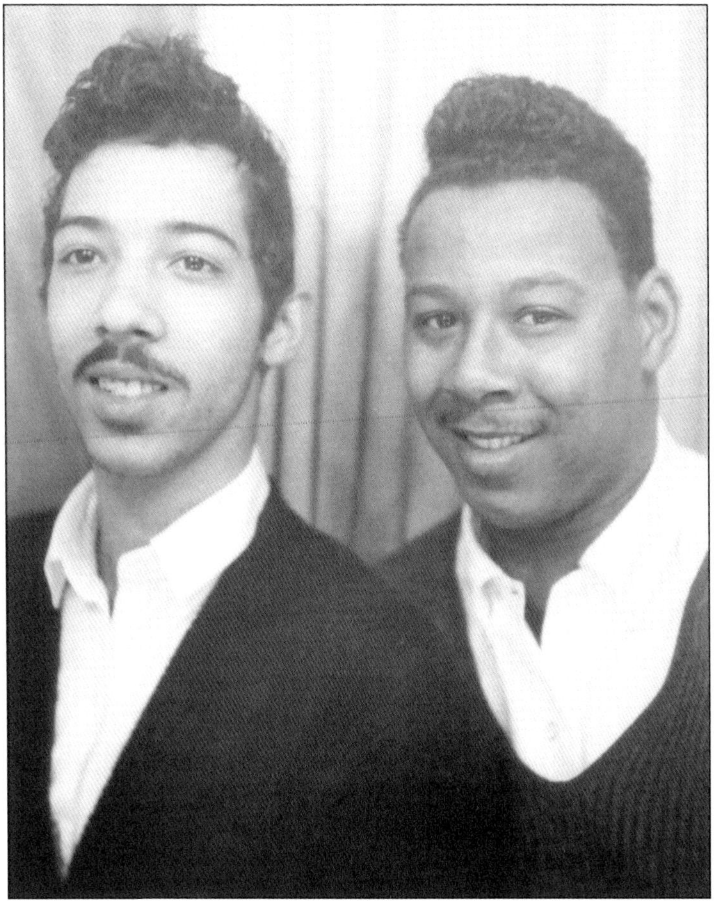

Johnny House (left) and Harry Blackwell are pictured here. House performed with the Crystals and signed a contract with Paramount Records in 1962. Blackwell, nephew of blues guitarist Francis "Scrapper" Blackwell who performed with Leroy Carr in the 1920s, sang with the Five Dots. (Indiana Historical Society.)

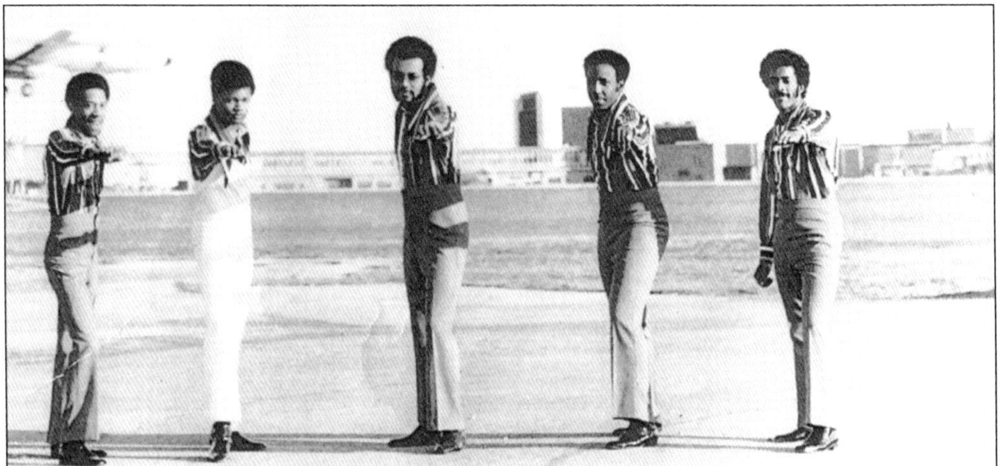

The Rhythm Machine was comprised of former members of the Highlighters. The original members were James Brantley, James Bell, "Baby Leon" Northern, Robert Dycus, Kevin Ferrell, and Donald Harris. They were the house band at the 20 Grand nightclub and backed up many of the touring Motown entertainers. They recorded the album *Rhythm Machine*, which was wildly popular in Great Britain. (Indiana Historical Society.)

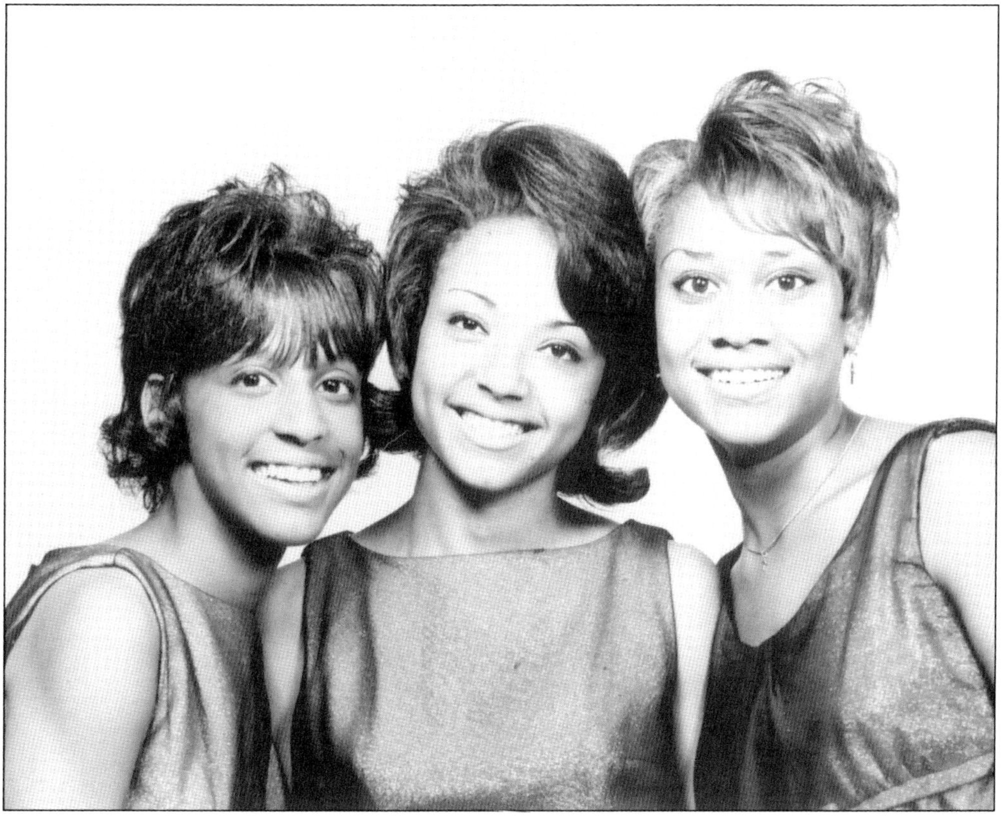

The Tri Dells—Karen Tanner, Tanya Terry, and Brenda Barnett—formed at Crispus Attucks High School and performed at many of the school's entertainment programs. (Indiana Historical Society.)

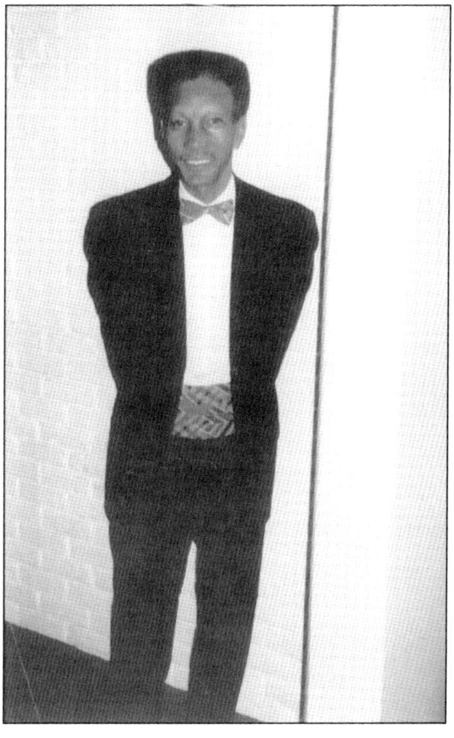

Pictured is a dapper William "Roach" Cochrum, lead guitarist of the Presidents.

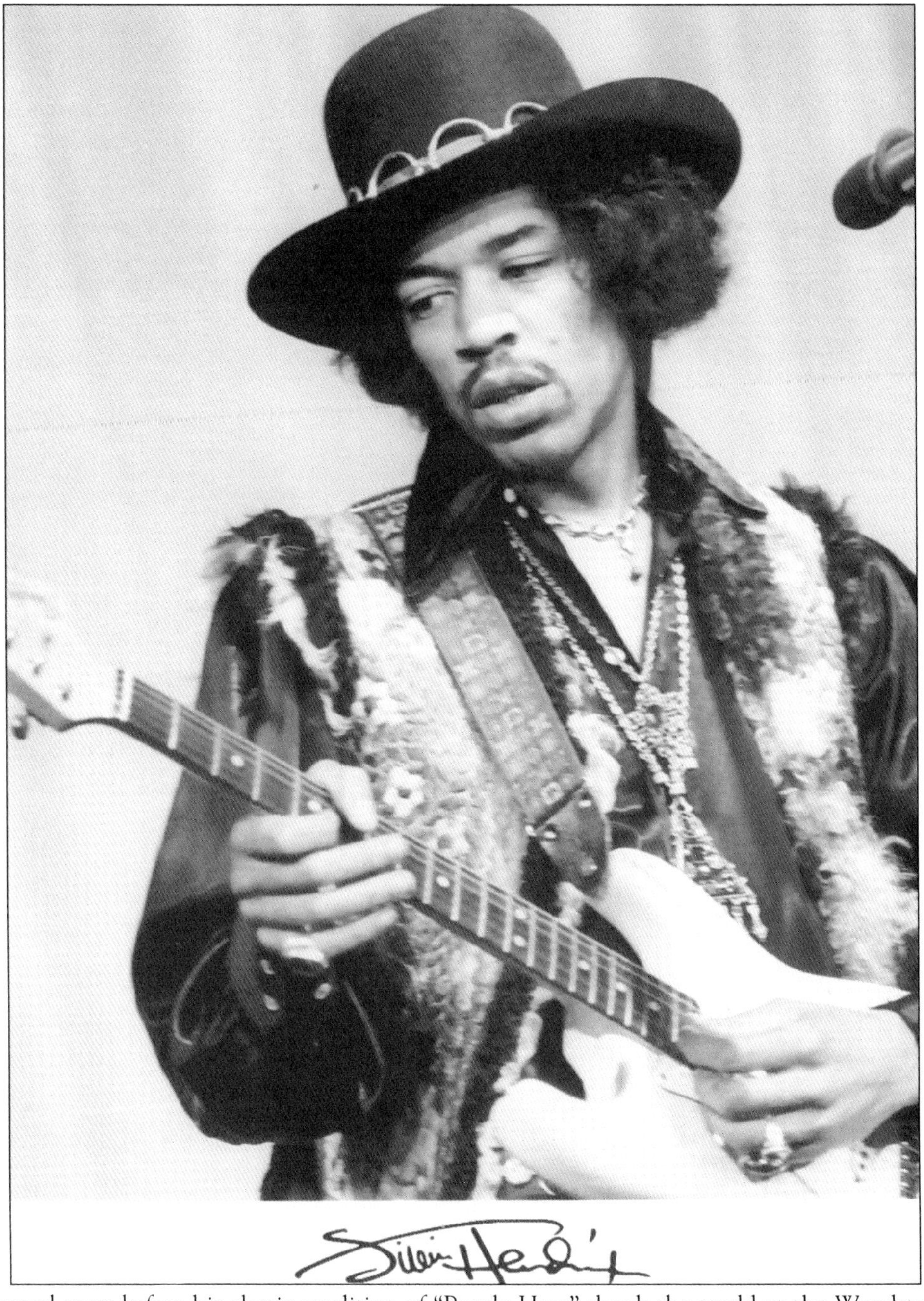

Several years before his classic rendition of "Purple Haze" shook the world at the Woodstock Festival in Bethel, New York, in August 1969, this unknown, left-handed guitarist appeared at George's Bar to participate in a "battle of the bands" competition. Accompanied by his hometown bandmate/drummer Billy Cox and a few local musicians, they lost the contest, and the Presidents, featuring Baby Leon and Mr. Tee, took home the grand-prize money. Hendrix and Cox, with their pockets bare, had to sleep in their car behind a vacant building on Indiana Avenue. A decade later, Hendrix garnered the attention of the country and became the psychedelic, rock and roll genius who is honored around the world.

One of the many Indiana Avenue rhythm-and-blues stars who hailed from the Lockefield Gardens public housing development was Debbie Nelson. She was a product of Norman Merrifield's music program and participated in the lead roles of many of the school's productions. She was discovered by blues legend and icon B.B. King at the Surfside Seven Night Club and was encouraged to tour with his revue. She refused his offer and continued to perform at many Indiana Avenue premiere venues such as George's Bar, the Place to Play, and the Blue Eagle Night Club. In 2001, she appeared in the Indy Jazz Fest with her band In Full Transition. (Deborah Nelson.)

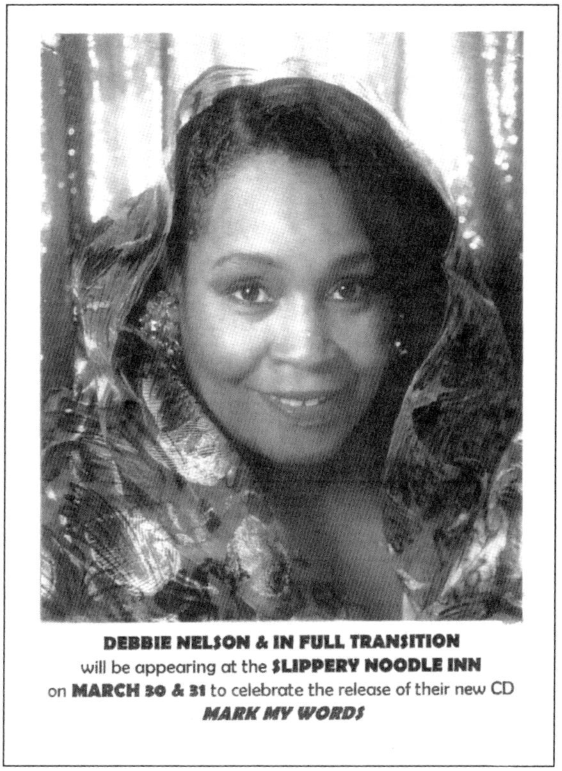

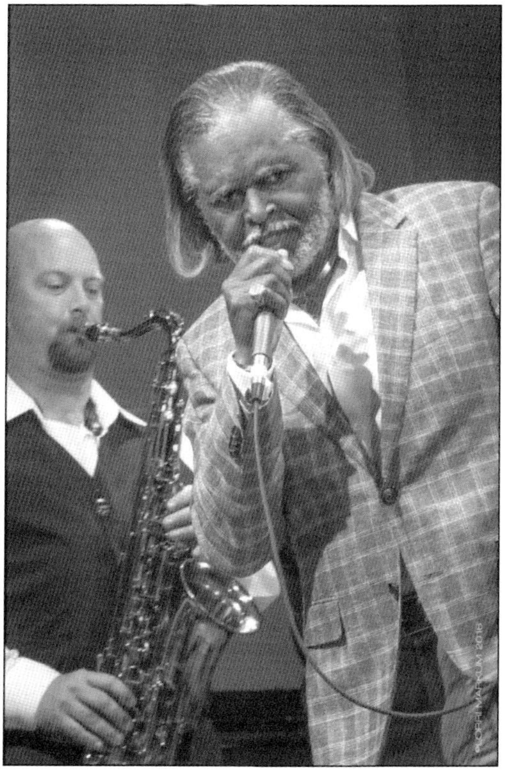

Missouri is known as the "Show Me State," and Lonnie Lester came to town from there and showed Indianapolis how one should truly sing rhythm and blues. Born in Dorena, Missouri, but raised in St. Louis, his earliest and fondest memories of his childhood were listening to Ella Fitzgerald sing her hit song "A-Tisket, A-Tasket" and crooner Billy Eckstein's hits on the local radio station. Later in life, he joined the Air Force and then relocated to Indianapolis. In 1965, his first performances were at Indiana University and the Antlers Hotel. A few years later, he teamed up with pianist/organist Jackie Ivory and appeared at the Honey Dripper Night Club. In the 1970s, he joined organist Roland Armour and saxophonist Tommy Wills and performed in many of the upscale nightclubs throughout the state. (Bill Myers.)

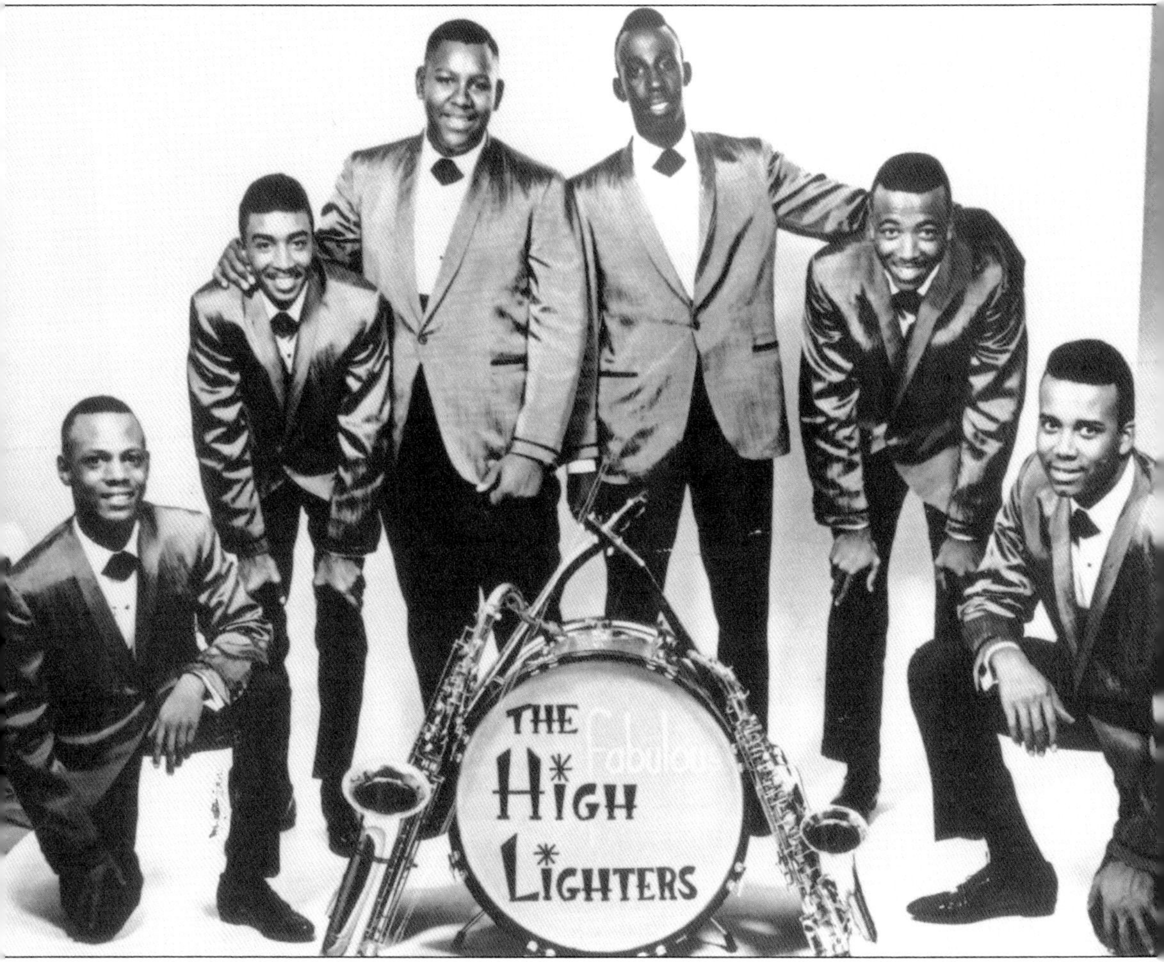

The Highlighters slipped back in the band room at Crispus Attucks High School after music teacher Russell Brown left the building and practiced rhythm-and-blues music for fear of the reprimand of Brown. The original members Richard "Boola" Ball, keyboards; James Edwards, drums; Clifford Ratliff and Clifford Palmer, trumpet; and Richard Corbin, bass. They backed up the Temptations, Martha and the Vandellas, the Marvelettes of Motown, Chess, Chicago song-stylist Jackie Ross, and Miss Fontella "Rescue Me" Bass. They performed at dances at Prince Hall Masonic Lodge, Place to Play, Blue Eagle, and the Walker Casino.

Although principally regarded as an Indiana Avenue trumpet great, Clifford Ratliff also dabbled in rhythm and blues. He performed with the Highlighters, Ebony Rhythm Funk Campaign, and Blue Note bands and played with the James Brown Revue Band at Victory Field. (Clifford Ratliff.)

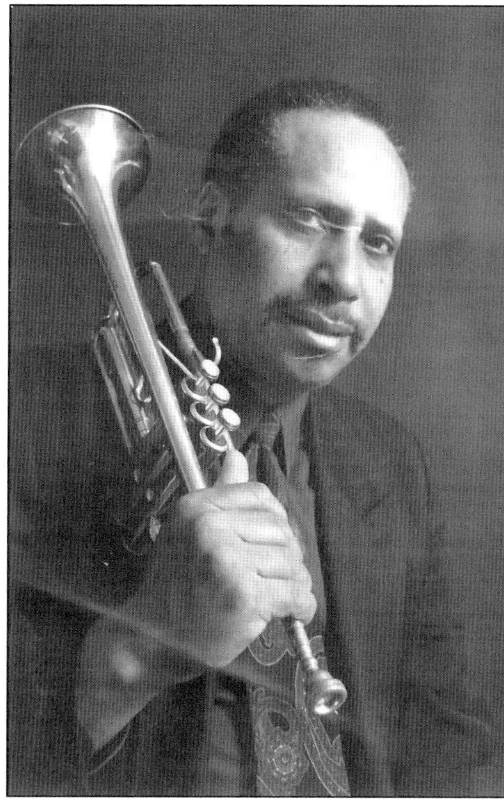

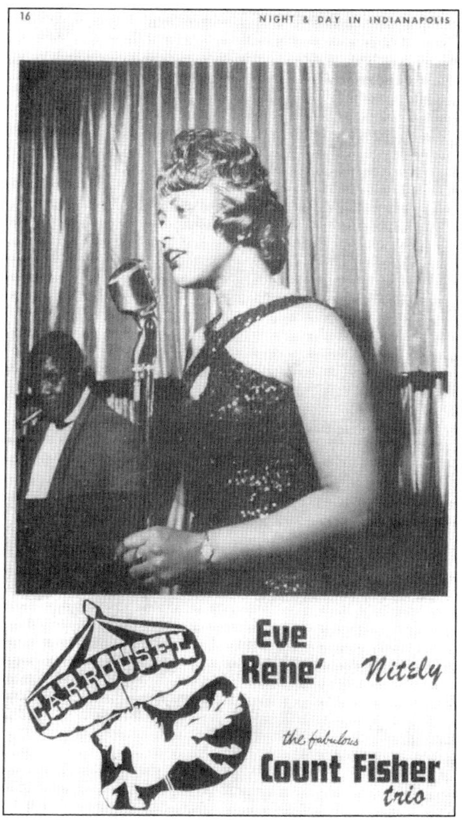

The Chateau de Count was the venue where song stylist Eve Renee "whooped things up," according to the *Indianapolis Recorder*. She was backed by the Count Fisher Trio. In 1952, she won female vocal honors in the Recorder Dream Band Contest. (Stanley Warren.)

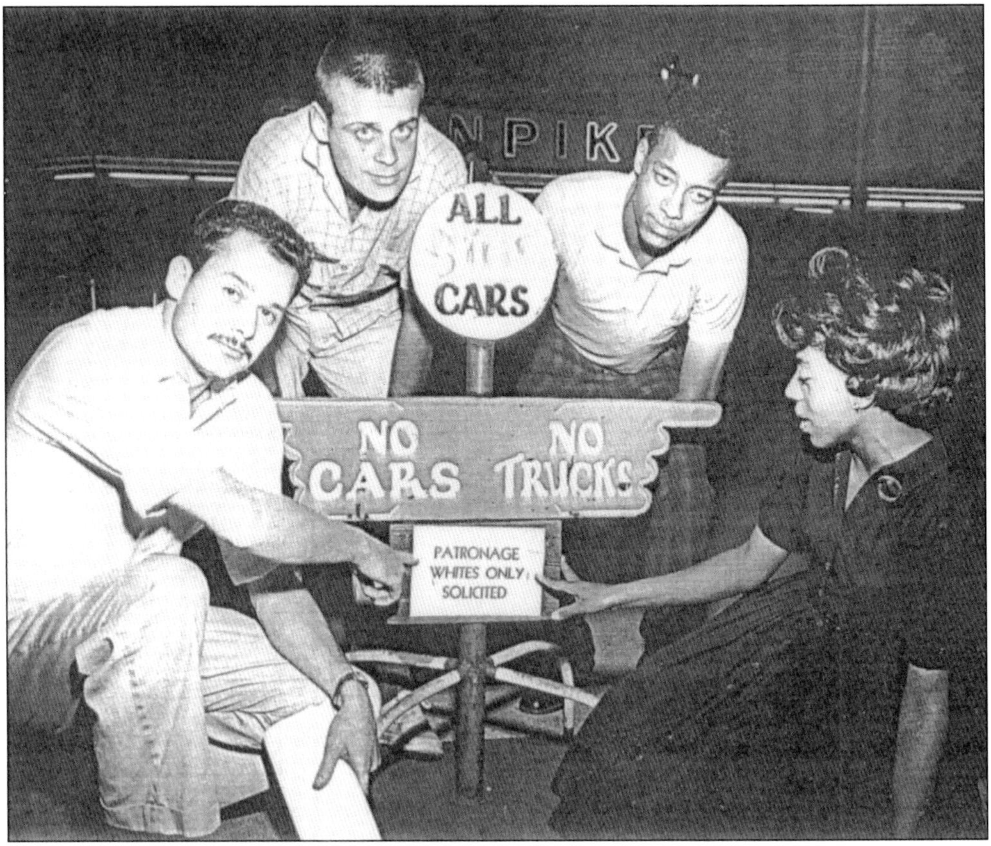

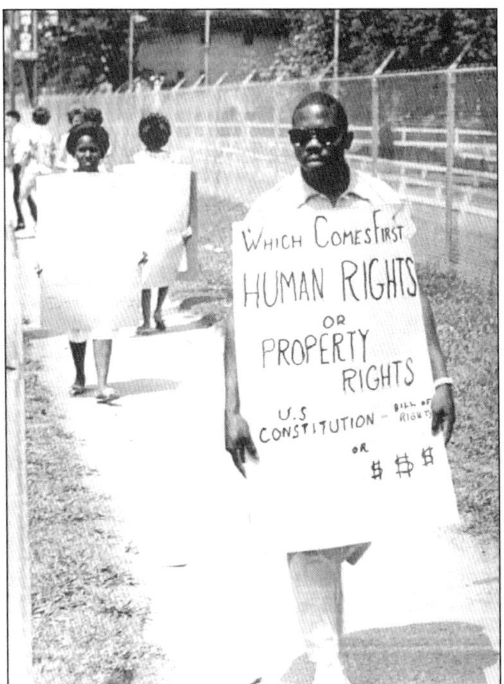

During the era of segregation and Jim Crowism in the 1940s and 1950s, there were many entertainment attractions that did not welcome African Americans. Pictured above are the signs posted at the Riverside Amusement Park. African Americans were allowed to attend only one day a year during the Polk's Milk Company Milk Top Day, when patrons could present milk bottle tops as proof that they supported the company and be allowed to enter the park. (Both, Indiana Historical Society.)

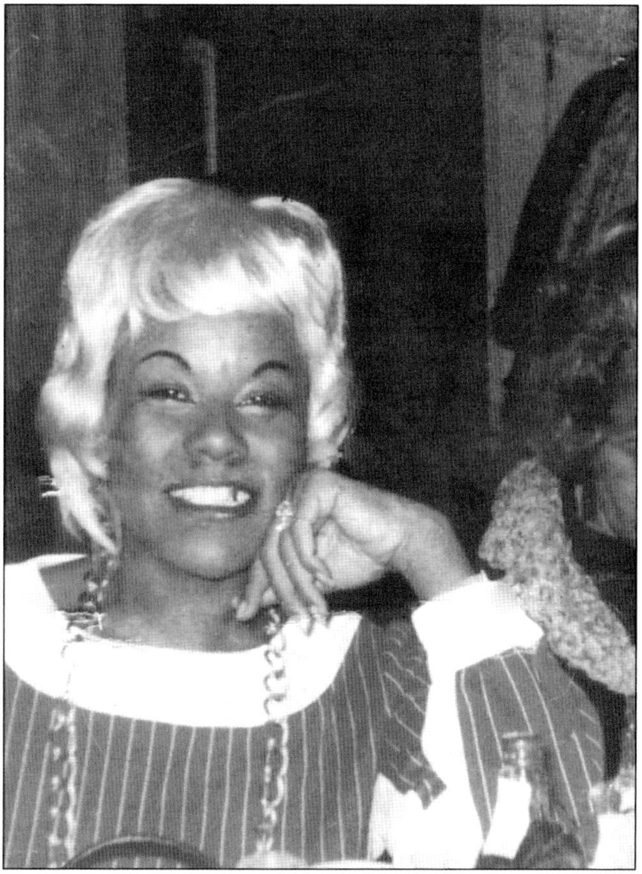

The queen of Indiana Avenue gospel music was Arlene Caldwell Manson, who owned and operated Arlene's Record Shop. (Winford Cork.)

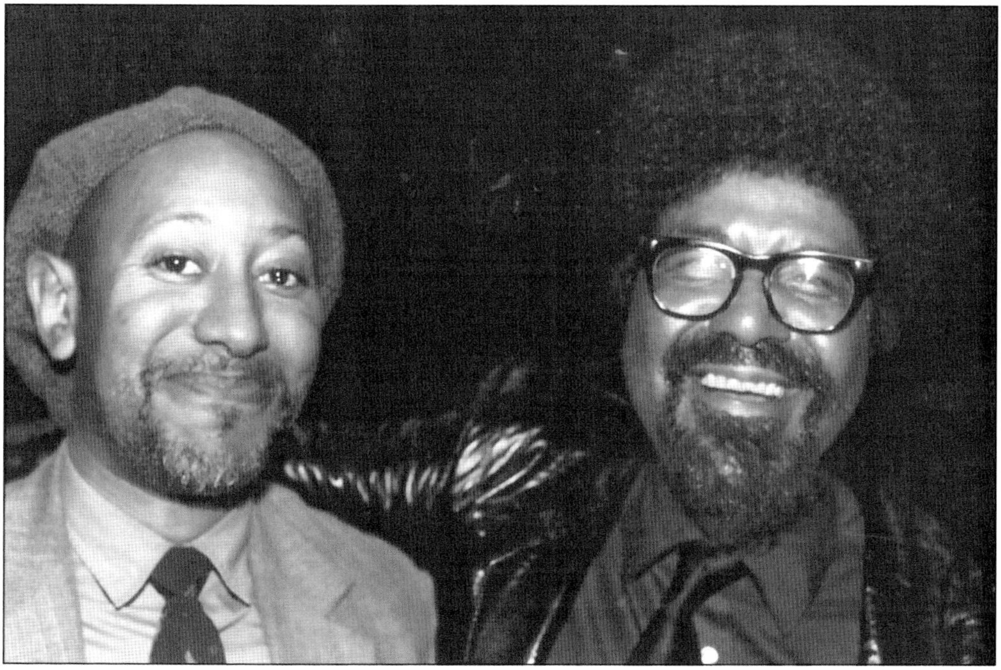

David Baker taught his prize student Gregory "Mousey" Scott at Indianapolis Public School 87. Baker established the jazz department at Indiana University and became a world-renowned jazz musician and educator. Scott performed with many of the rhythm-and-blues groups on Indiana Avenue, including the Moonlighters. (Gregory Scott.)

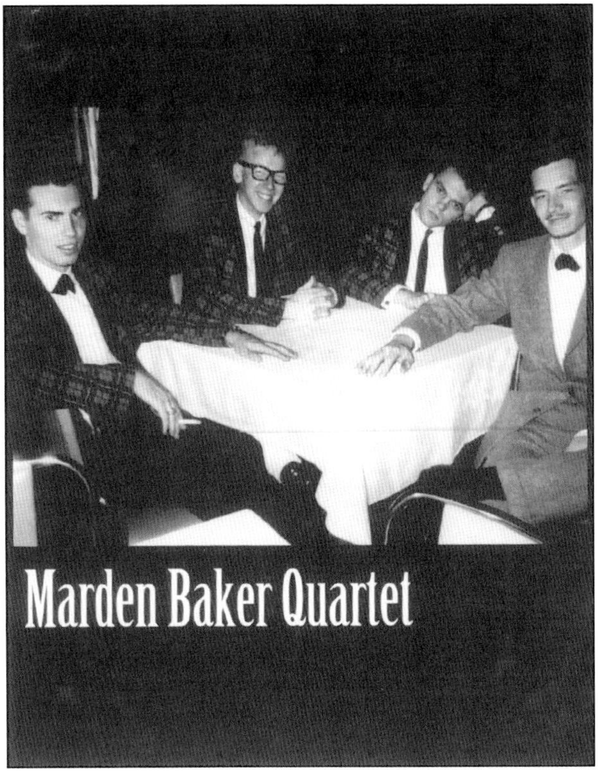

Contrary to conventional thought, Indiana Avenue welcomed entertainers regardless of race or religion. According to an old Naptown adage, "If you're black, white, blue or polka dot, if you could play, you could stay." The Marden Baker Quartet—from left to right, Gary Thaxton, bass; Larry Goshen, drums; Jimmy Ganzberg, keyboards; and Marden Baker, saxophone—performed at Sea Ferguson's Cotton Club in 1960. Goshen was particularly dynamic on the drums and had been a student of Indiana Avenue drummer extraordinaire Sonny Johnson. (Larry Goshen.)

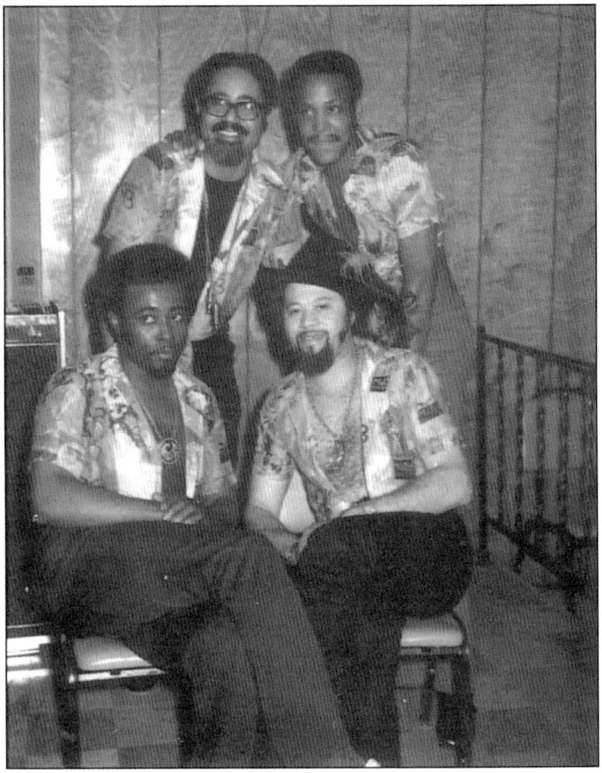

A 1955 graduate of Crispus Attucks High School and distinguished student in Russell Brown's music department, Walton, seated far right, studied the piano, bassoon, and saxophone. During his teen years, he played with the Monarchs, which included James Spaulding, Eugene Manning, Allen Moore, Virgil Jones, and David Hardiman. They regularly backed rhythm and blues groups at the Walker Casino in the 1950s.

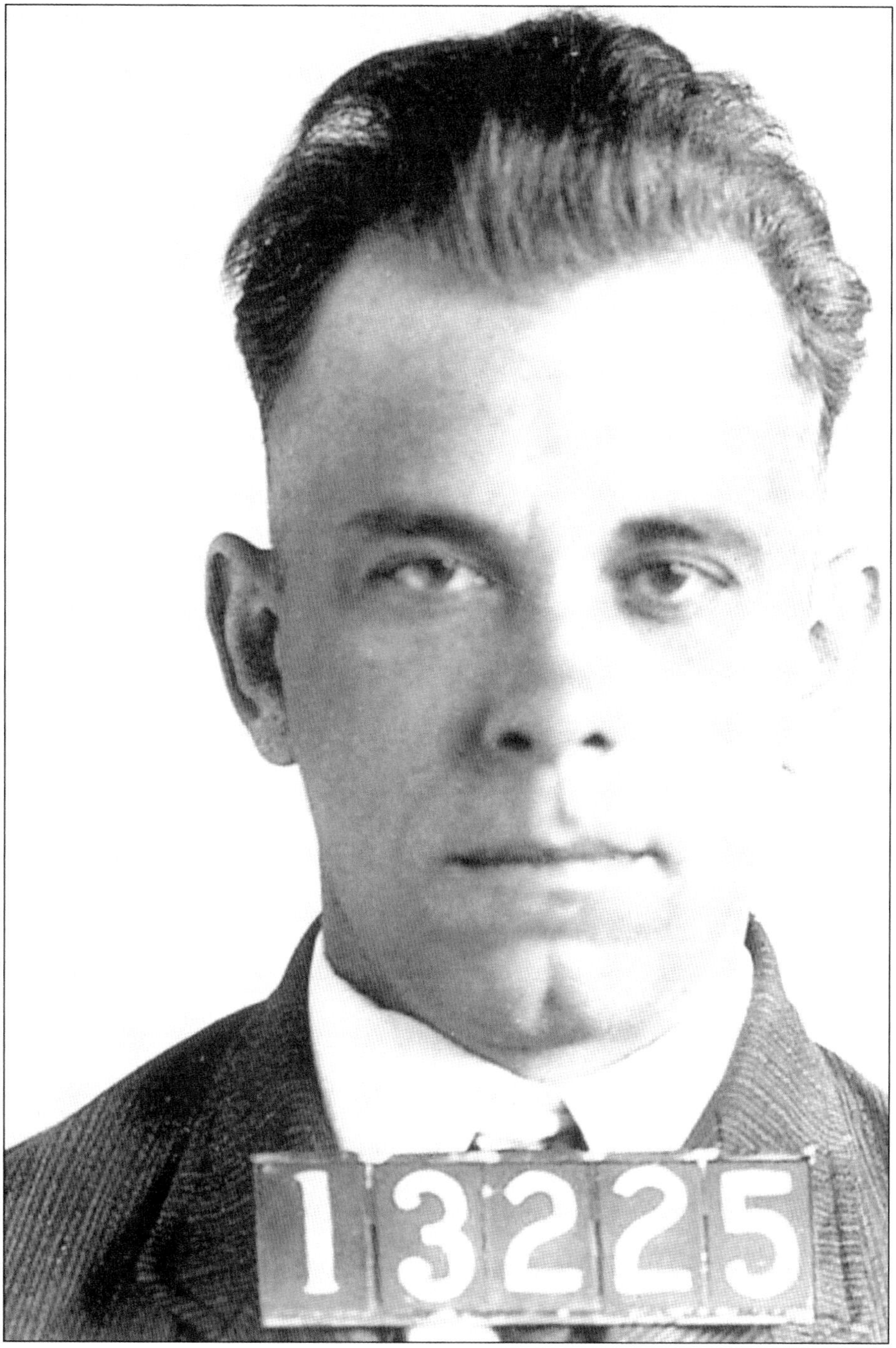

American gangster and Mooresville native John Dillinger frequented Indiana Avenue in the late 1920s. Legend has it that Dillinger was on the run from Chicago authorities and, en route to West Baden, Indiana, stopped briefly on Indiana Avenue to relax and hide out. He entered the Hole in the Wall Tavern in Rag Alley, the most dangerous area of Indiana Avenue, to purchase a drink. After looking around the establishment and spotting a few dangerous characters, he decided to exit immediately.

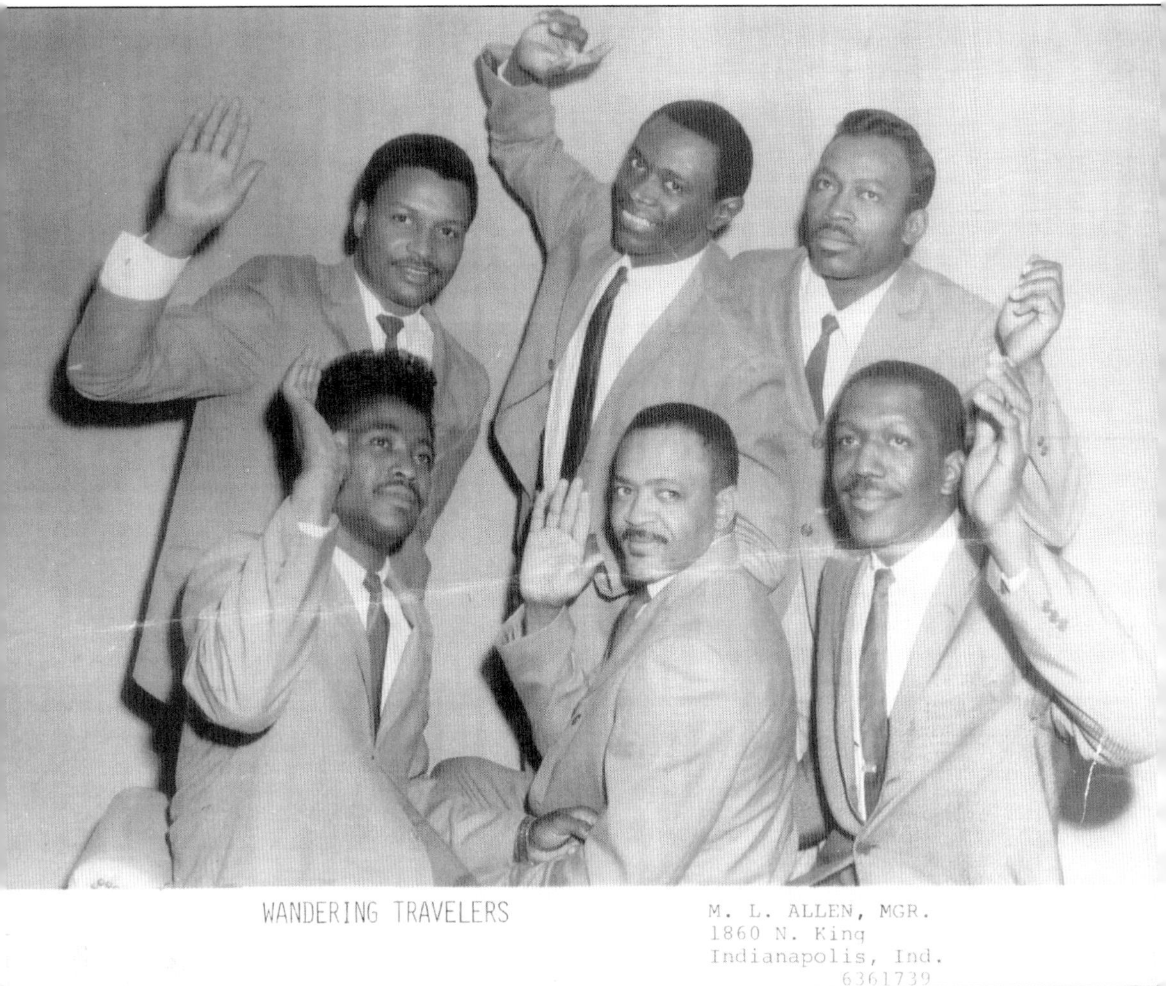

The Wandering Travelers were one of the most popular gospel groups on Indiana Avenue during the 1950s. They appeared at many churches and revivals. The original members were M.L. Allen, Percy Gowdy, Jerry Bond, Robert Malone, and James Alexander. Their signature hit was "Jesus is the Heavyweight Champ." (M.L. Allen.)

The rhythm-and-blues scene was a hot commodity during the late 20th century, and one of the stars who shone so brilliantly in its constellation was Kenny "Baby Face" Edmonds. Nicknamed by funk icon William Earl "Bootsy" Collins because of his youthful appearance, his professional career has been nothing short of amazing. Edmonds has written or produced more than 26 No. 1 rhythm-and-blues hits and won 11 Grammy Awards.

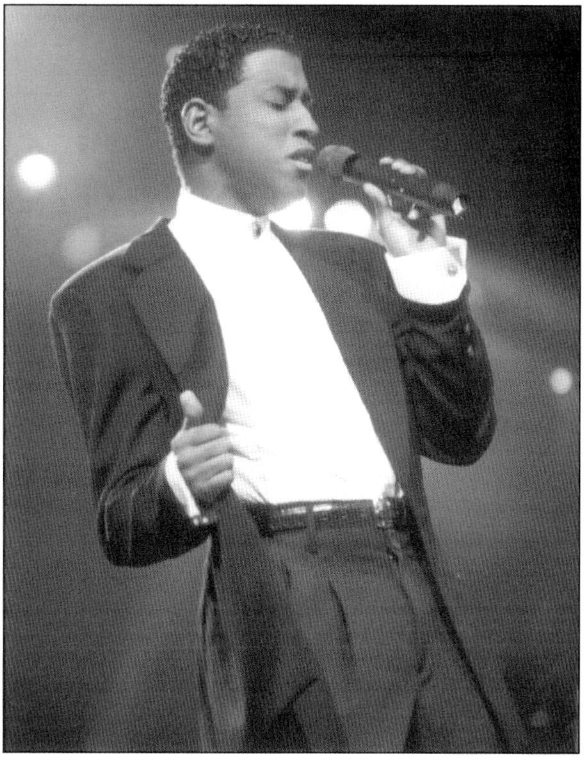

Manchild, which featured Grammy Award–winning Kenny "Baby Face" Edmonds, recorded several albums and appeared on many rhythm-and-blues programs.

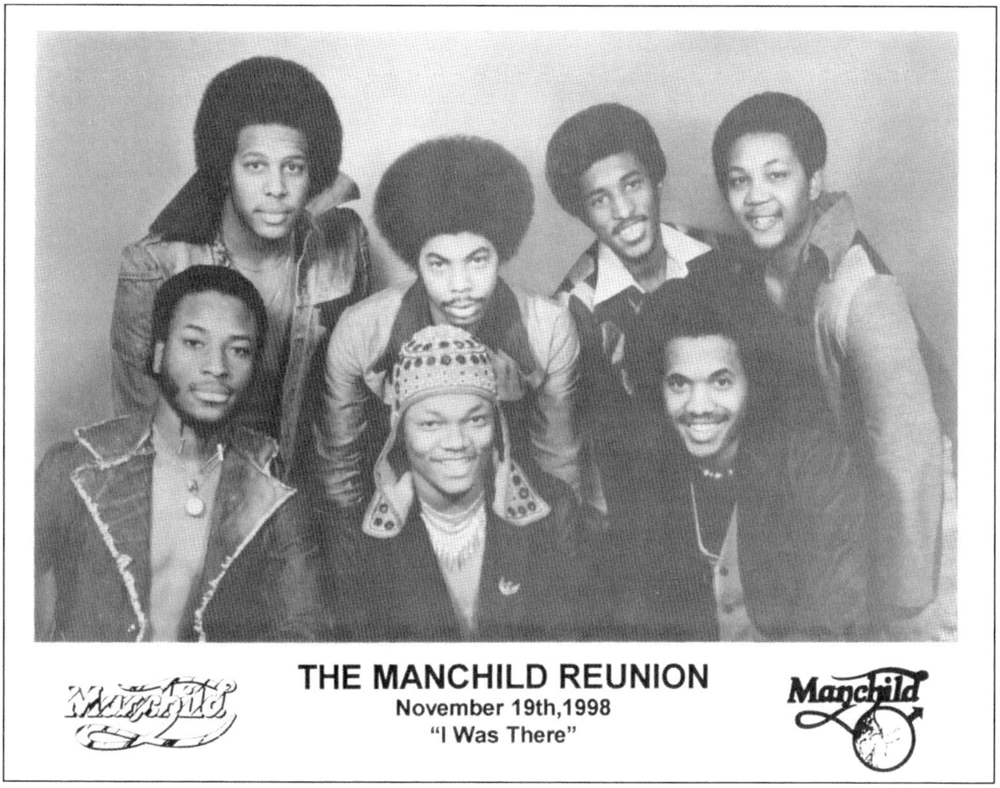

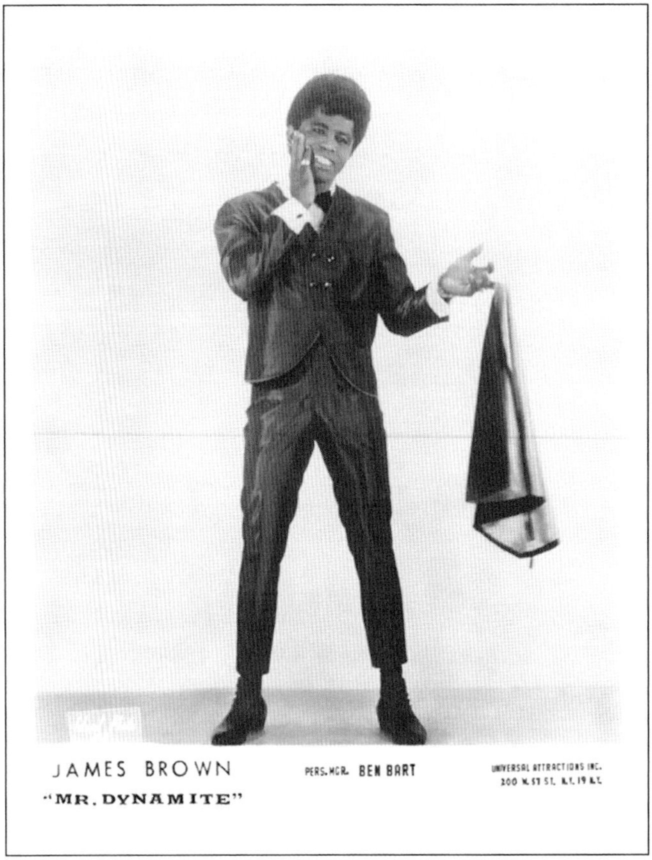

Sunday, August 21, 1966, was the day the earth stood still and stopped revolving around the sun. Many Indiana Avenue rhythm-and-blues lovers flocked to nearby Victory Field to see "the hardest working man in show business," James Brown. To add more excitement to the concert, one patron won a $1,000 door prize.

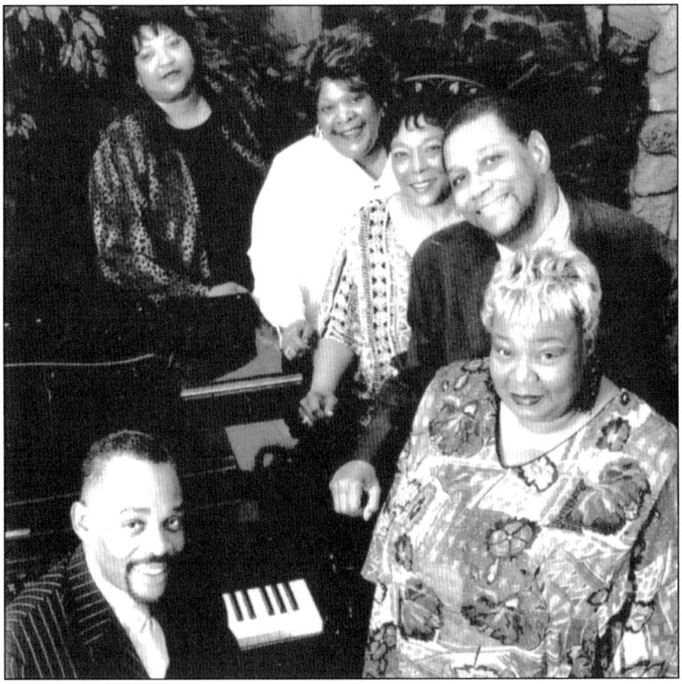

Robert Turner, leader of the Silver Heart Singers (pictured), appeared on the gospel-music radar as a young four-year-old tyke standing on a chair in front of his church singing the old gospel tune "Let God Abide." In 1958, he heard the world-famous Clara Ward Singers perform at a local church, and that experience was his baptism into the world of gospel. Some of the original singers were Will T. Edmonds, Lilly Mae Farr, Edna McCombs, and Brenda Miles. For many years, Turner hosted an all-gospel radio program on WTLC radio.

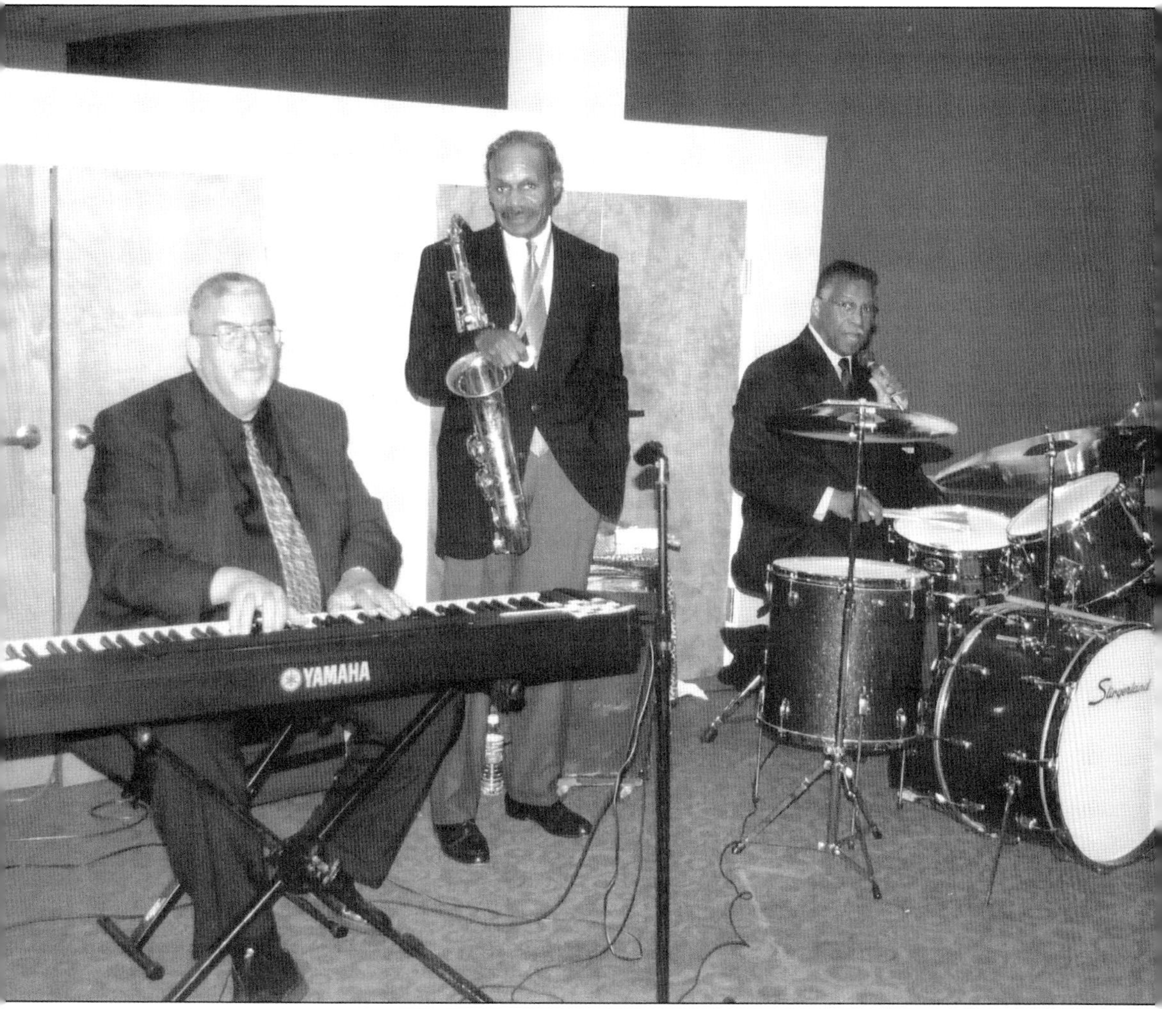

Many of the Indiana Avenue entertainers were not only products of the Indianapolis Public School System, but educators as well. Carl Hines, a North Carolina native, taught mathematics at Crispus Attucks High School by day and jammed by night. He appeared at the piano at many of the entertainment venues and also penned "Two Jazz Poems," which was published in the *American Negro Poetry* magazine, receiving rave reviews. From left to right are Hines on keyboards, Bill Penick on saxophone, and Ray Cumberland on drums. (Carl Hines.)

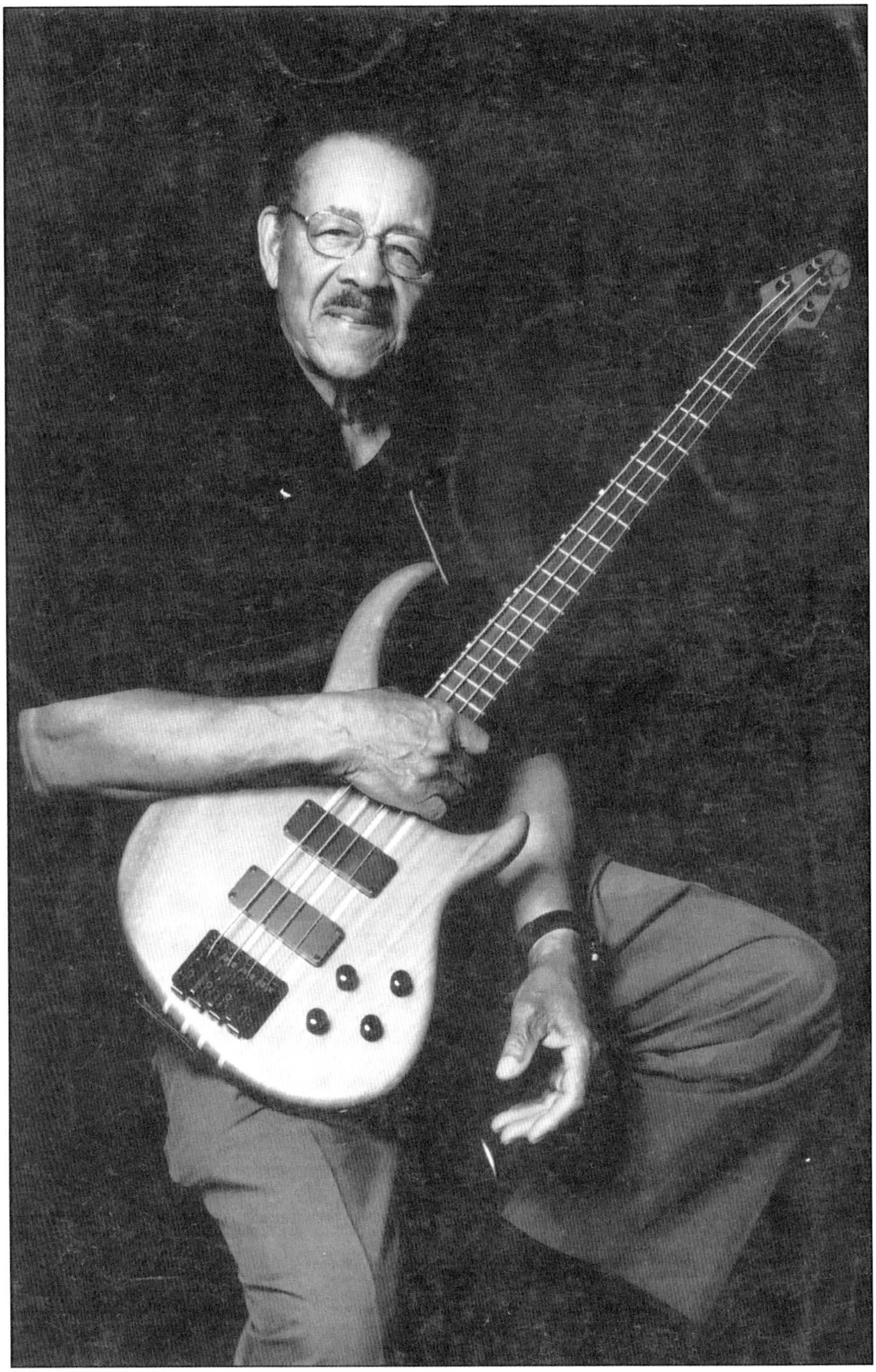

Al Finnell was a principal and Indianapolis Public School administrator during the day and an exceptional Fender bassist during the night. Overshadowed by his contemporaries such as James Spaulding, Virgil Jones, and Larry Ridley, who relocated to New York and received greater exposure, Finnell was a fantastic vocalist and musician. He was known for putting his school materials away in the evening and picking up his bass at night and heading straight to Indiana Avenue to wow the crowds. He performed with the James Dupee Orchestra. (Mark Sheldon.)

Three

Music on Parade

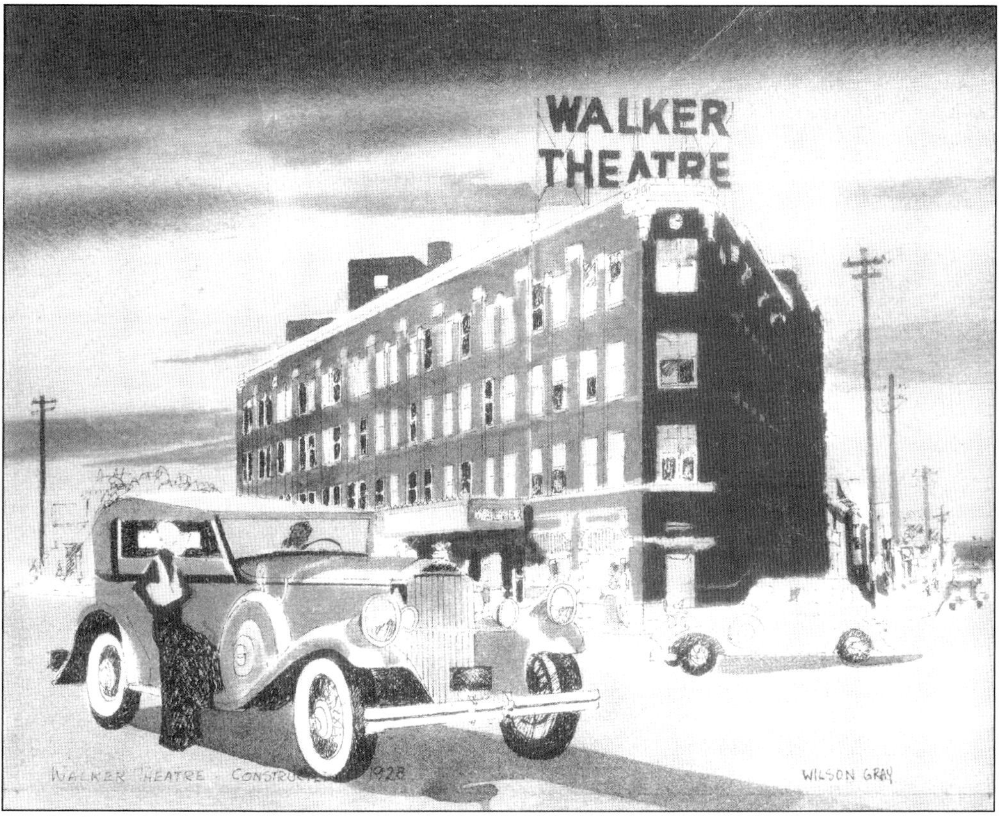

Pictured is a charcoal rendering of the Walker Theatre from the intersection of Indiana Avenue with West and North Streets.

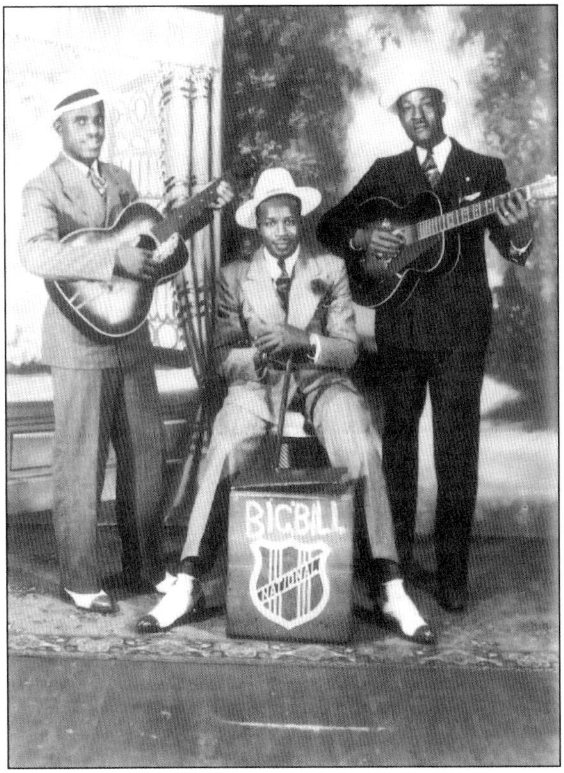

The blues were an expression of sadness and exasperation, and no one could articulate those emotions through song better than Big Bill Broonzy. Blues lovers on Indiana Avenue loved Big Bill Broonzy. The November 15, 1958, edition of the *Recorder* reported some of Big Bill's final words about the blues: "Back in my day people didn't know nothing else to do, but cry. They couldn't say about things that hurt 'em. But now, they talks and get lawyers. They don't cry no more."

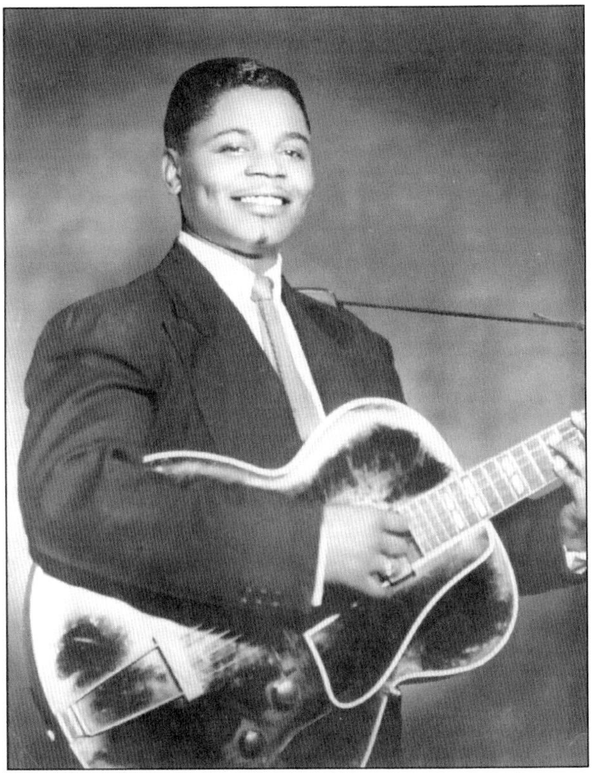

Although Indiana Avenue music historians consider Alec Stephens one of the major influences of a young Wes Montgomery, he also blazed a trail in the rhythm-and-blues genre. He performed with Hank Lyman and the Boys, which featured Stephens on guitar. The July 5, 1947, edition of the *Indianapolis Recorder* reported, "Alec Stephens Swing Trio featuring Snookum Russell at the piano." Stephens also played with trumpeter Blue Mitchell and saxophonist Julian "Cannonball" Adderley. Stephens relocated to Miami and, according to his relative Winford Cork, never returned to Indianapolis to perform on Indiana Avenue. (Alec Stephens, Jr.)

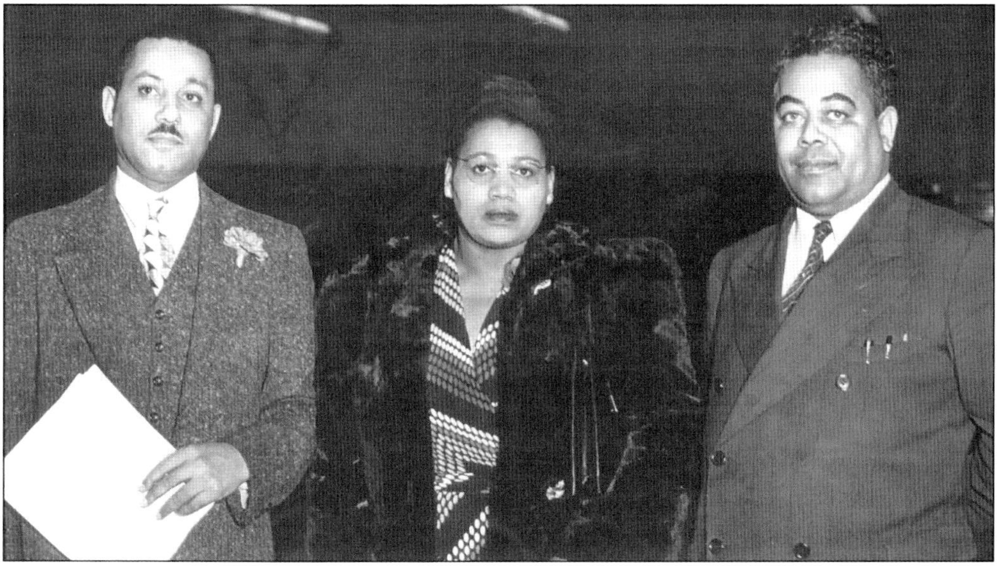

Brothers Sea (left) and Denver Ferguson, seen here with their sister Blanch, are considered by many Indiana Avenue old-timers as the "Fathers of Indiana Avenue Entertainment." During the 1940s, both operated the Ferguson Booking Agency and were instrumental in bringing many stars of international and national acclaim to town. Sea owned the Cotton and Trianon Clubs and Denver owned the Sunset Terrace Ballroom. They also owned real estate and baseball ticket enterprises that employed many Indiana Avenue residents. (Carole Ferguson-Finnell.)

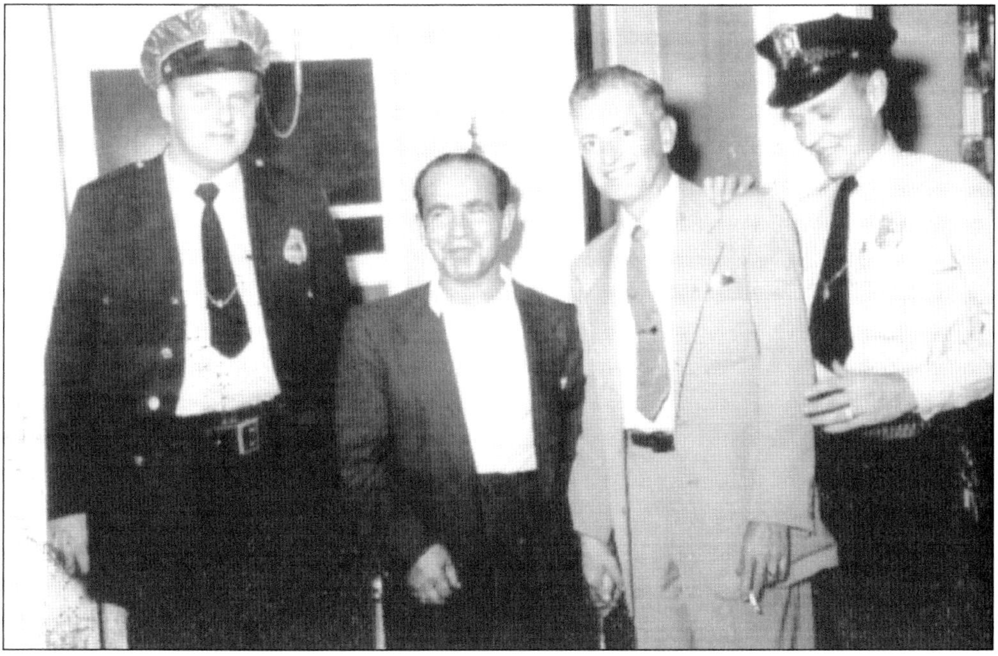

Isaac "Tuffy Mitchell" and his brother Joseph Mitchell owned and operated nightclubs and booking agencies and were in direct competition with the Fergusons. Tuffy owned the Pink Poodle, and Joseph owned the Mitchellyne Tavern. Tuffy was also involved in baseball tickets and the numbers enterprises. In this photograph, Mitchell comically poses with members of the Indianapolis Police Department. (Joe Cunningham.)

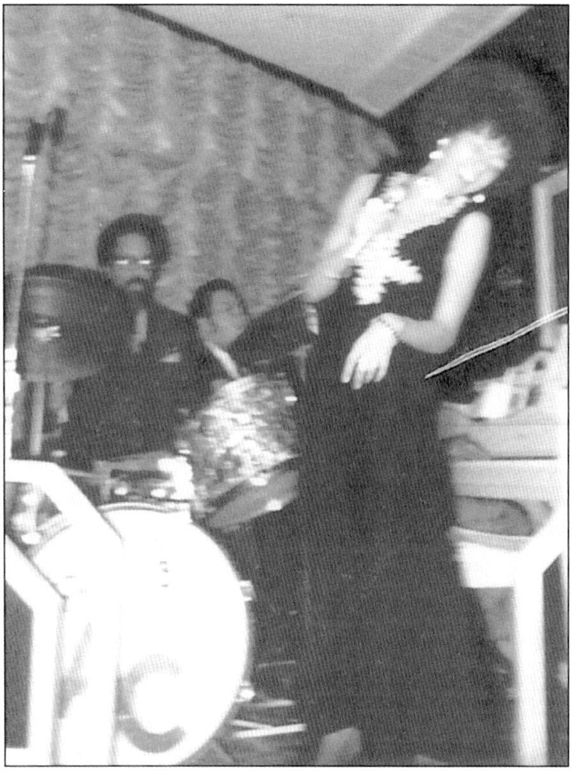

Vocalist Ruth Woods performs on stage at Al Coleman's British Lounge. (Al Coleman.)

Michael Jackson and the Jackson Five rehearse in their Gary, Indiana, home. (Charlotte Mayfield.)

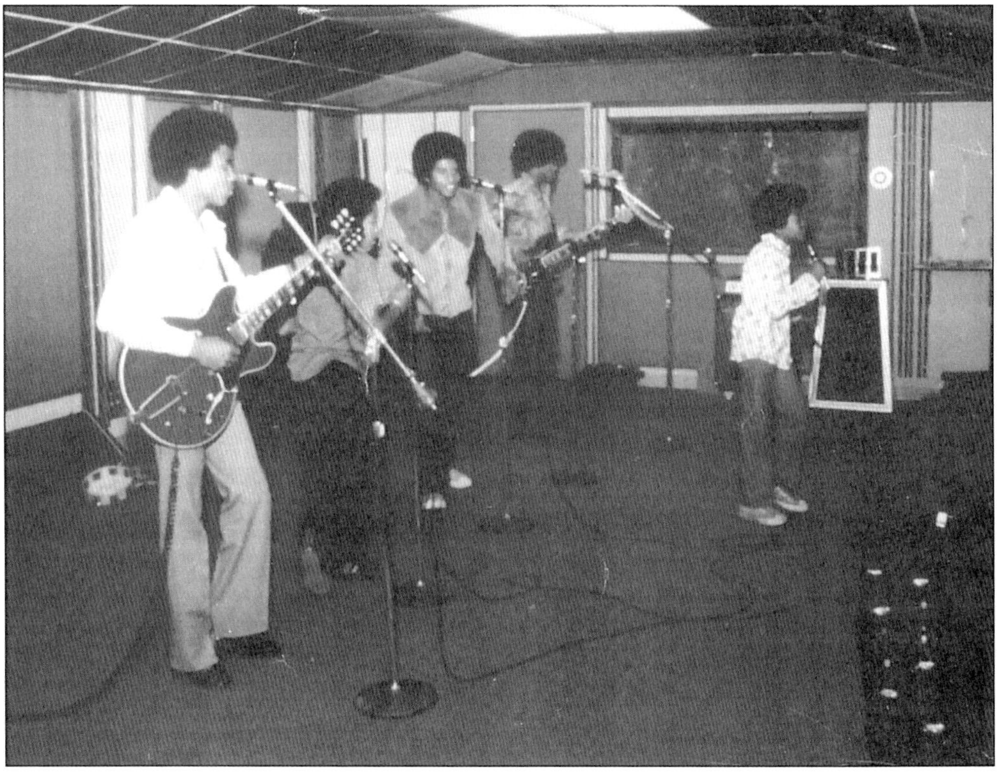

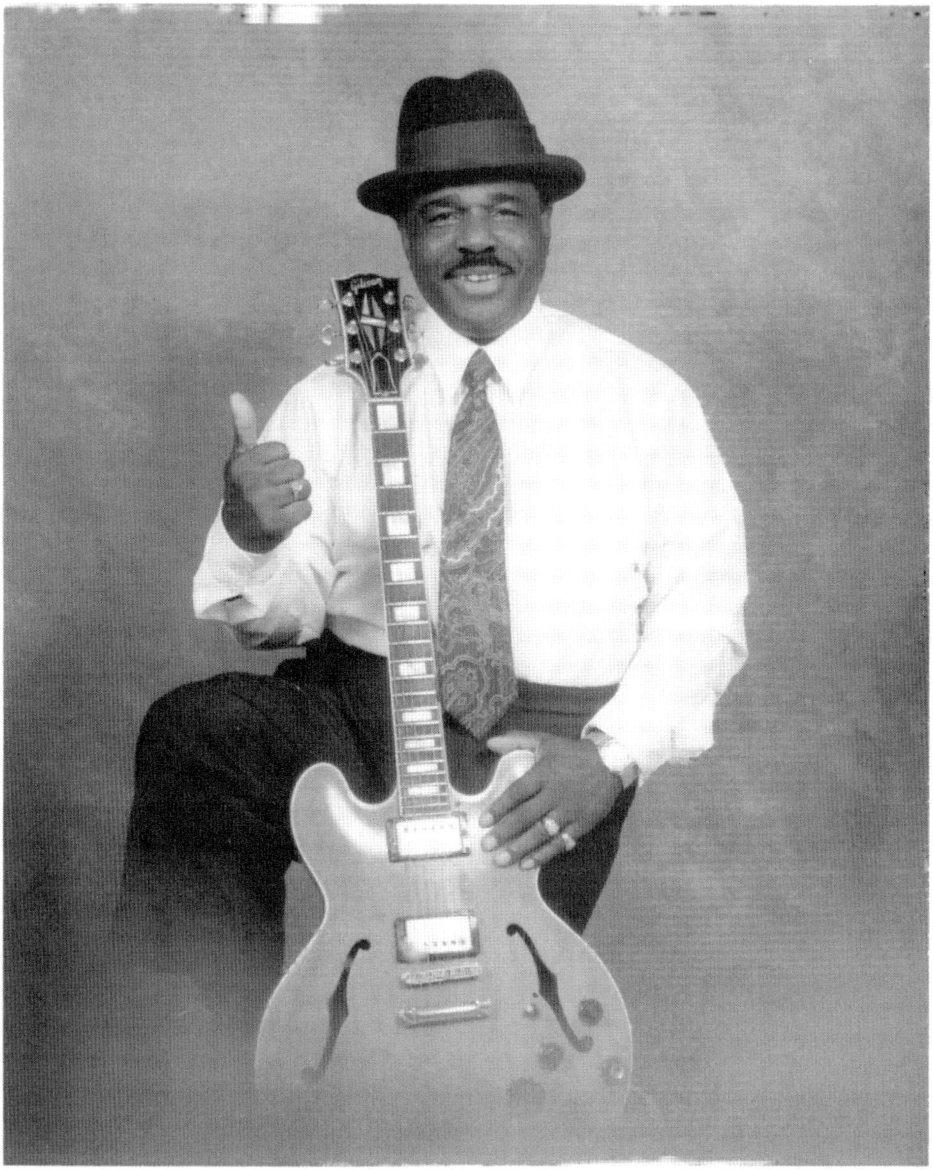

HARVIE C.

Harvey Cook, son of sharecroppers on the L.T. Cutts plantation of Grenada County, Mississippi, was born in the birthplace of the blues. As a child, he worked the cotton fields during the day and, at night, listened to the blues played in his Baptist Town neighborhood. In 1960, he organized his first band, Harvey & the Blue-Tones, which consisted of Lester Johnson on bass and Henry Hart on drums. Their first engagement was at Club Paradise and they later performed at the Place to Play, Al Coleman's British Lounge, the Famous Door, and the Flame nightclubs. On July 15, 2009, the *Greenwood Commonwealth Newspaper* of Greenwood, Mississippi, reported that the tiny section of the city called Baptist Town, known for its strong sense of community and its blues heritage, honored several of its native blues personalities; the names on the plaque were bluesmen Robert Johnson, "Sonny Boy" Williams, "Honey Boy" Edwards, and Harvey Cook. (Harvey Cook.)

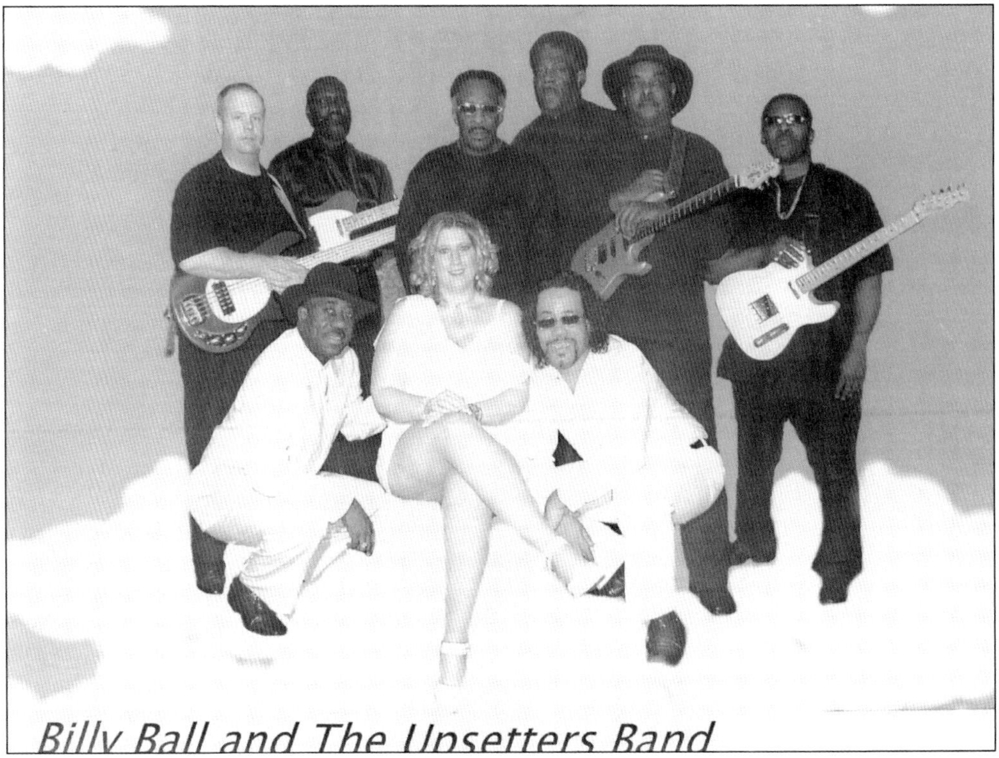

Ponotoc, Mississippi, was the birthplace of Billy Ball. As a young child, he traveled with his father's gospel group, the Ball Quartet, throughout the South. In the late 1950s, Ball visited Indianapolis and realized that there was an absence of the blues on Indiana Avenue. He organized Billy Ball & the Upsetters and performed at venues such as Dave's Lounge, the Clown's Playhouse, the Barrington Lounge, and the Blue Eagle Tavern. (Billy Ball.)

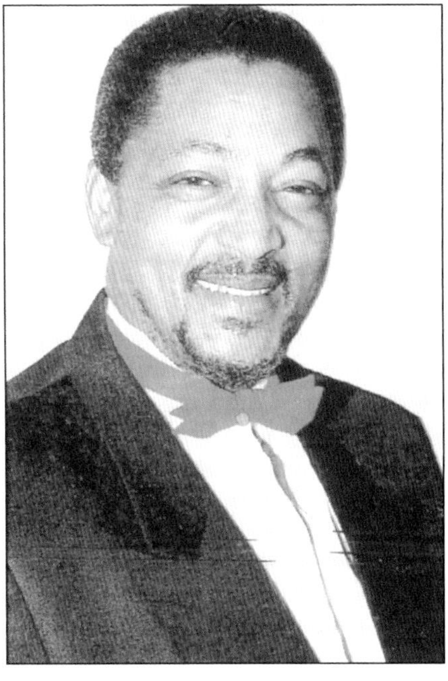

The South produced more than the blues, and occasionally, a strong tree of promise and determination broke forth through the soil and yielded precious fruit. Charles "Chubby" Massey, a native of Ardmore, Tennessee, appreciated the cultural significance of the blues and what it meant to his region but decided to follow his dream in the world of rhythm and blues. In 1957, Massey relocated to Indianapolis and tested his chops on Indiana Avenue, obtaining a gig at the popular Club Thirteen. There, as a vocalist, he teamed with his brother Howard Dixon on lead guitar and piano, William Crawford on bass, Roy Nelson on drums, and James Stewart on tenor and alto saxophone. Massey performed on every Indiana Avenue entertainment stage, made a name for himself, and set the bar of excellence on a higher plane. He was dynamic! (Charles Massey.)

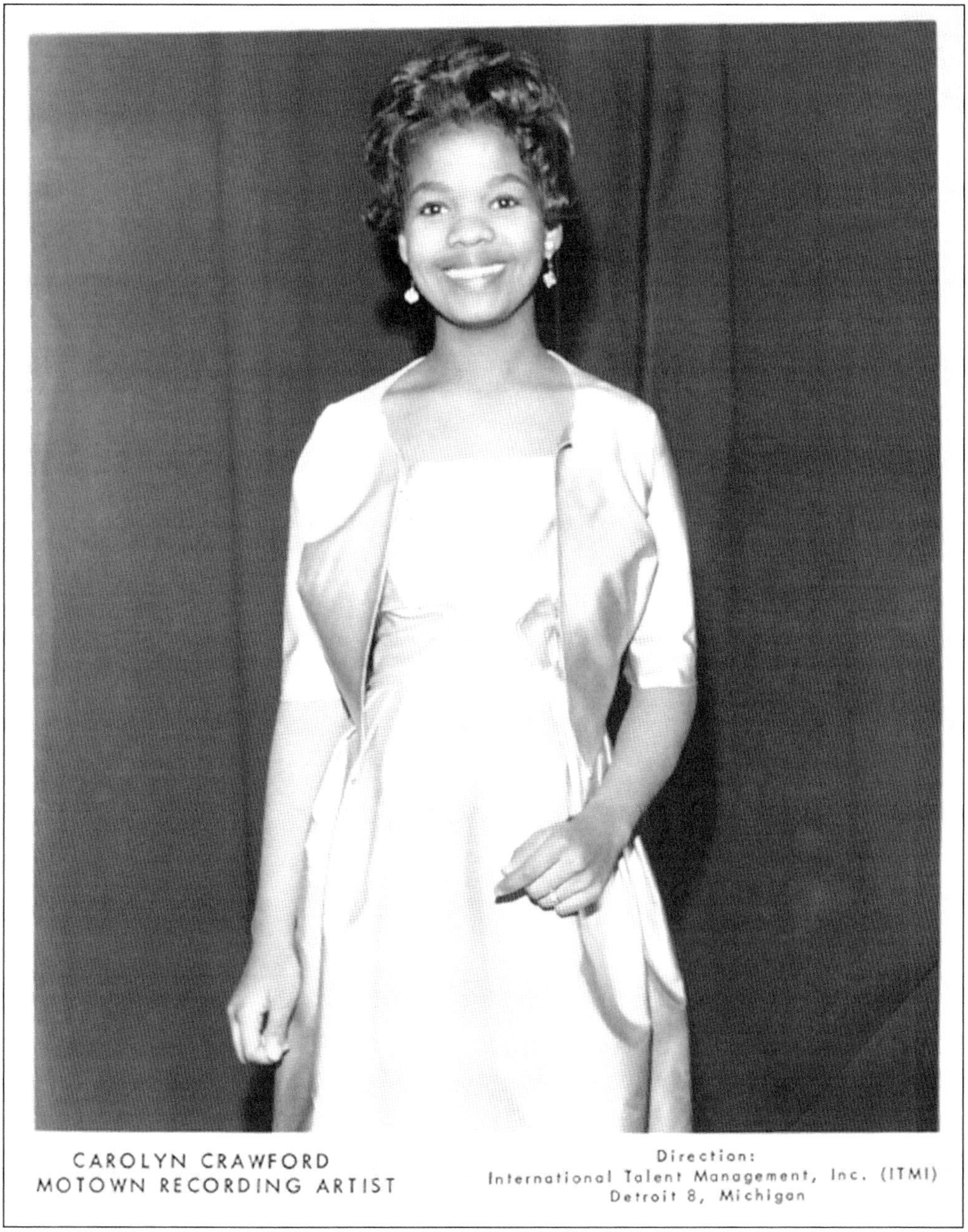

Early Motown singing sensation Carolyn Crawford stopped by the Twenty Grand nightclub in August 1969 for an engagement. Having released her first two songs, "I'll Come Running" and "My Smile Is Just a Frown (Turned Upside Down)," she wowed the audience. The *Indianapolis Recorder* reported, "This newly opened club is going like a house afire with such hot numbers as Carolyn Crawford, Motown vocalist . . . and she's real fine." (Julia Harris-Conner.)

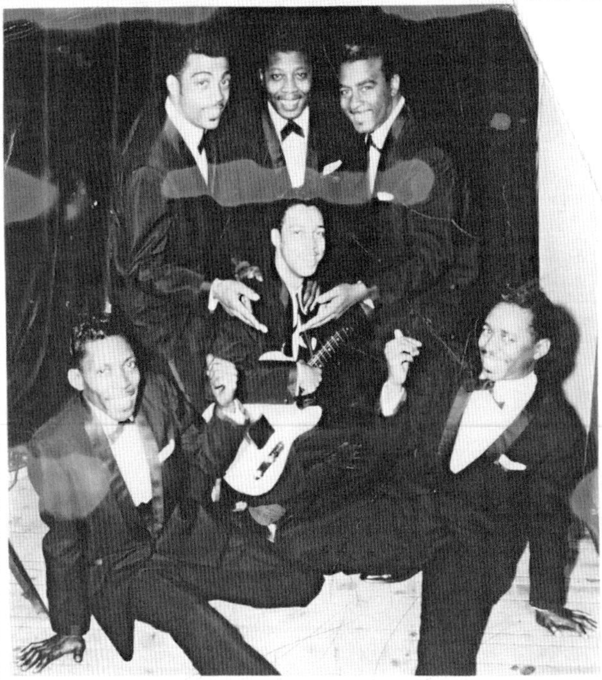

PAM'S RECORDING ARTISTS THE SHEPPARDS

Indiana Avenue rhythm-and-blues fans tuned into the radio stations to hear the Shepards of Chicago with their hit "Island of Love." Many of the Chicago area rhythm-and-blues singers, such as Pookie Hudson and the Spaniels, Jerry Butler and the Impressions, Gene Chandler, Jackie Ross, Barbara Acklin, Donald Jenkins & the Delighters, the Dells, the Five Stair Steps, and Denise Williams, received considerable airplay on Indianapolis radio and television stations.

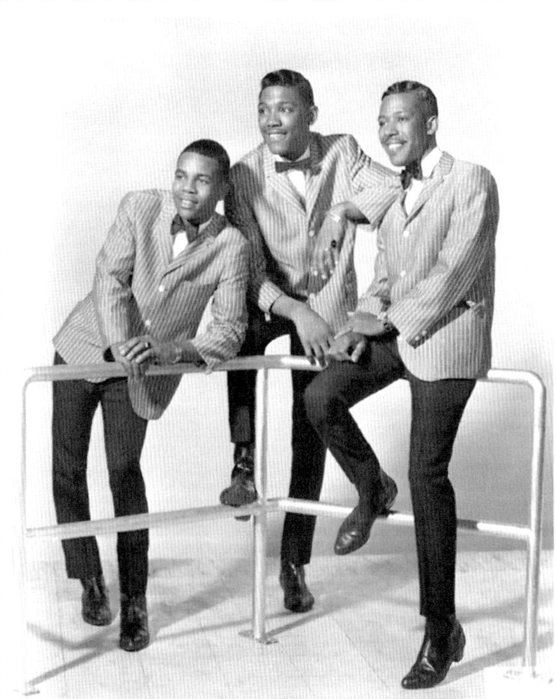

THE CAPITOLS Personal Management OLLIE McLAUGHLIN

During the mid-1960s, many Indianapolis music lovers crowded into the popular Dave's Lounge on Northwestern Avenue to dance "the Jerk." It was popularized by the record "Cool Jerk" by the Capitols of Detroit. The song received considerable air play on the Nashville rhythm and blues stations.

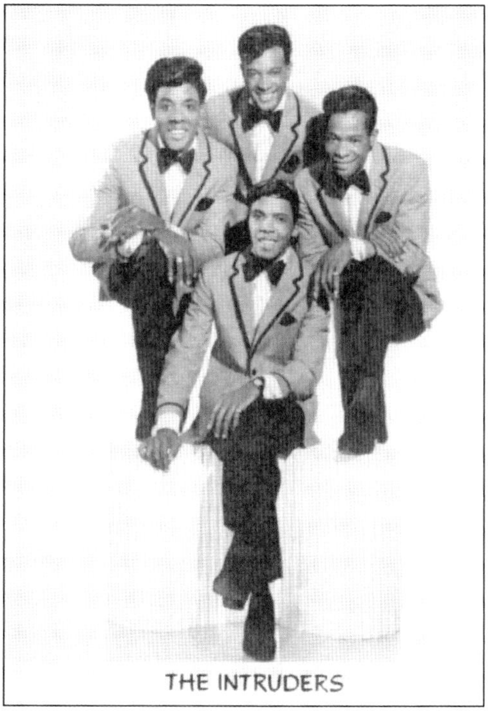

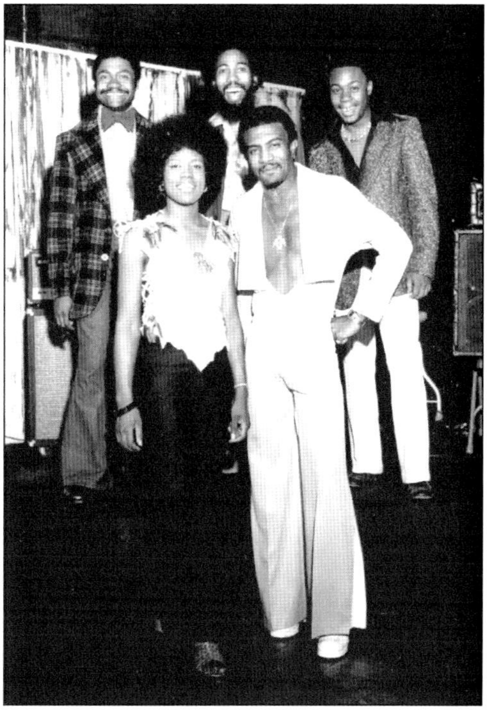

"Cowboys to Girls" was the mega-hit produced by the Intruders of Philadelphia (left). On Saturday, September 18, 1971, they appeared at the Twenty Grand nightclub, with proceeds donated to the Operation Bread Basket program. At right are, from left to right, (first row) June Smith and Walter Webb: (second row) Richard Corbin, Larry Clark, and Steve Weakley. Weakley became one of the top guitarists in the country and was greatly influenced by Wes Montgomery.

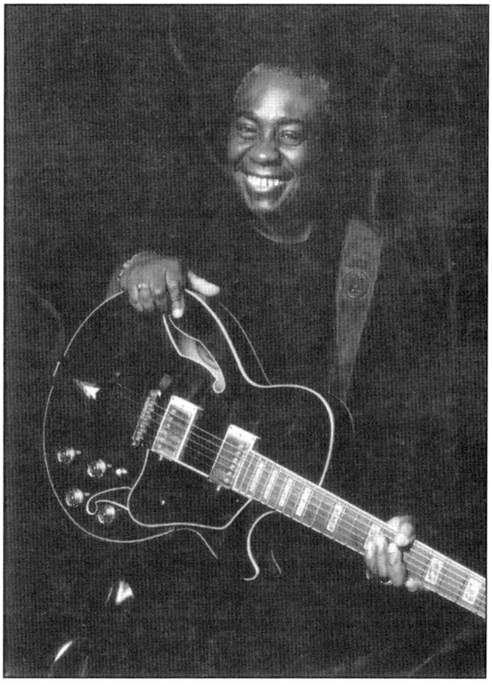

The Avenue has long been a launching pad for some of the world's greatest guitarists. Names like Wes Montgomery, Alec Stephens, Paul Weeden, Johnny Blanchard, Specs Maynard, Bill Jennings, Mopps Marshall, and Al Finnell come to mind. Another name to add to that august list is Steven James Weakley, pictured here. Weakley performed on and off the Avenue for several decades and distinguished himself as one of the contemporary greats. Jazz radio host and historian Chuck Workman joyfully gave him the name "Little Wes." (Steve Weakley.)

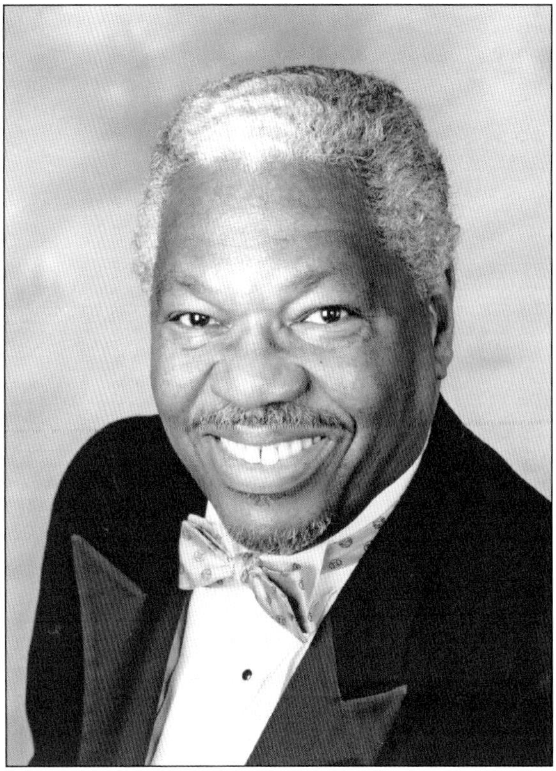

Everett Francis Greene, who was primarily known as a popular music stylist, began his performance career singing doo-wop music. Born to musically inclined parents, different genres of music constantly reverberated in his home in Washington, DC. His mother was an accomplished gospel singer, and his father was a drummer with the Byron Doty All-Star Band, which performed in venues in Washington and northern Virginia. Relocating to Indianapolis in 1955, Greene's great baritone voice was celebrated by many in the jazz community, and he performed in the leading jazz and popular music clubs in the area. In February 1983, Greene traveled to Chicago and auditioned for and won a role in the production of *Little Dreamer*, which chronicled the life of blues legend Bessie Smith. Smith was played by internationally known folk singer Odetta. In 1988, Greene won an Emmy for *Precious Memories*. (Everett Greene.)

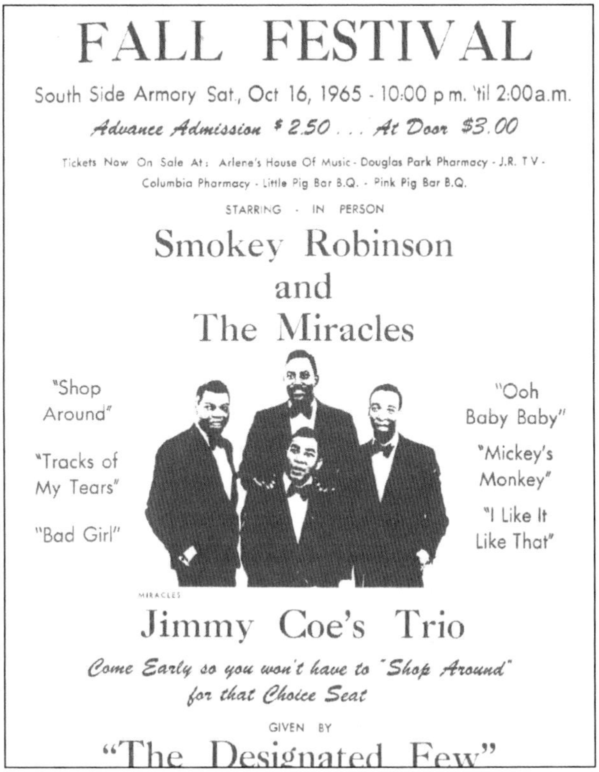

One of Motown's top acts, Smokey Robinson and the Miracles, were backed by the Jimmy Coe Trio at the Southside Armory on Saturday, October 16, 1965. (Everett Greene.)

The Sentimentals—Josephine Cheatham and Henry Hinch—and Ray Johnson toured with the stars of the Designated Production promotional group.

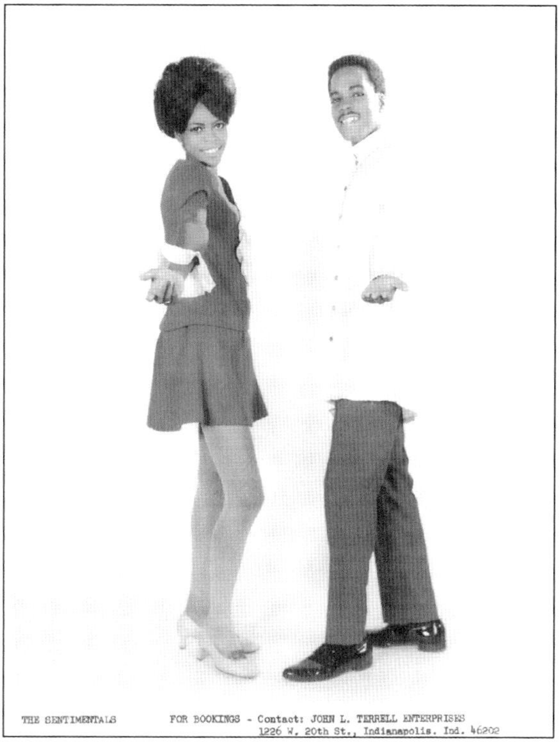

Designated Productions was an enterprising promotional group in the 1960s that showcased local talent on college campuses and nightclubs around the state. Allen King and the Pearls consisted of King, Donald Alexander, Valerie Ross, Mardeen McCorkle, and Rebecca Locke. (Guy Russell.)

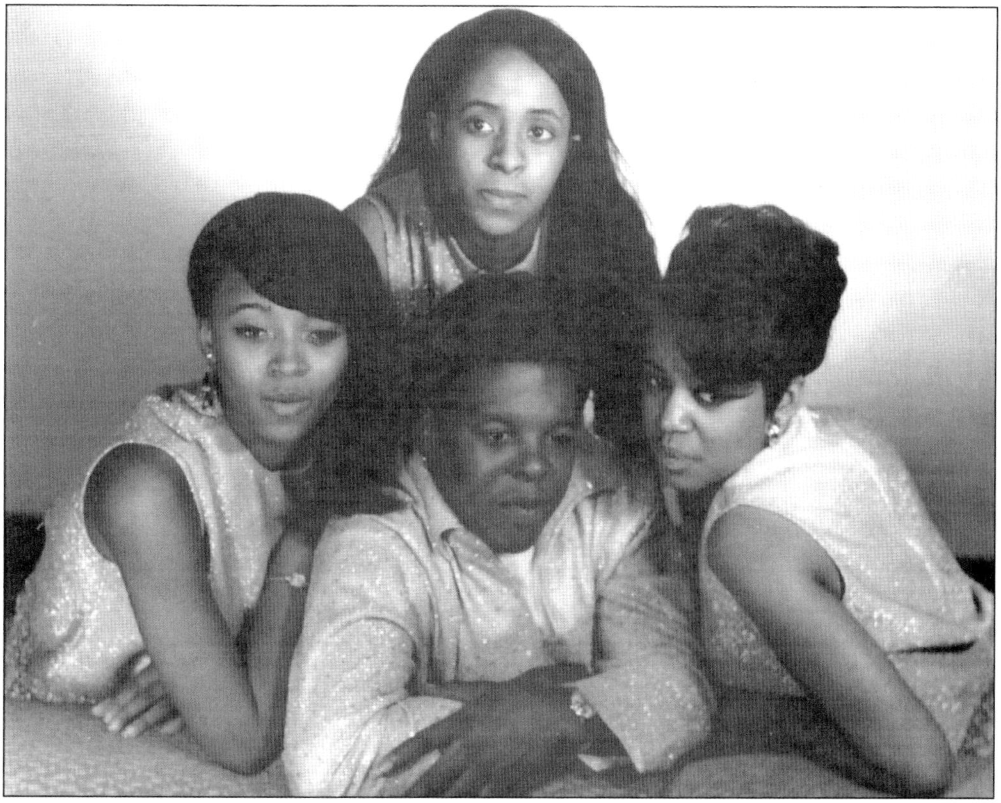

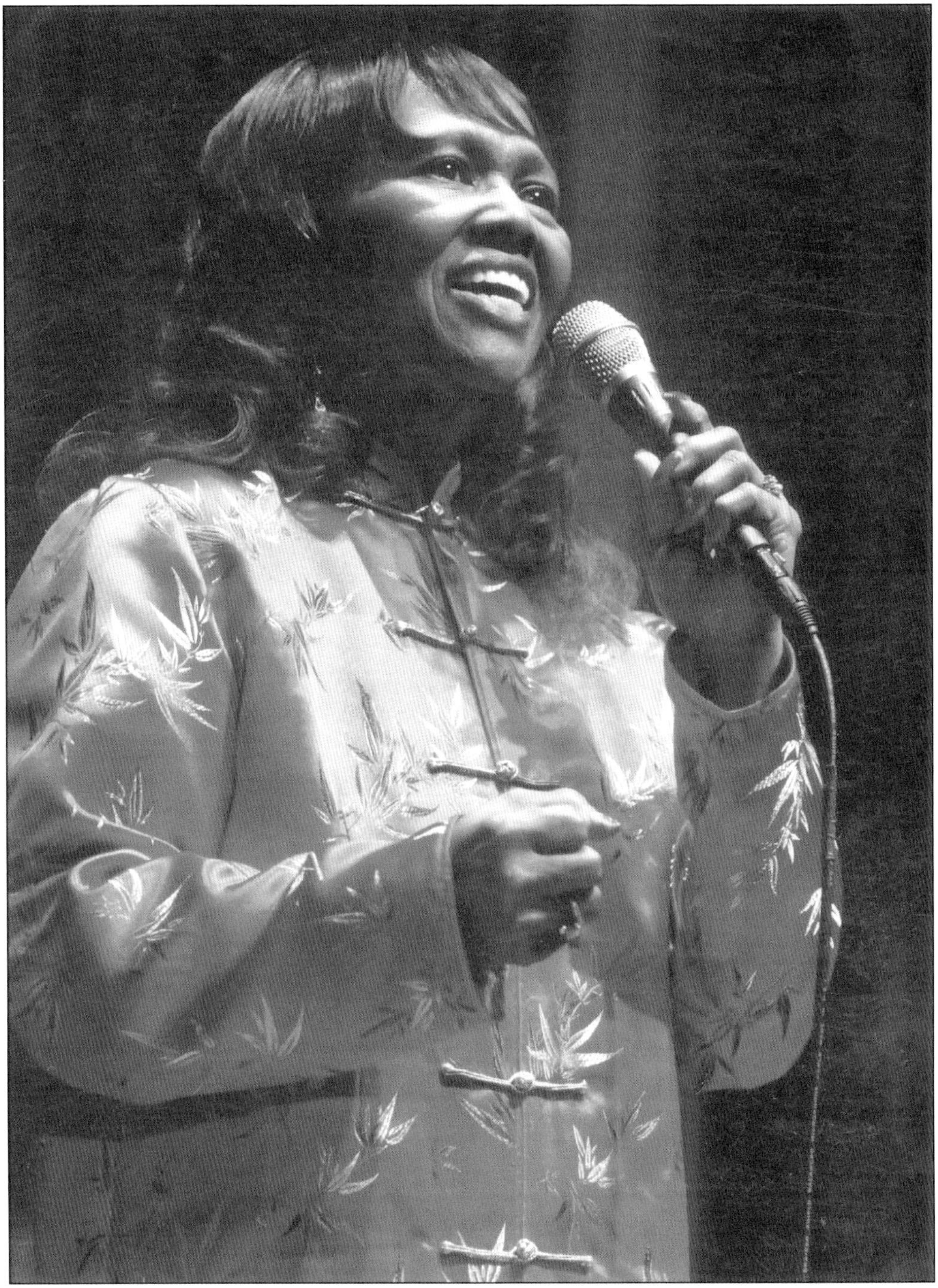

Mary Moss was a fantastic vocalist and entertainer who performed in many of the top venues in Indianapolis. In 1958, she relocated from Kentucky, married King Moss, and appeared with her husband as King and Mary. The *Indianapolis Recorder* reported that on Friday, June 3, 1988, the Mary Moss Trio performed at the Indianapolis Museum of Art. (Larry Goshen.)

Known as "the voice," Hazel Johnson-Strong was a proud member of Norman Merrifield's music department at Crispus Attucks High School. She performed in many of the top venues and received thunderous applause with her great voice. (Mack Strong.)

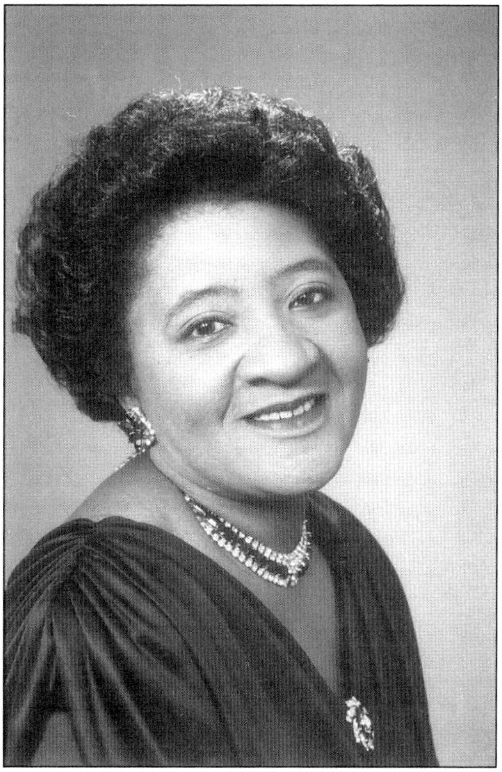

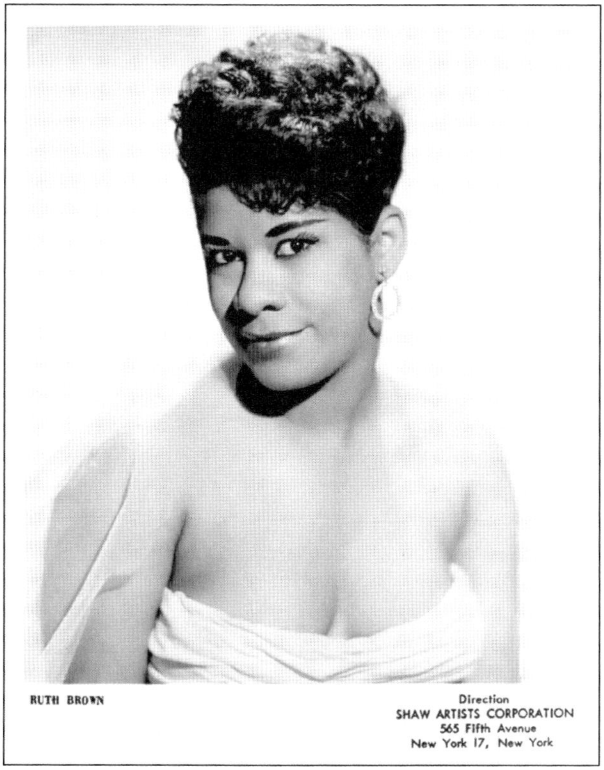

"Queen of Rhythm and Blues," Atlantic Records recording star Ruth Brown and rhythm-and-blues vocalists Charles Brown and Bobby Blue Bland appeared at the Skatarena Skating Rink on Monday, October 3, 1955. Ruth Brown's chart-topping song was "Mama He Treats Your Daughter Mean."

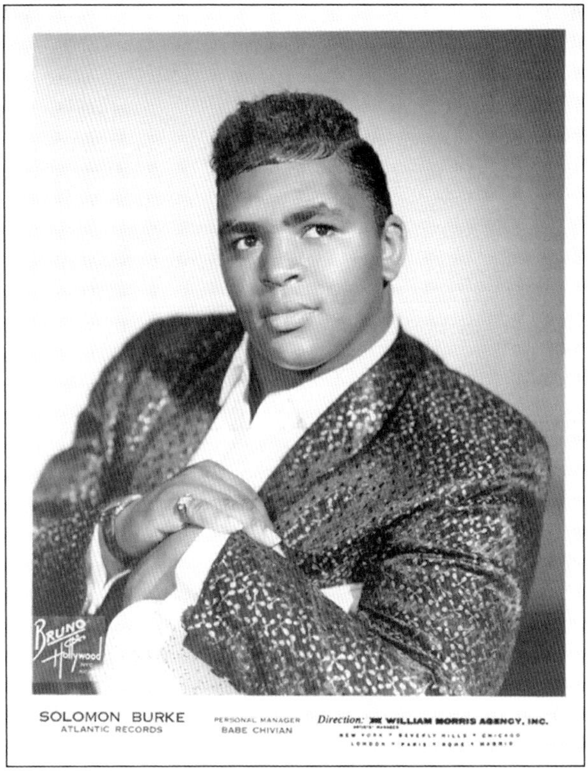

Twelve-year-old Philadelphia-born child-preaching sensation Solomon Burke left gospel music in the pulpit and carved out a musical career in rhythm and blues. He appeared Tuesday, June 12, 1962, at the Murat Theatre, where he belted out his hit "Cry to Me" and stole the show.

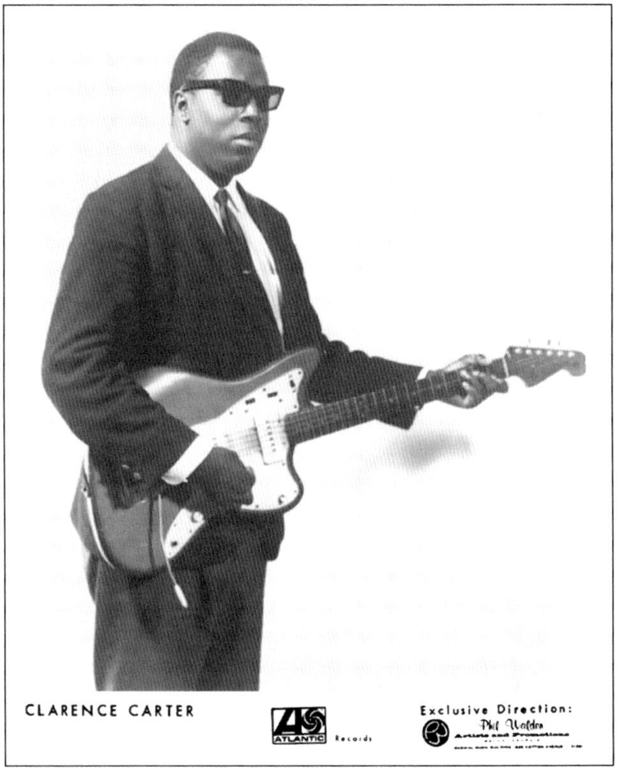

Although born blind in Montgomery, Alabama, in 1936, Clarence Carter turned this apparent disability into an ability to achieve stardom in the world of music. He attended the Alabama School for the Blind and received a bachelor's degree in music from Alabama State College in 1960. He recorded "Tell Daddy" in 1967, which reached No. 35 on the *Billboard* Hot 100. His greatest hit was his 1970 release of "Patches," which sold more than one million units and won the Grammy for Best Rhythm and Blues song of 1971.

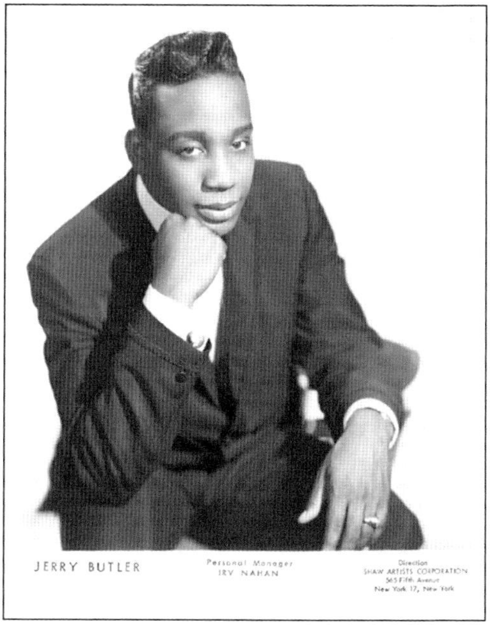

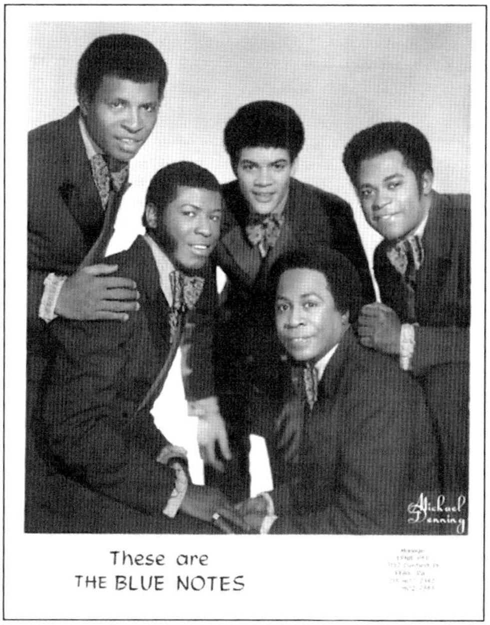

The original lead singer of the Chicago-based rhythm-and-blues group the Impressions was Jerry Butler (left). He co-wrote his signature song "For Your Precious Love" in 1958, which reached No. 11 on the *Billboard* chart. One of the legendary rhythm and blues groups from Philadelphia, Harold Melvin and the Blue Notes (right) were the toast of the town during the 1970s with their hits "If You Don't Know Me by Now," "The Love I Lost," "Wake-Up Everybody," "Bad Luck," and "I Miss You."

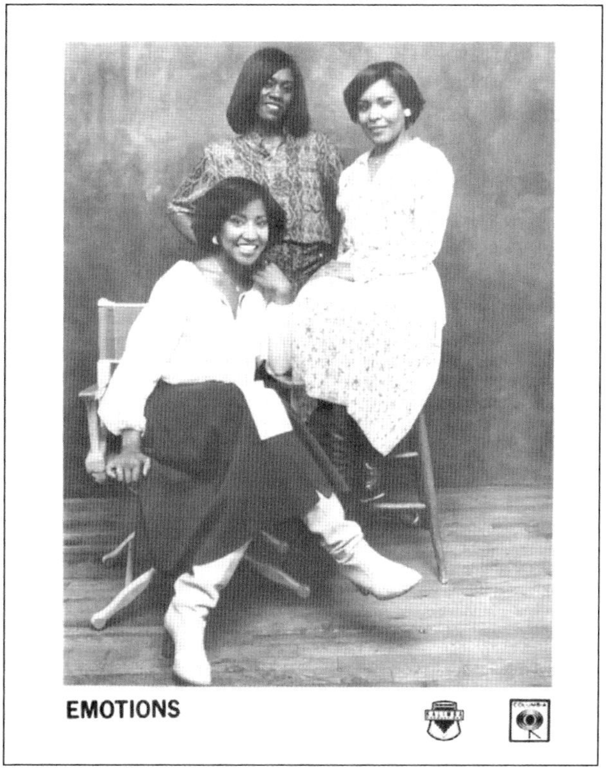

Sisters Wanda, Sheila, and Jeanette Hutchinson—the Emotions—scored a mega-hit with "Best of My Love," which topped the *Billboard* chart for five weeks in 1977 and won the Grammy for Best R&B Performance by a Duo or Group with Vocals. On Saturday, July 17, 1999, they appeared at the Indiana Black Expo Celebration.

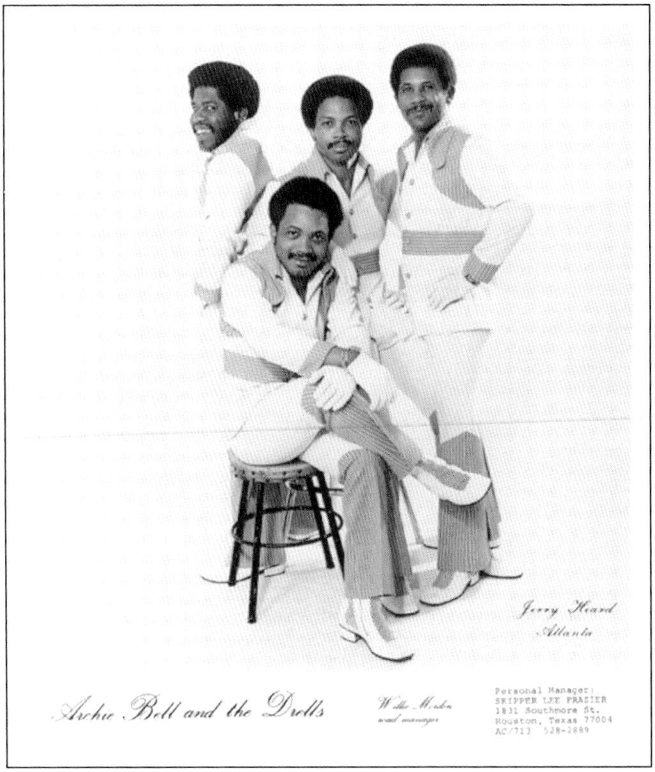

Naptowners piled into their cars and raced over to Riverfront Stadium in Cincinnati to see Archie Bell & the Drells at the Kool Jazz Festival on Friday, July 23, 1976. Their big hit was "Tighten Up."

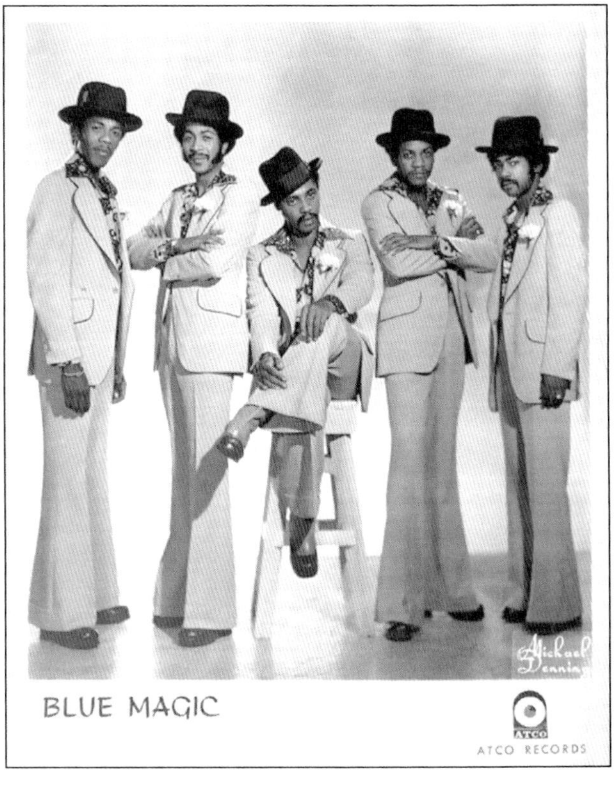

Philadelphia-based Blue Magic, with their hit "Sideshow," appeared at the Indiana Black Expo Celebration on Sunday, July 22, 1976.

Motown stars the Contours, with their hit "Do You Love Me," graced the stage at RCA Hall on July 13, 1963.

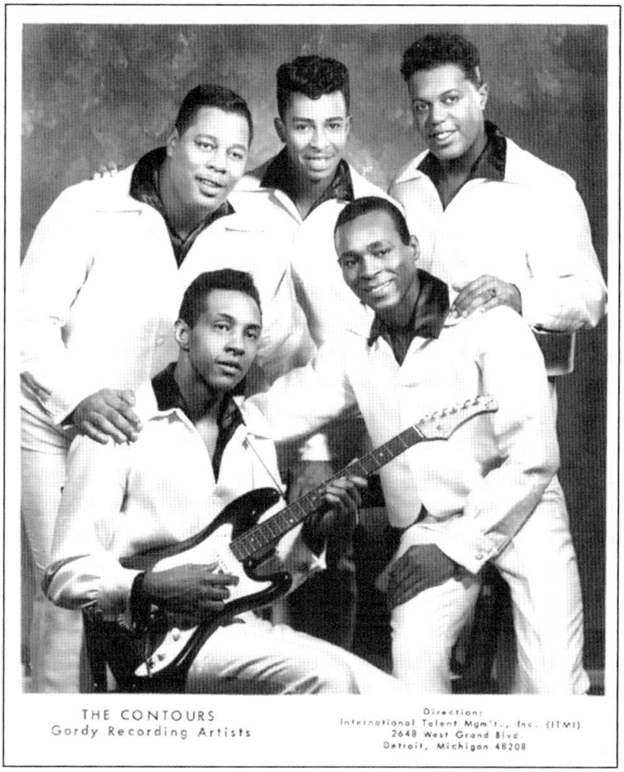

Super-masculine baritone crooner and ladies' man Arthur Prysock hit the stage at the Murat Theater on Monday, September 26, 1966.

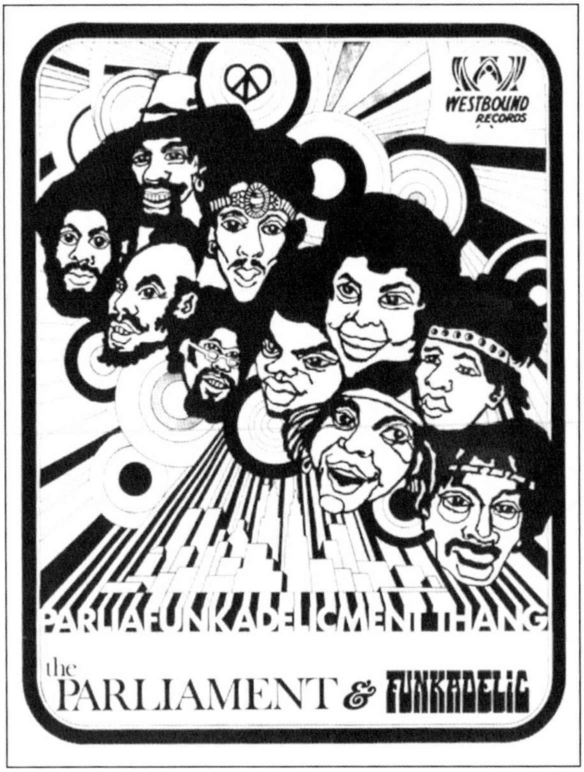

Parliament Funkadelic, along with Bootsy's Rubber Band, played the Murat Temple on Wednesday, May 19, 1976.

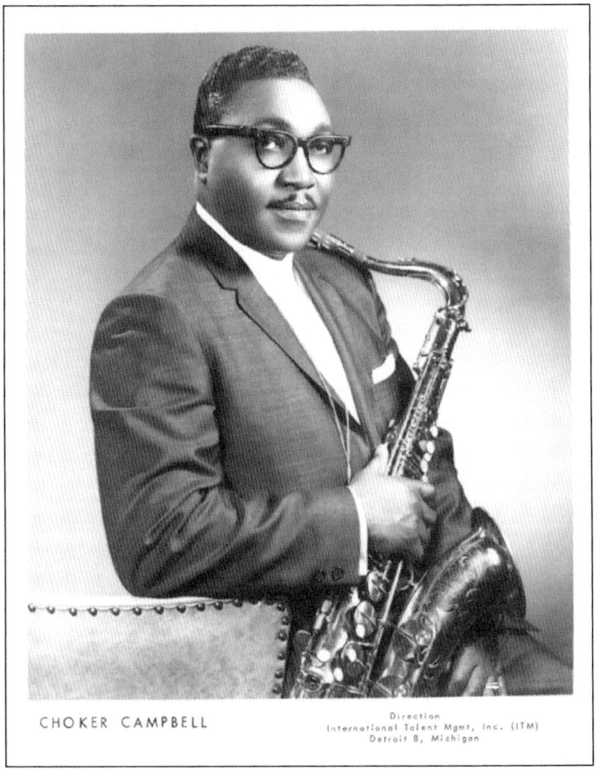

Bandleader extraordinaire Choker Campbell led his aggregation on stage at Tomlinson Hall on April 14, 1956. His orchestra backed singers Ruth Brown, the Clovers, and Little Richard.

"Tear on My Pillow," one of their greatest hits, brought Little Anthony and the Imperials to the Southside Armory on Saturday, February 12, 1966.

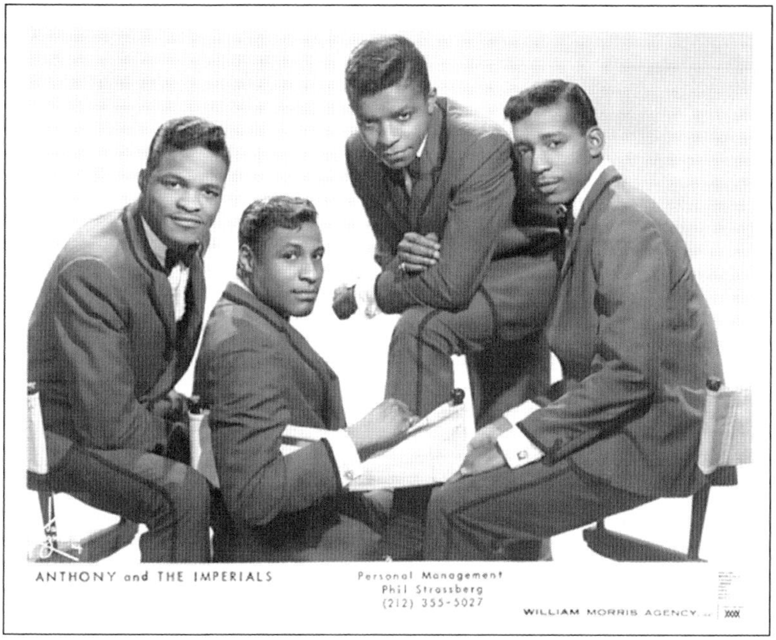

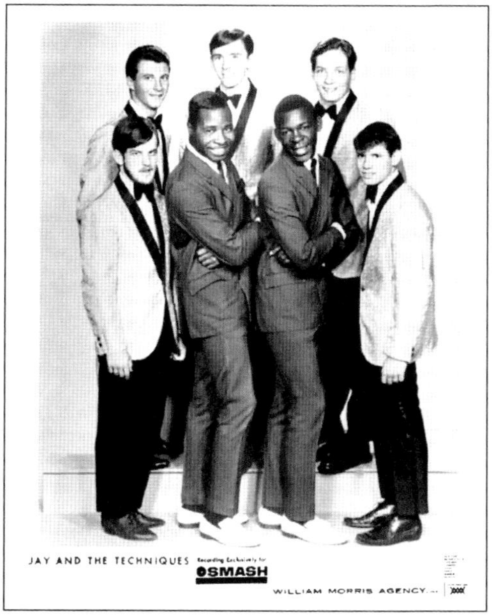

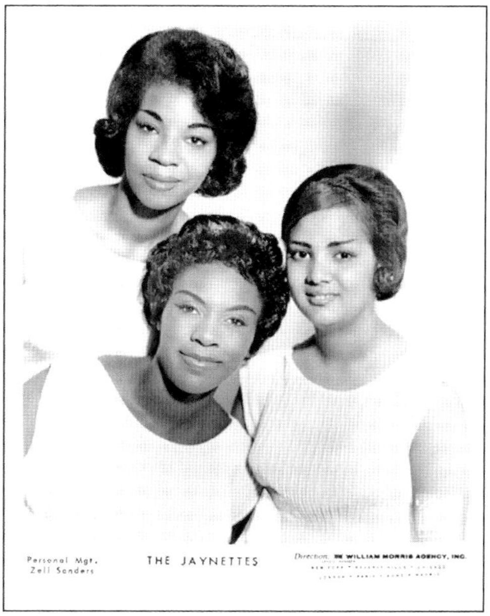

Jay and the Techniques (left), from Allentown, Pennsylvania, recorded "Apple, Peaches, Pumpkin Pie" in 1967, which climbed to No. 6 on the *Billboard* Hot 100. It sold one million units and was certified gold. At right, one-hit wonder the Jaynettes was comprised of Selena Healey, Marie Hood, Marlene Mack, Louise Harris, Lezli Valentine, and Iggy Williams. Their sole hit was "Sally Go 'Round the Roses," which reached the No. 2 spot on the *Billboard* Hot 100.

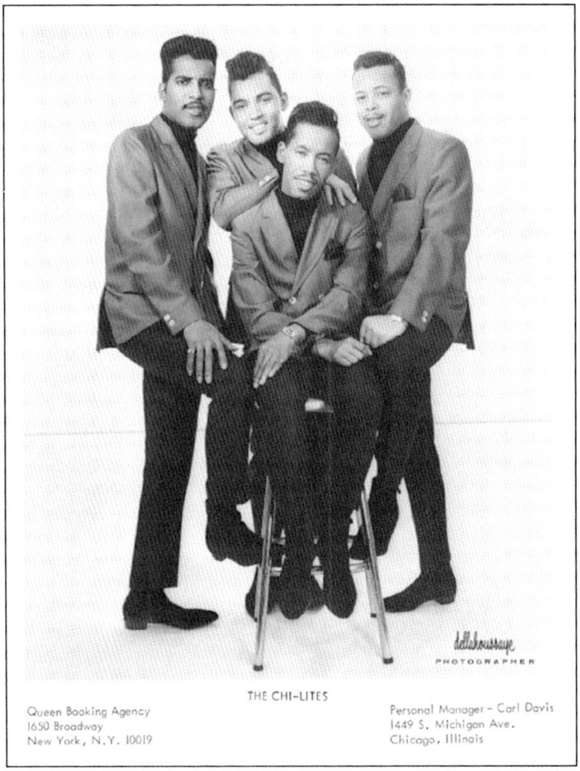

"Oh Girl" and "Have You Seen Her?" were performed by the Chi-Lites at "A Night of Golden Memories" at the Indiana Black Expo of 1986.

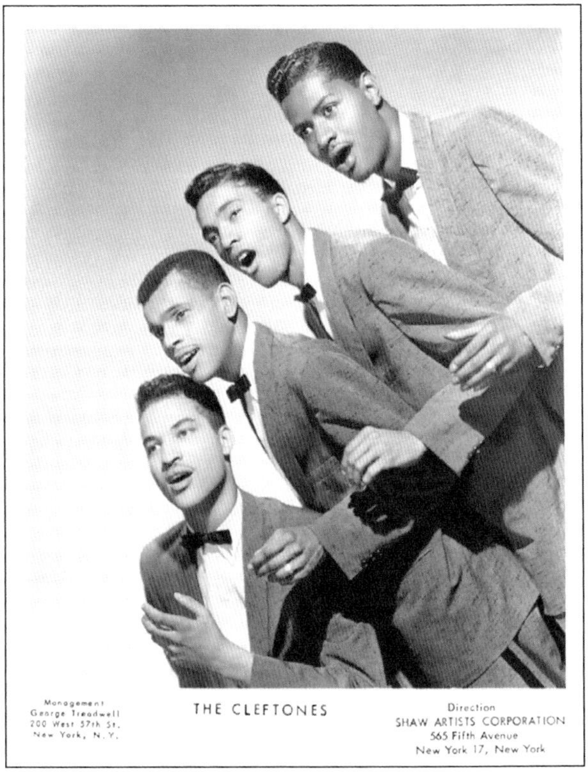

The smooth-stepping, fast-dancing Cleftones visited the Skatarena Skating Rink on Saturday, November 25, 1961. Their big hit was "Heart and Soul."

"It looks like raindrops," is the first line of Dee Clark's 1961 million-seller "Raindrops," which propelled him to the top of the rhythm-and-blues charts. He appeared at the Murat Theater on Tuesday, June 6, 1962.

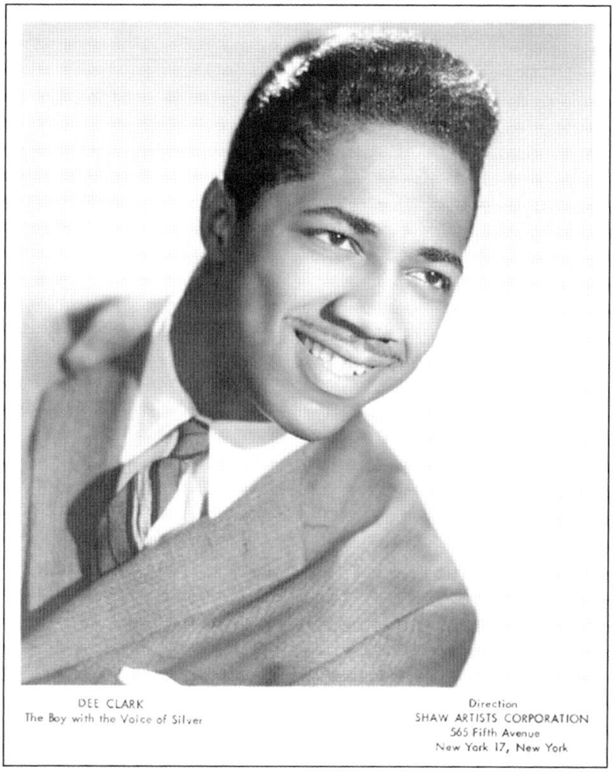

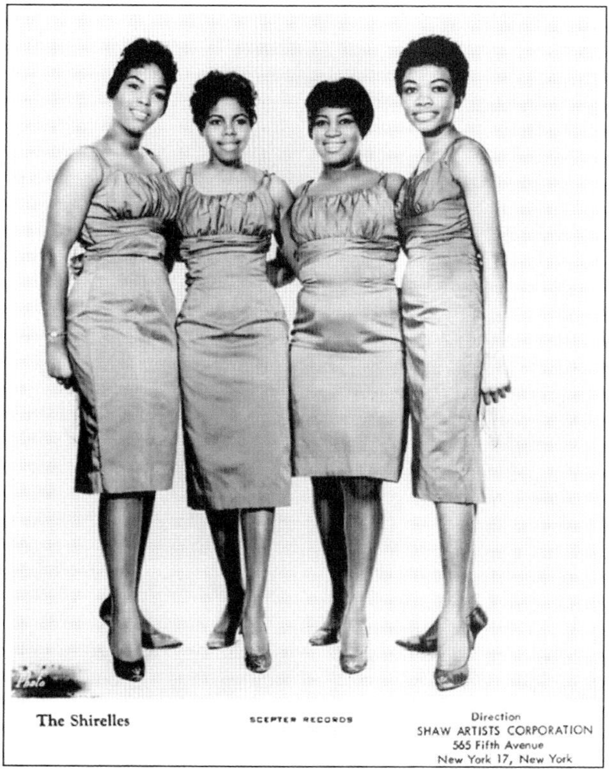

Jimmy Reed and the Shirelles headlined a rock and roll show at the Skatarena Skating Rink in the early 1960s.

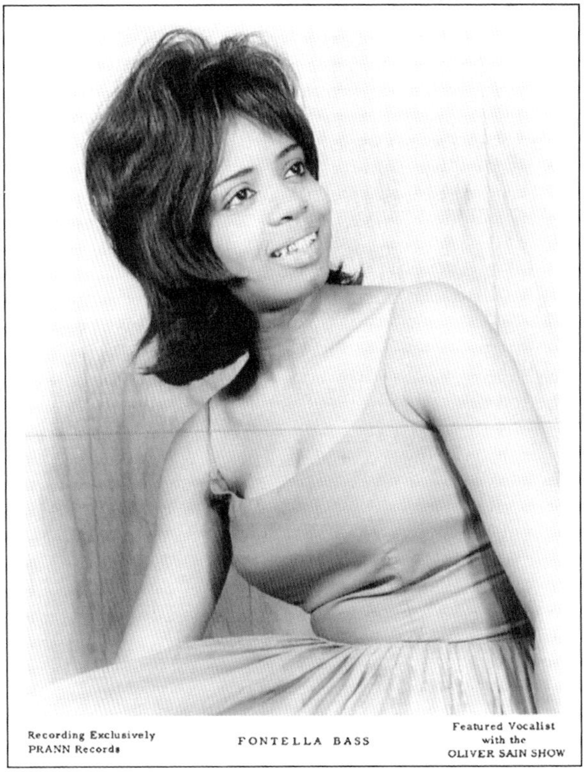

This St. Louis-born daughter of a famous gospel mother and member of the Clara Ward Gospel Singers was destined for a fabulous musical career in the church, but fate stepped in. An article in the April 15, 1995, *Indianapolis Recorder* titled "The Gospel According to Fontella Bass" illuminated her struggle between secular and gospel music. As old church folks said back in the day, "You can't worship two masters." Bass went on to record the 1965 mega-hit "Rescue Me," which reached No. 4 on the US pop charts and No. 11 on the UK pop charts.

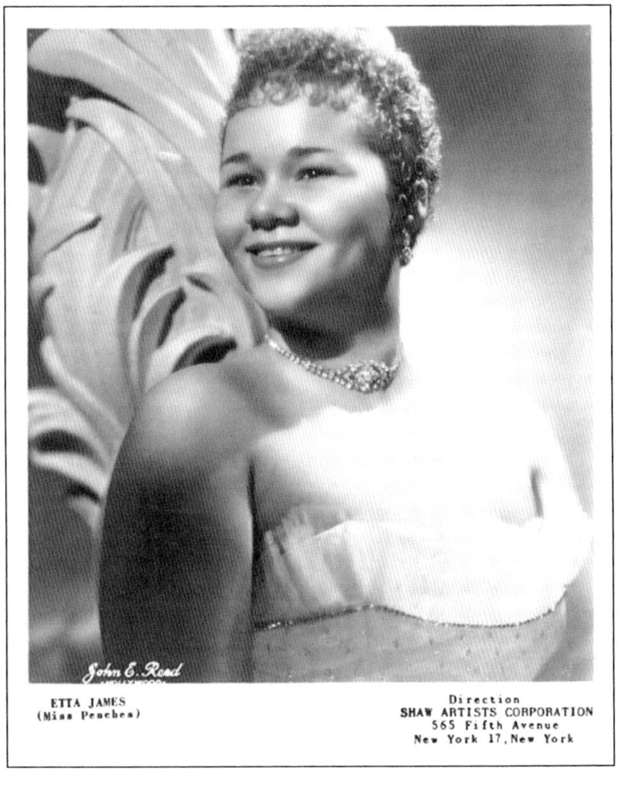

Six-time Grammy Award–winner and Rock and Roll Hall of Fame inductee Etta James was loved by Indiana Avenue blues lovers. Her signature hit, "At Last," released in 1960, sent her fans to the land of "Spellboundonia." She frequently appeared at the Pink Poodle to standing room–only crowds.

Eighteen-time Grammy Award–winner "the Queen of Soul," Aretha Franklin, is one of the most highly esteemed and universally recognized rhythm-and-blues singers in the world. Her song "Respect" was an inner-city anthem during the turbulent 1960s. She frequently headlined shows at the Pink Poodle.

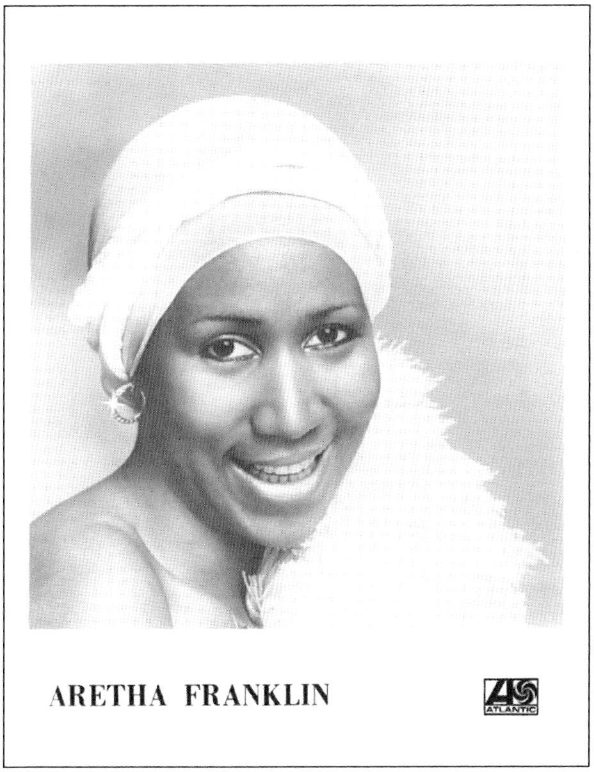

Baby Leon of the Presidents is pictured on stage at the Place to Play around 1960. (Larry Goshen.)

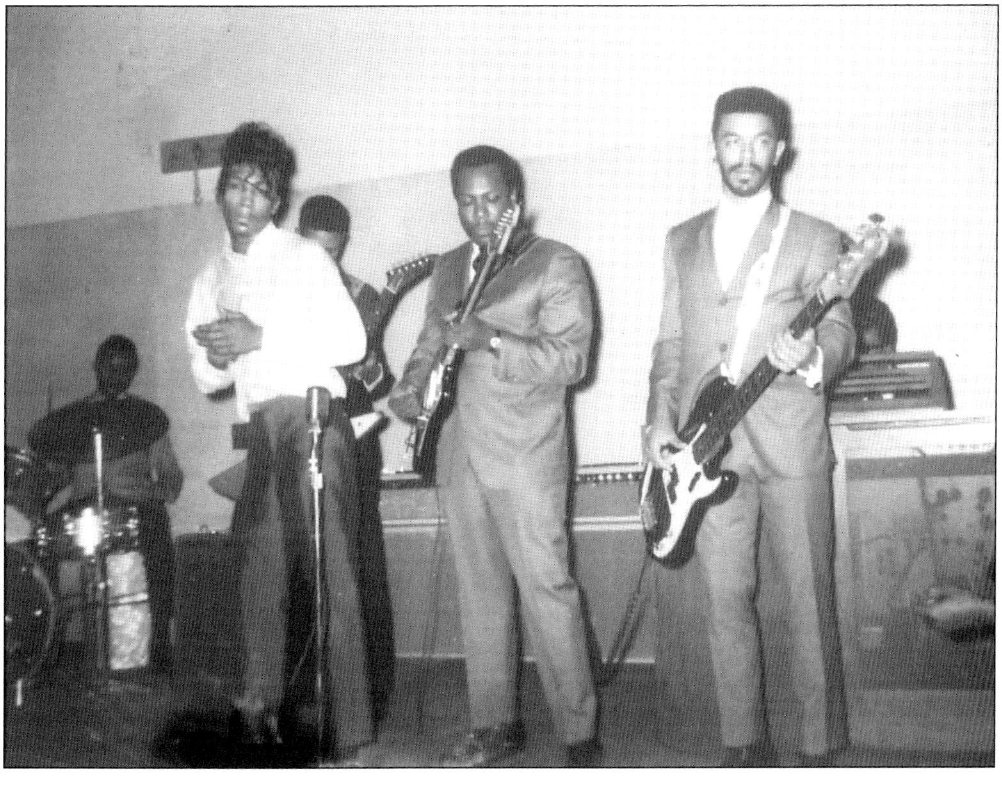

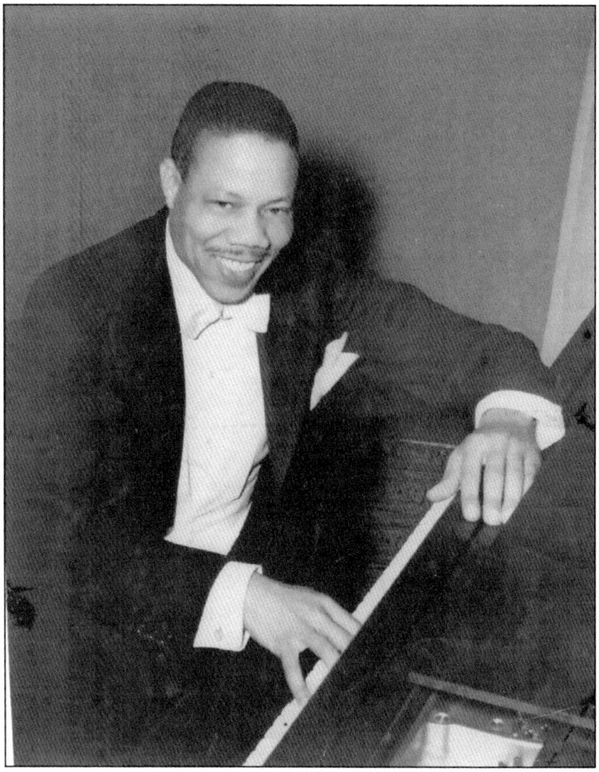

The name Belford Hendricks must go down in history as the greatest arranger of rhythm-and-blues hits of all times. This Evansville native arranged and composed songs performed by everyone from James Brown and Elvis Presley to Tammy Wynette and Dolly Parton. (Jeffery Bibbs.)

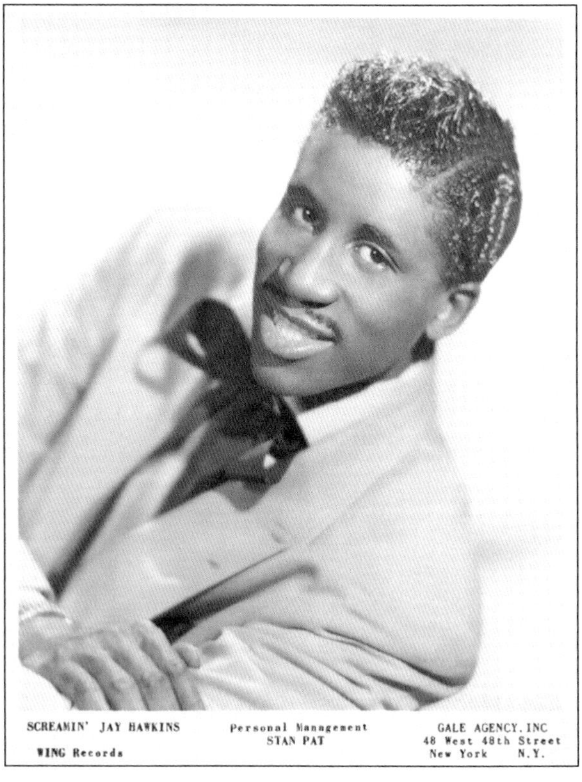

"Screamin' Jay" Hawkins brought the house down during his appearance at the Big All-Star Show at the Circle Theater on Thursday, August 15, 1957. As the curtain rose, there was a casket on center stage. The lights dimmed, and background music from his signature hit, "I Put a Spell on You," began to play. Slowly, the lid of the casket began to open, and the music intensified to a heightened crescendo. Hawkins slowly climbed out of the casket. Dressed in a long black cape and stovepipe hat, Hawkins smiled and then hollered in a ghoulishly sardonic voice, "I Put a Spell on You," as audience members screamed; some exited the theater. Hawkins pulled out a walking stick and struck the floor, and a flame shot out of the tip as he continued singing his song. Folks talked about the concert for many years.

A distinguished music educator in the Indianapolis Public School System who trained many of the jazz and popular music greats, Larry Liggett founded the Meridian Recording Company in his basement and introduced many of the local groups to the radio airwaves. Among the groups were the Creations, with their hit "The Wedding," and the Esquires with their hits "When I Fall in Love" and "The Bells;" both recordings featured the fantastic voice of Rudd Kenneth Williams.

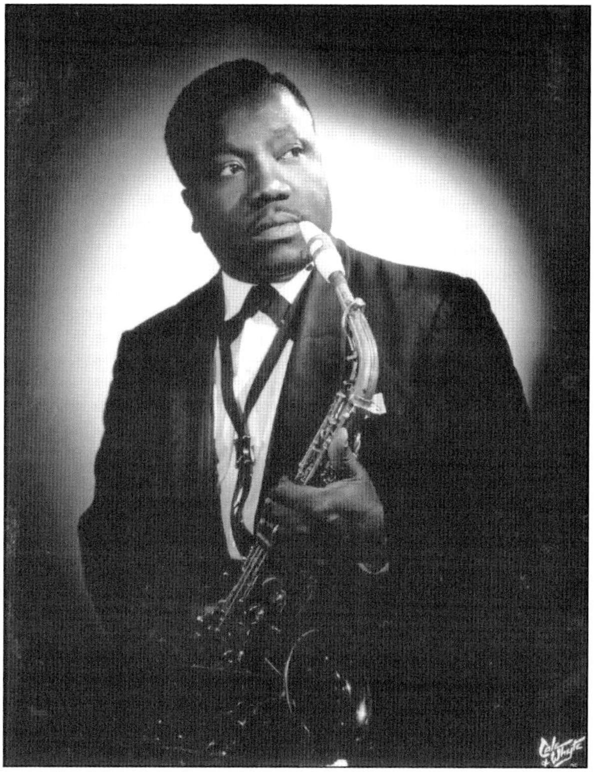

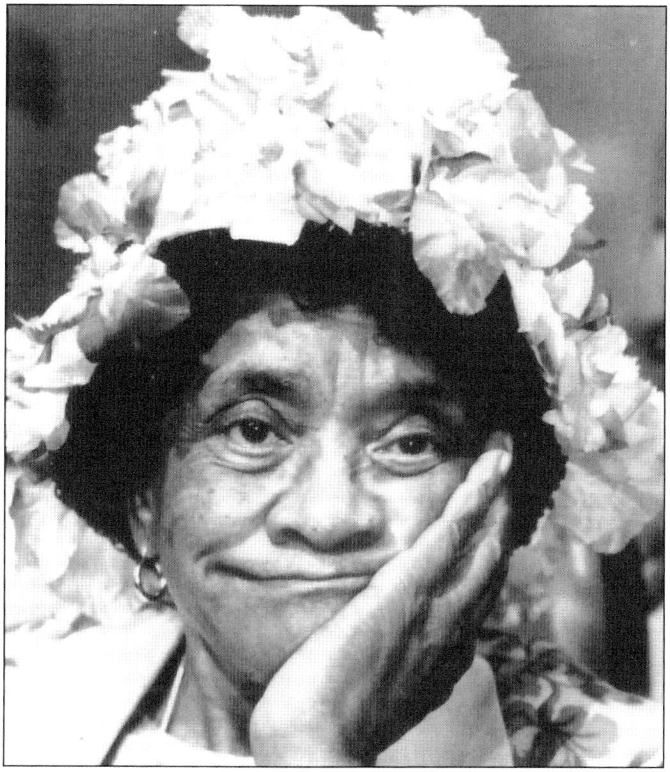

Born Loretta Mary Aiken in Brevard, North Carolina, on March 19, 1894, Jackie "Moms" Mabley became one of America's leading female comedians. She was the first female comedian to headline a show at the world-famous Apollo Theater and was a frequent performer for many years. She appeared in Hollywood motion pictures *The Big Timers* (1945), *Boarding House Blues* (1948), and the musical revue *Killer Diller* (1948), co-starring Nat King Cole and Butterfly McQueen. On Friday, May 8, 1964, she brought the Jackie "Moms" Mabley All-Star Show to the Circle Theater.

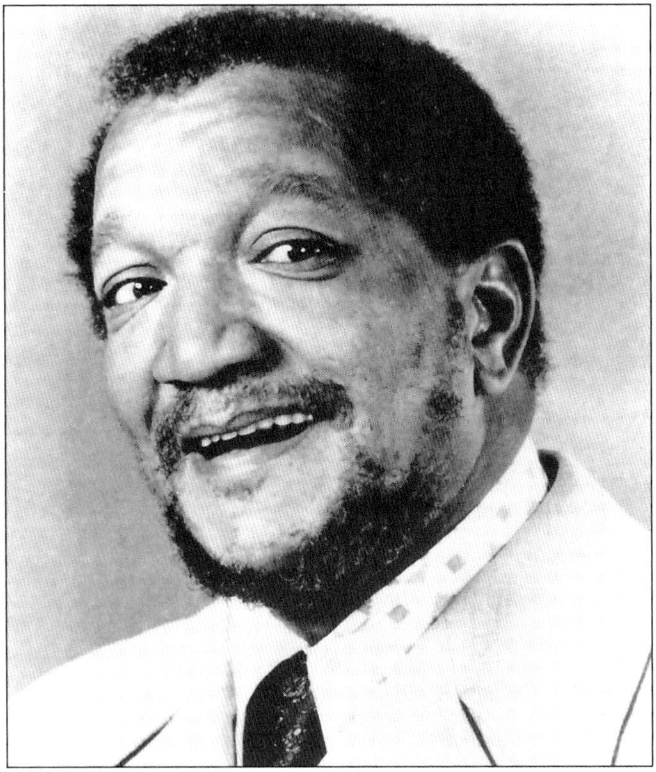

Redd Foxx was one of America's premier stand-up comedians for many decades. Born John Elroy Sanford on December 9, 1922, in St. Louis, he mastered the comedy-club stage as well as television. His television situation comedy show *Sanford and Son* was one of television's chart toppers from January 14, 1972, to March 25, 1977. On May 4, 1975, he brought the *Sanford and Son* comedy show to the Convention-Exposition Center.

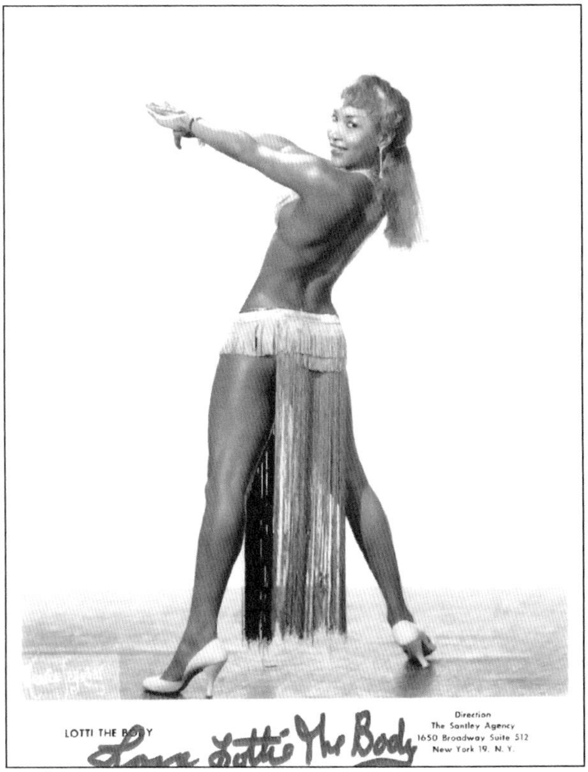

Statuesque, curvaceous "Lottie the Body," an ecdysiast (an erotic dancer who removes their clothes as a form of entertainment), was not an exotic dancer or a stripper (both categories popular in the clubs), but a creatively artistic dancer who maintained a degree of decorum and professionalism in her act. On Friday, May 3, 1963, she appeared in the Louis Jordan Show, and on May 25, 1963, in the Redd Fox Comedy Show at the Pink Poodle.

Vanilla Wafer was an exotic dancer who performed in many of the clubs around town. In January 1964, she danced in the Big Maybelle Show at the Club 16 Night Club and on Friday, January 19, 1962, she appeared on the Ruth Brown Show at the Pink Poodle.

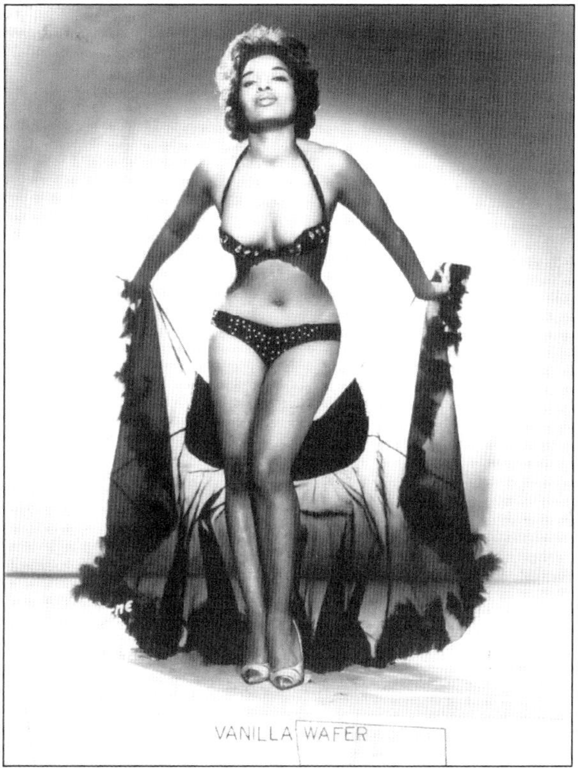

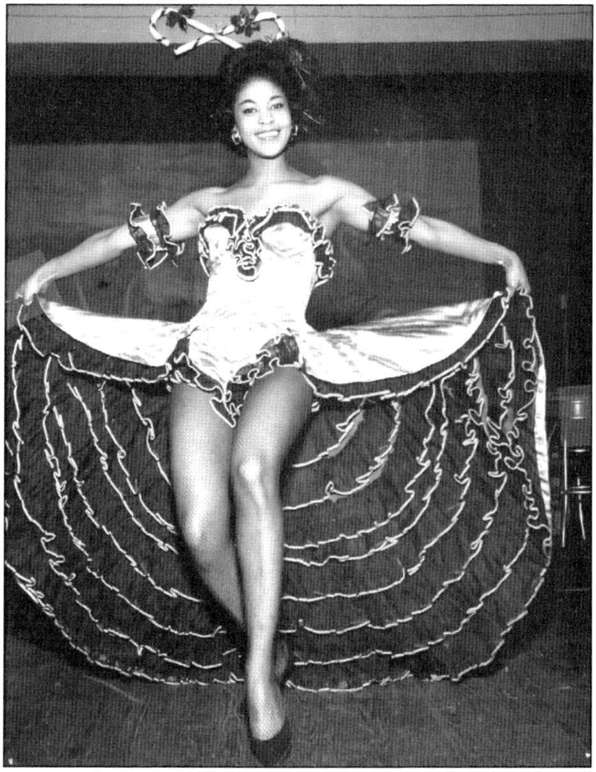

The Arthur Braggs Idlewild Review show took place in the Paradise Night Club in Idlewild, Michigan, 250 miles northwest of Detroit during the era of racial segregation in the 1950s and 1960s. It showcased Hollywood-caliber entertainment for prosperous blacks from surrounding states, featuring musicians, singers, dancers, showgirls, models, comedians, choreographers, and makeup artists. Headliners such as Jackie Wilson, the Four Tops, Roy Hamilton, T-Bone Walker, and Della Reese often appeared there. Pictured is Carleen Gill, a pretty showgirl who delighted the crowds nightly. Indianapolis native Joella Keough, one of the beautiful dancers who sparkled under the lights on stage, later became a nationally-renowned bowler.

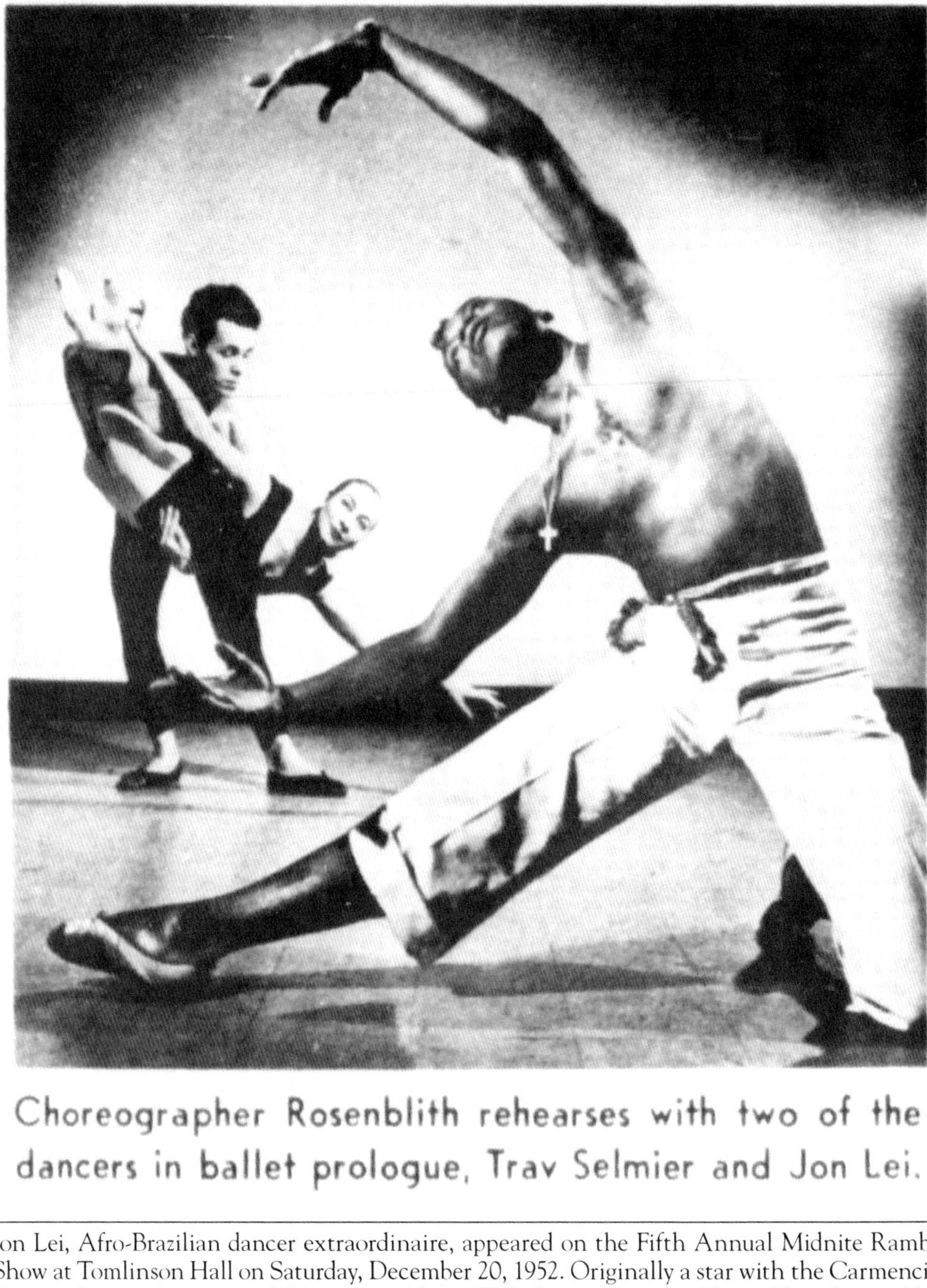

Choreographer Rosenblith rehearses with two of the dancers in ballet prologue, Trav Selmier and Jon Lei.

Jon Lei, Afro-Brazilian dancer extraordinaire, appeared on the Fifth Annual Midnite Ramble Show at Tomlinson Hall on Saturday, December 20, 1952. Originally a star with the Carmencita Romero Dance Company of Chicago and New York, he distinguished himself in the world of dance. In April 1945, he joined the internationally acclaimed New York–based Katherine Dunham Dance Company and performed throughout Europe and South America. He danced six months in the Prince of Wales Theater in London and was the head of the dance department at the Mac Arthur Conservatory of Music.

Four

Performers around the Country

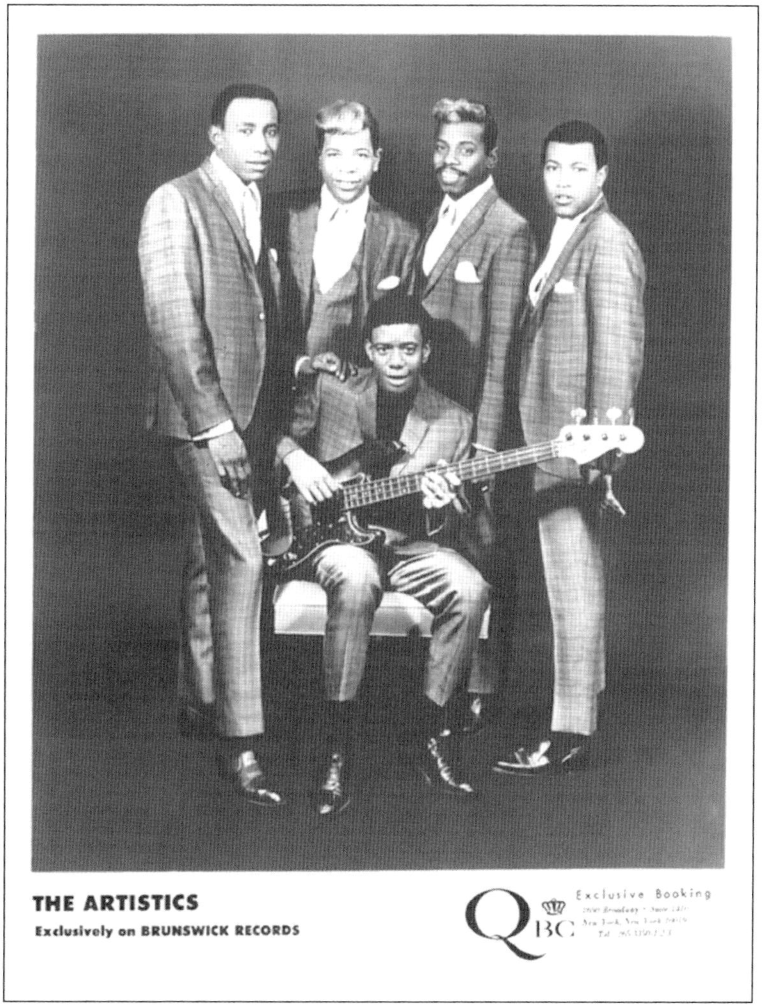

Formed at Marshall High School in Chicago in 1958, the Artistics were the talk of the town. With Curt Thomas, lead; Larry Johnson, first tenor; Jesse Bolian, second tenor; and Aaron Floyd, baritone/bass, their greatest hit, "I'm Gonna Miss You," topped the charts in 1966.

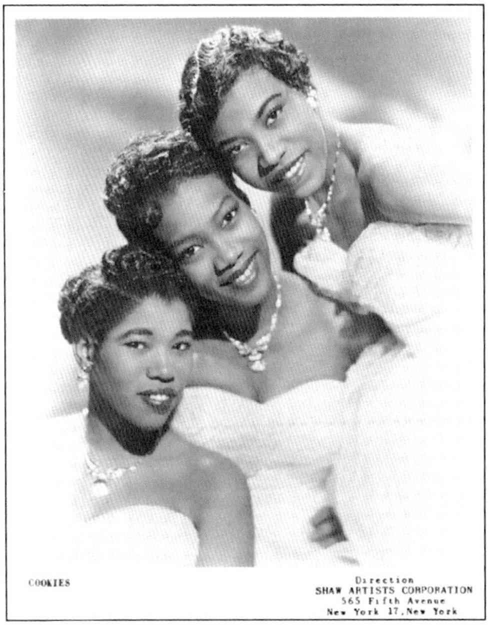

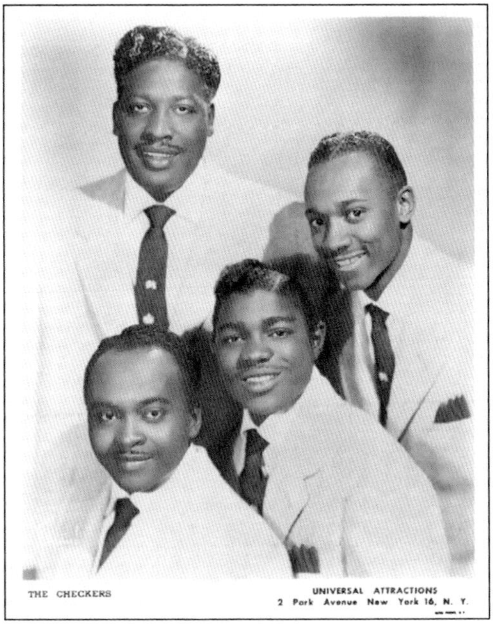

The Cookies (left)—Dorothy Jones, Darlene McRea, and Beulah Robertson—formed in Brooklyn, New York. Later, some members became the Raelettes, who were background singers for Ray Charles; they were also the background singers on Little Eva's 1962 hit "Locomotion." When bass Bill Brown of Billy Ward and his Dominoes left the group, he formed the Checkers (right). The members were Brown, Charlie White, Eddie Harris, John Carnegie, and Perry Heyward. Their hit was "White Cliffs of Dover."

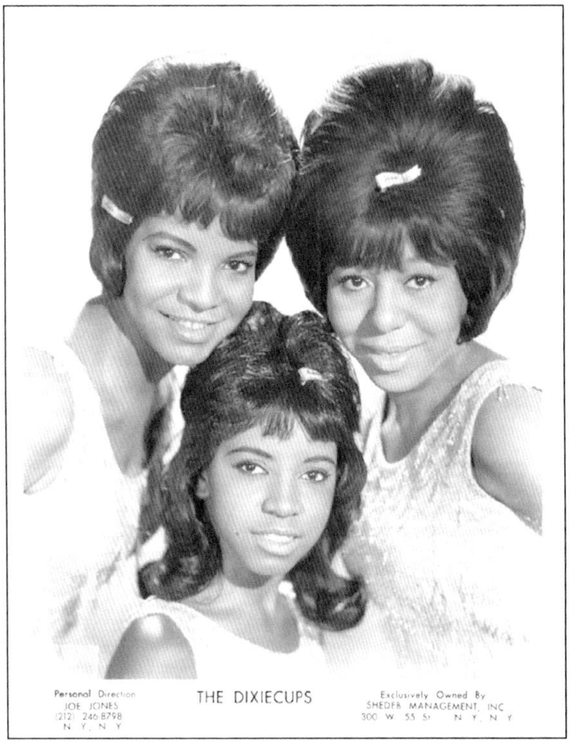

The Dixie Cups' 1964 hit "Chapel of Love" was showcased on Dick Clark's *American Bandstand*. Originally called Little Miss and the Muffets, the group consisted of sisters Barbara Ann and Rosa Lee Hawkins and their cousin Joan Marie Johnson.

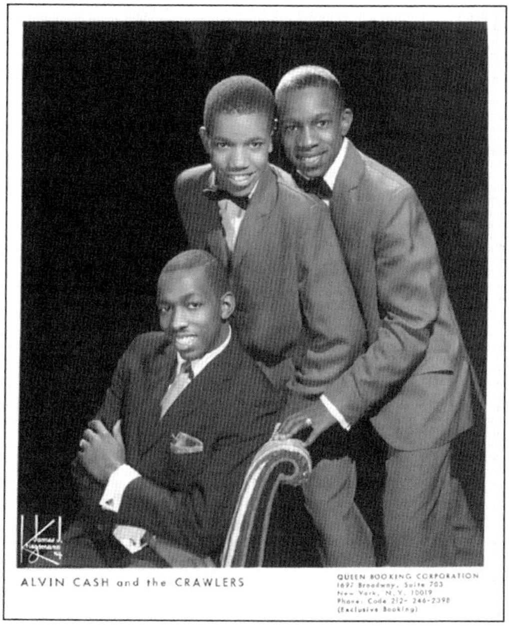

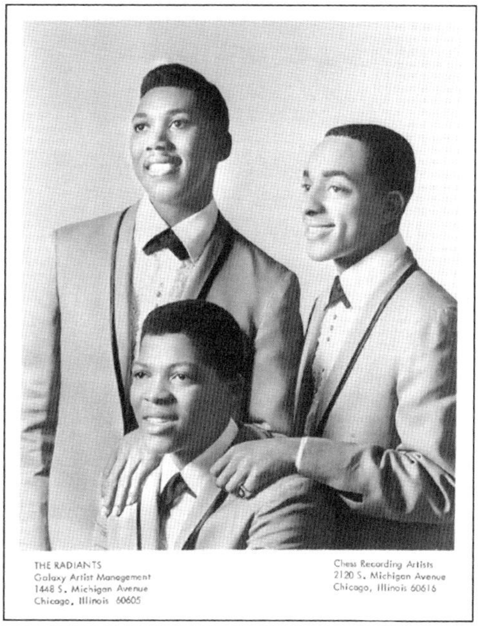

Alvin Cash (left), whose given name was Alvin Welch, had a mega-hit in 1965 titled "Twine Time." Later, he appeared in blaxploitation movie *Petey Wheatstraw*. "Voice Your Choice," recorded by the Radiants (right) in 1964, was a rhythm-and-blues favorite on college campuses across the country. Group members were Maurice McAllister, Wallace Sampson, Leonard Caston, and James Jameson.

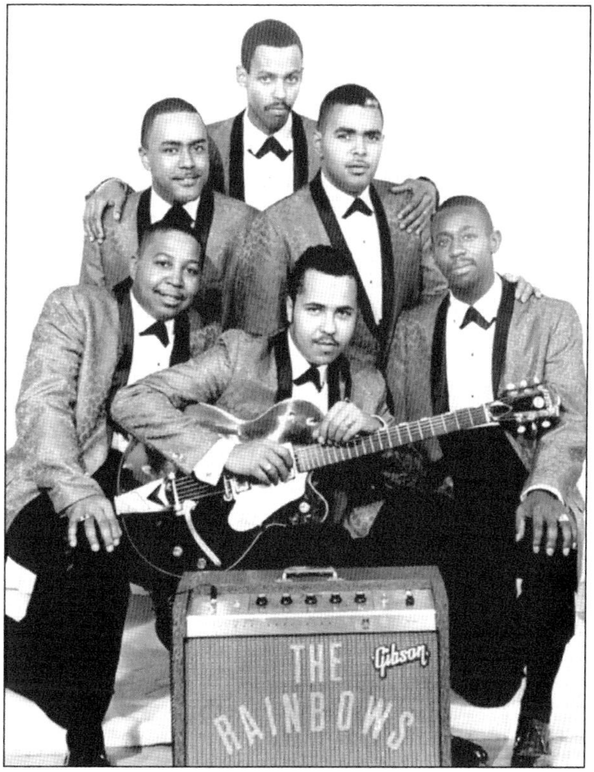

The Rainbows, one of the most popular groups out of Washington, DC, recorded their songs with female names. "Mary Lee," "Shirley," and "Minnie" were their hits. The members were Ronald "Posie" Miles, John Berry, and Chester Simmons.

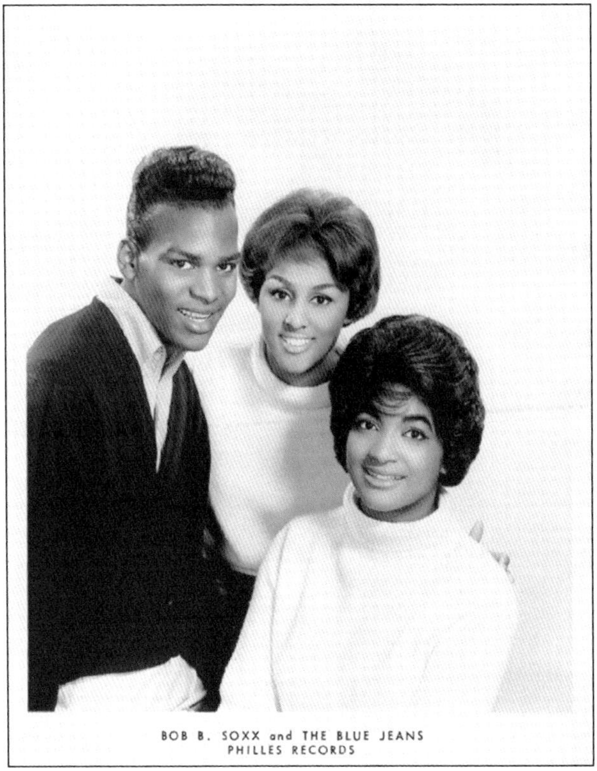

Bob B. Soxx & the Blue Jeans—Bobby Sheen, Darlene Love, and Fanita James—had a hit in 1962 titled "Zip-a-Dee-Doo-Dah," based on the title song from the 1946 Disney movie *Song of the South*. Love and James were also members of another rhythm-and-blues group, the Blossoms.

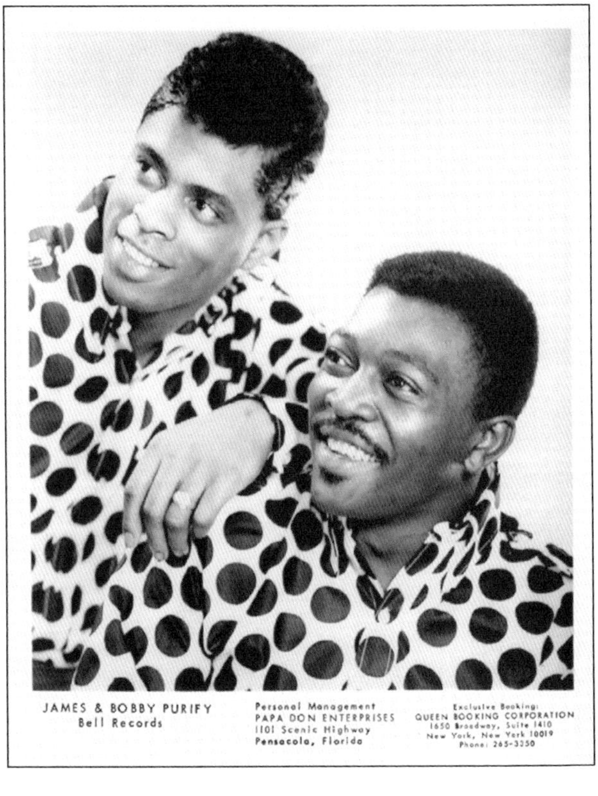

James & Bobby Purify were James Lee Purify and Robert Lee Dickey. Their two big hits, "I'm Your Puppet" and "Shake a Tail Feather," reached No. 6 in 1966 and No. 25 in 1967, respectively, on the *Billboard* Hot 100.

"Silver Fox of the Blues" Buddy Ace, whose given name was Jimmie Lee Land, was a Texas crooner of the blues. He sang in a gospel group with bluesman Joe Tex. His greatest hit, "Nothing in the World Can Hurt Me," reached No. 25 on the *Billboard* Hot 100 in 1966.

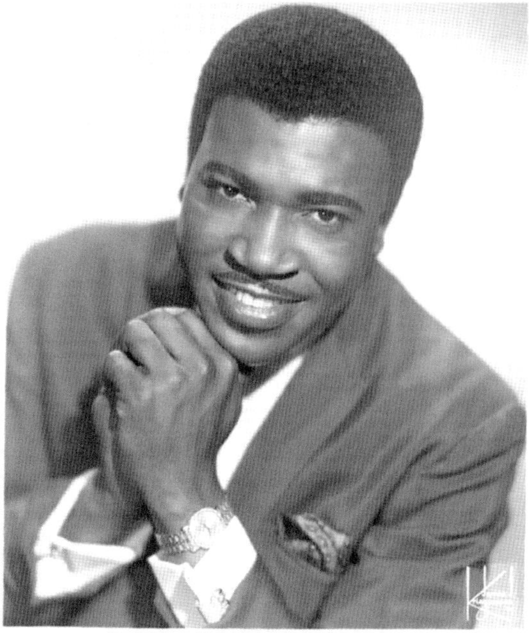

BUDDY ACE

Management:
Buffalo Booking Agency

The younger brother of Jerry Butler of the Impressions of Chicago, Billy Butler formed the Chanters, which included Erroll Batts and Jesse Tillman. Their greatest hit was "I Can't Work No Longer," which ascended to No. 6 on the *Billboard* Hot 100 in 1965.

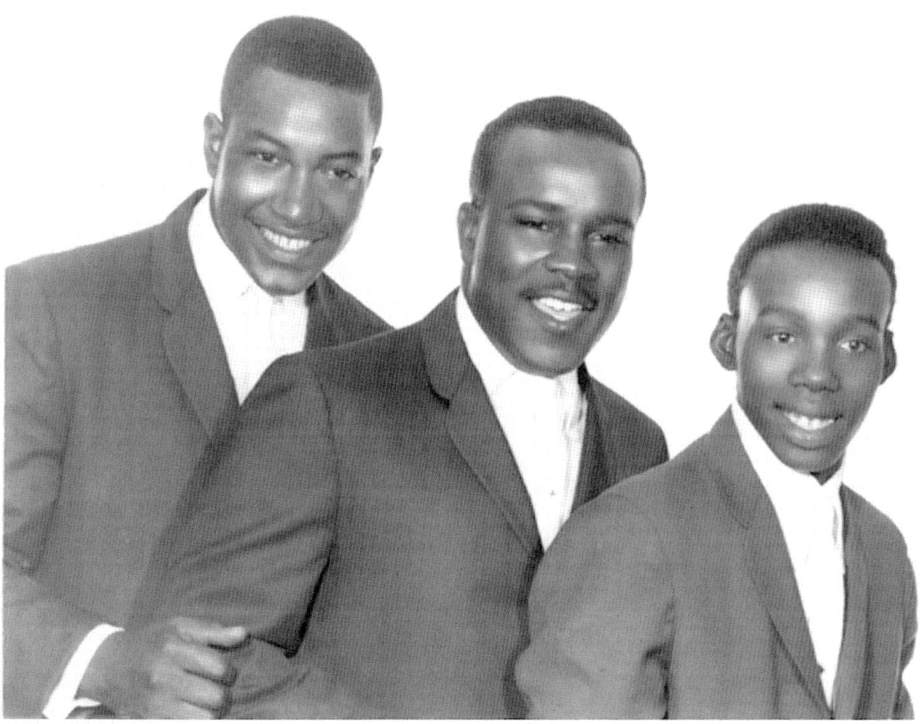

BILLY BUTLER and
The CHANTERS

Personal Mgr.
Irv Nahan

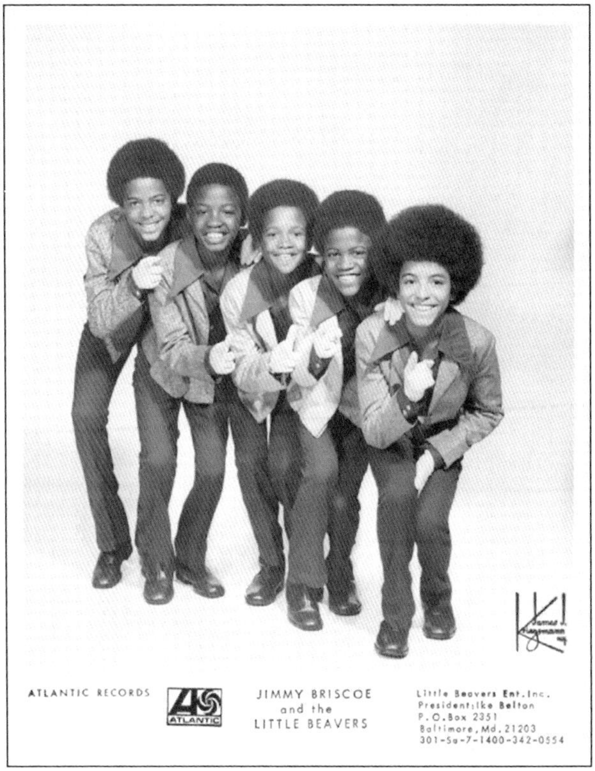

Jimmy Briscoe & the Little Beaver formed in the shadow of the Jackson Five when young male groups around the country wanted to emulate this great family of music. The members were Briscoe, Stanford Stansbury, Kevin Barnes, Maurice Pulley, and Robert Makins, who was later replaced by Robert Finch.

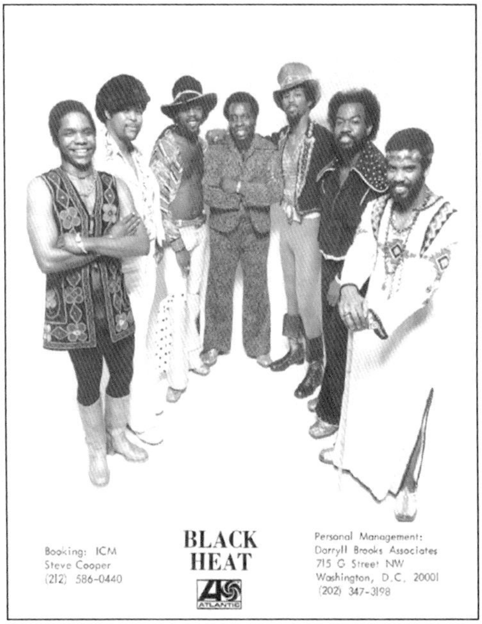

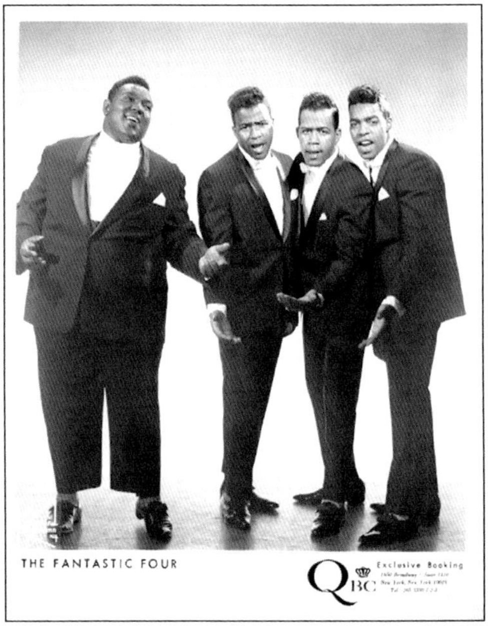

Black Heat (left) was a 1970s funk band formed by Phillip Guilbeau. Their biggest hit was "No Time to Burn." The Fantastic Four (right) organized in 1964, comprised of James Epps, brothers Ralph and Joseph Pruitt, and Wallace "Toby" Childs. Childs and Ralph Pruitt exited and were replaced by Cleveland Horne and Ernest Newsome. Their greatest hit was "The Whole World is a Stage," which climbed the *Billboard* rhythm and blues chart in 1967.

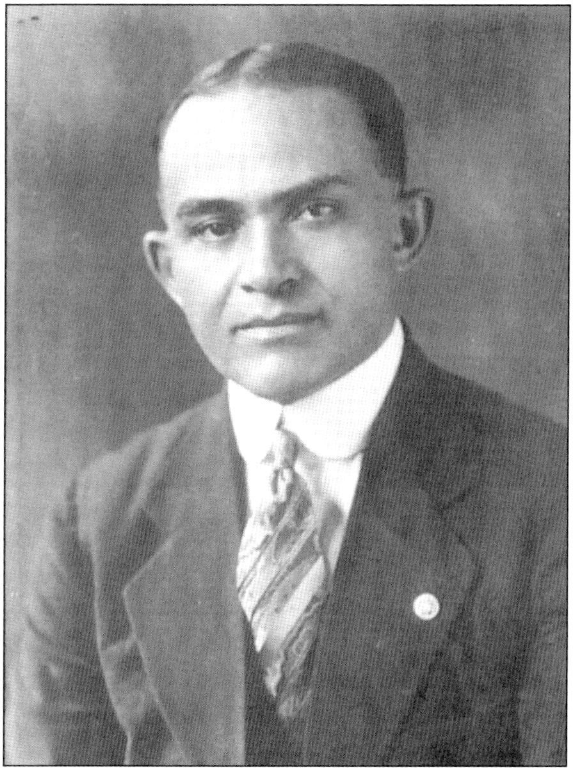

Mathias Nolcox was born in Lyles Station, Indiana, in 1886, received his bachelor's and master's degrees from Indiana University and Harvard University respectively, and became the first principal of Crispus Attucks High School in 1927. (Both, Indiana Historical Society.)

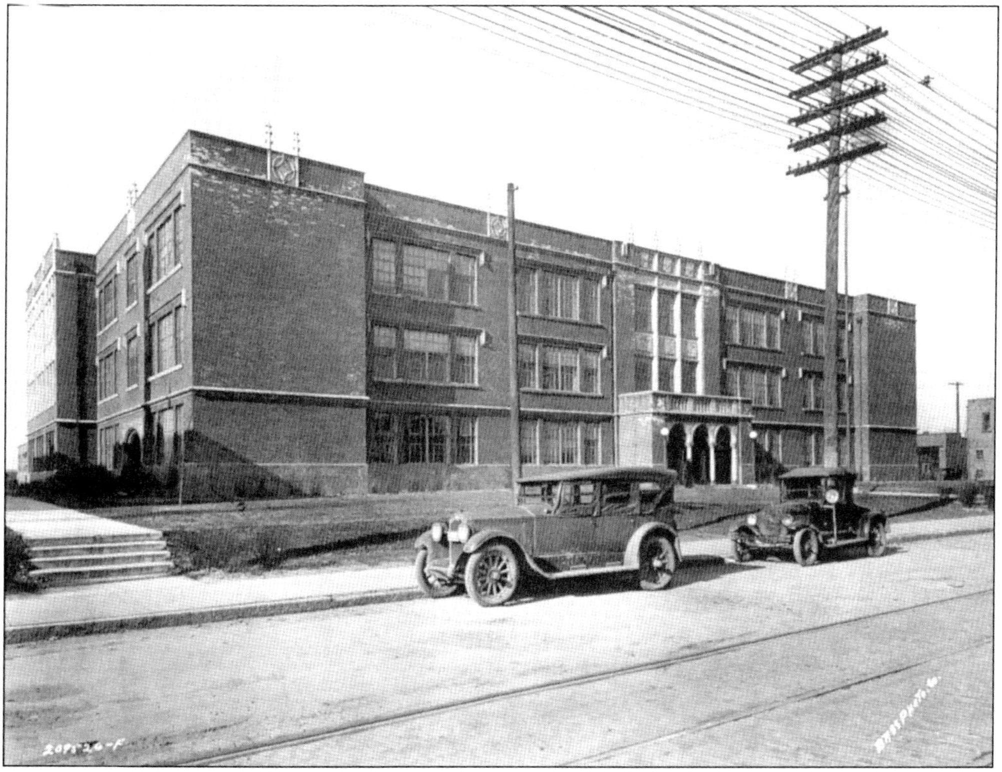

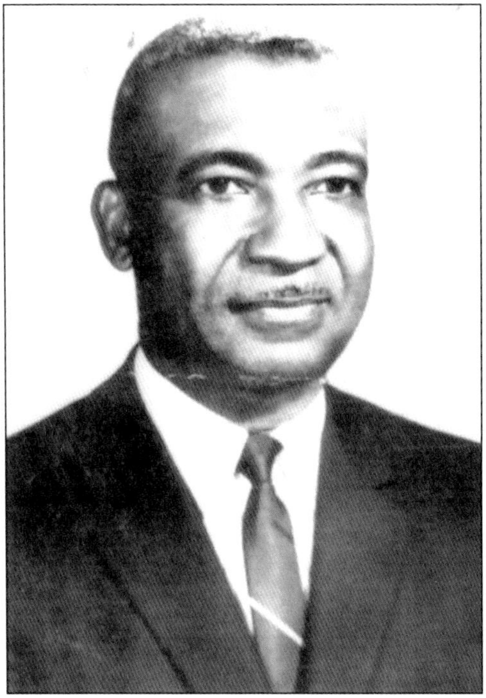

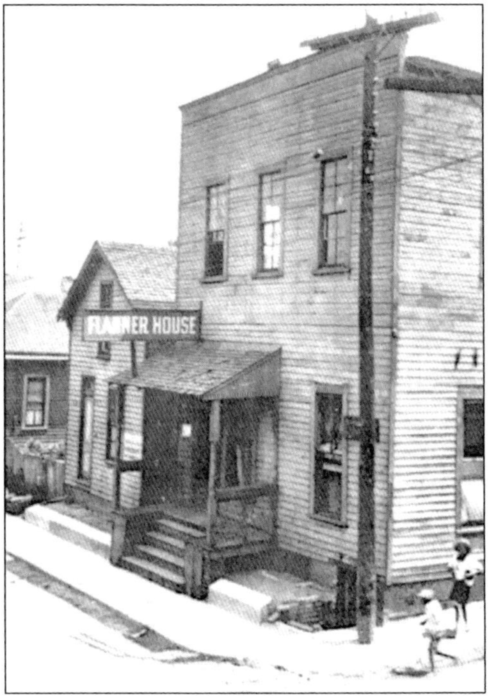

Dr. Cleo Walter Blackburn, a native of Port Gibson, Mississippi, relocated to Indianapolis in 1935 to assume the position of superintendent of the Flanner House Social Service Agency. This agency served African Americans in the areas of health care, housing, education, and employment. It was established by funeral home director Francis "Frank" Flanner in the late 19th century. (Both, Indiana Historical Society.)

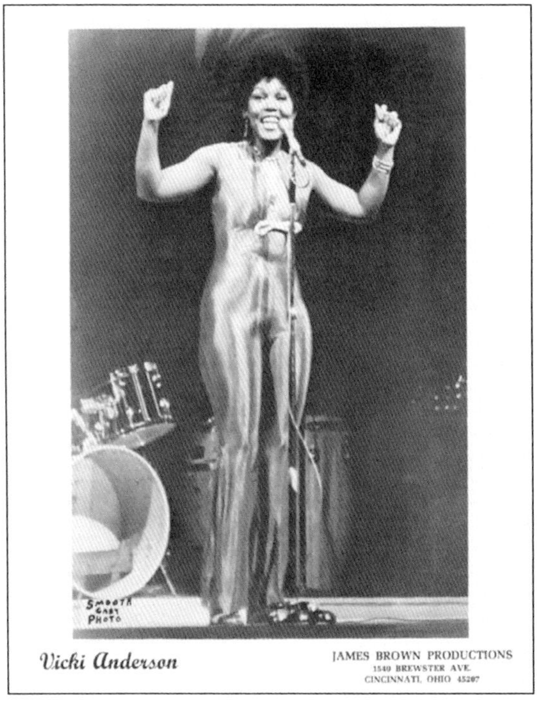

Born Myra Barnes, Vicki Anderson sang in the James Brown Revue. She was the widow of Bobby Byrd, one of the original founders of Brown's Famous Flames.

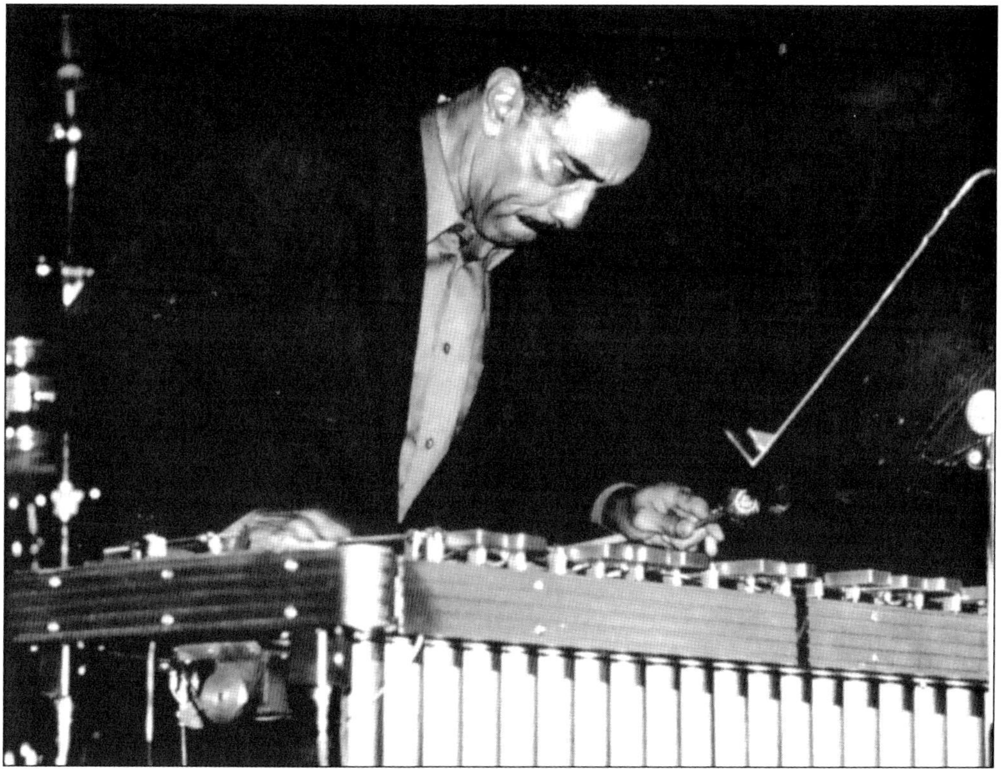

New York–born xylophonist Billy Wooten thrilled many fans at the Nineteenth Hole night club. He appeared with world-renowned guitarists Floyd Smith and Grant Green, organist Jimmy McGriff, and rhythm-and-blues composer Odell Brown. He performed with the rhythm-and-blues group Care Package and hosted the television program *Billy Wooten's Partytime* on the American Cable Network in the late 1980s.

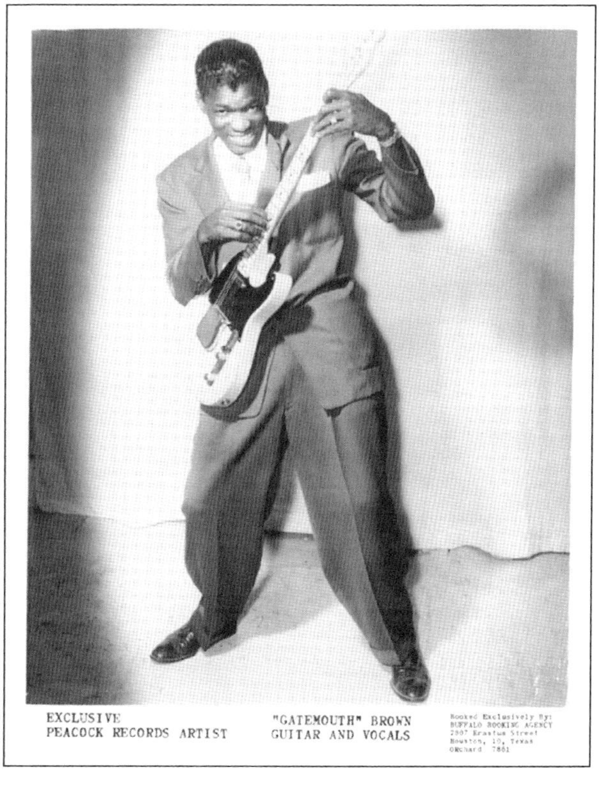

The blues master Clarence "Gatemouth" Brown was one of the originators of the Texas down-home blues singing style. He won a Grammy for the best traditional blues album in 1983.

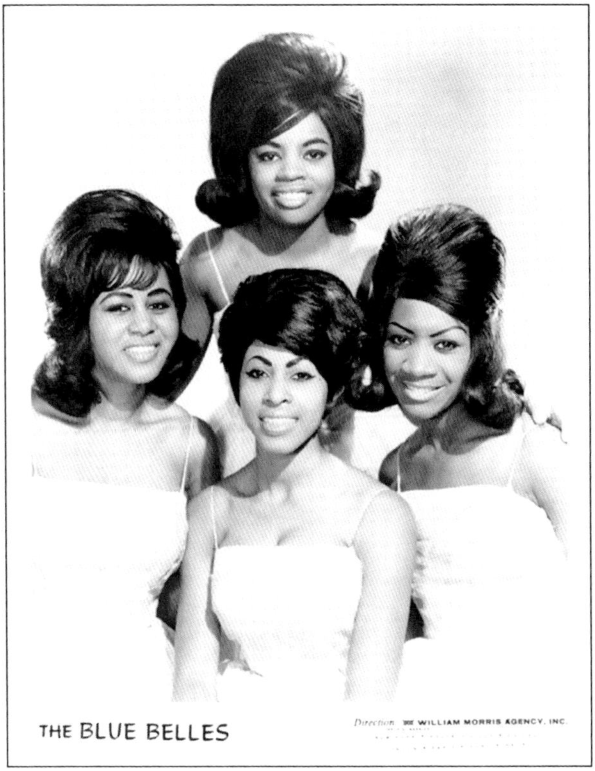

This Philadelphia all-female group dominated the record charts in the 1960s and were the toast of the town in inner-city neighborhoods across the country. The members were Patti LaBelle (Patricia Louise Holt), Cindy Birdsong, Nona Hendryx, and Sarah Dash. With Patti's stratospheric, soaring notes on "You'll Never Walk Alone," "Down the Aisle," and "Over the Rainbow," this group took rhythm and blues to a distant galaxy. In 1976, the group disbanded with each member going their separate ways. Hendryx and Dash launched very successful solo careers in avant-garde genres and Birdsong replaced Florence Ballard of Diana Ross and the Supremes. LaBelle headlined the Indianapolis Black Expo Music Heritage Festival on July 2, 1993.

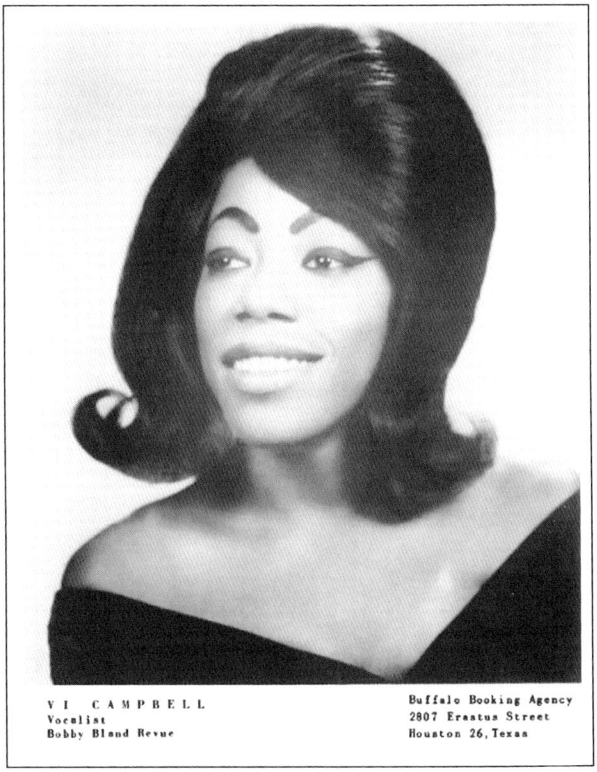

Vi Campbell, a Duke/Peacock recording artist, was a member of the Bobby Bland Revue in the 1960s.

Many Crispus Attucks High School teenagers made a beeline home after school to watch Dick Clark's *American Bandstand* on television. During the early 1960s, one of their favorite female groups were the Chiffons. This Bronx, New York, trio of Judy Craig, Patricia Bennett, and Barbara Lee appeared numerous times on the program. Their number one hit "He's So Fine" topped the charts and sold more than one million units.

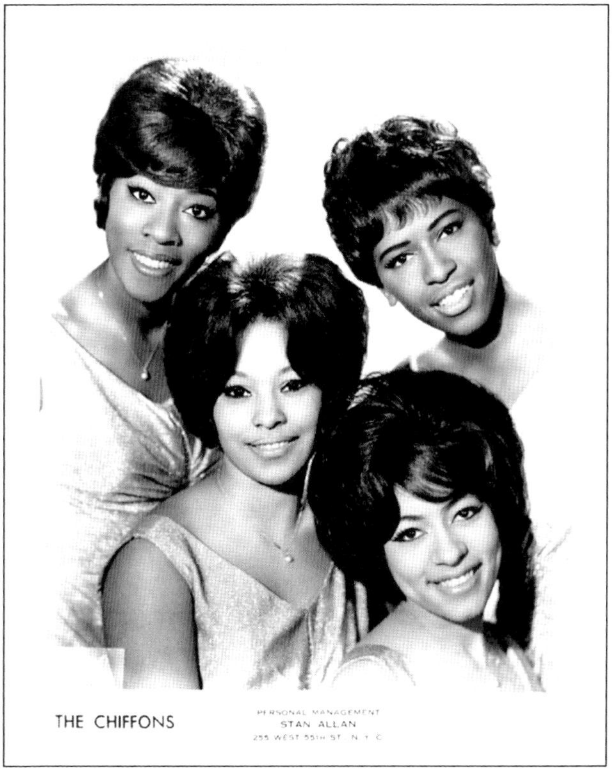

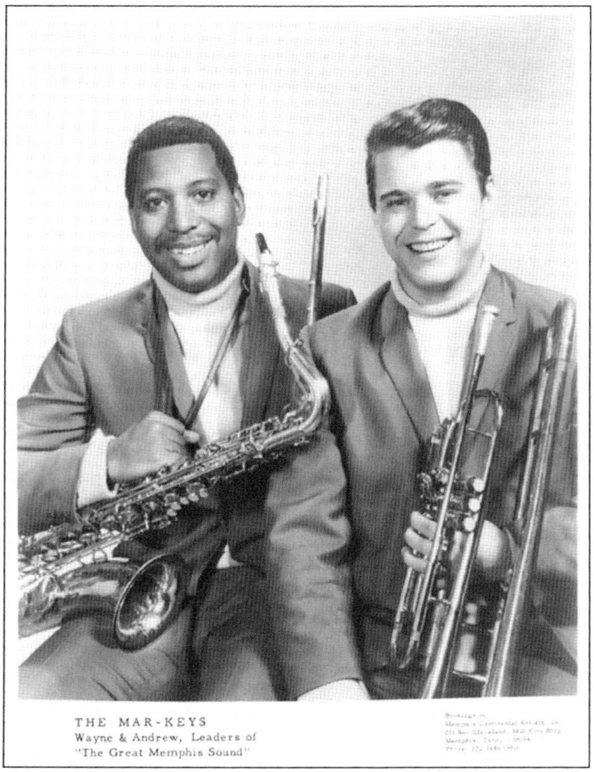

A studio session band for Stax Records in Memphis, the Mar-Keys backed many of the great soul songs of this company. They were the originators of the famed "Stax Sound."

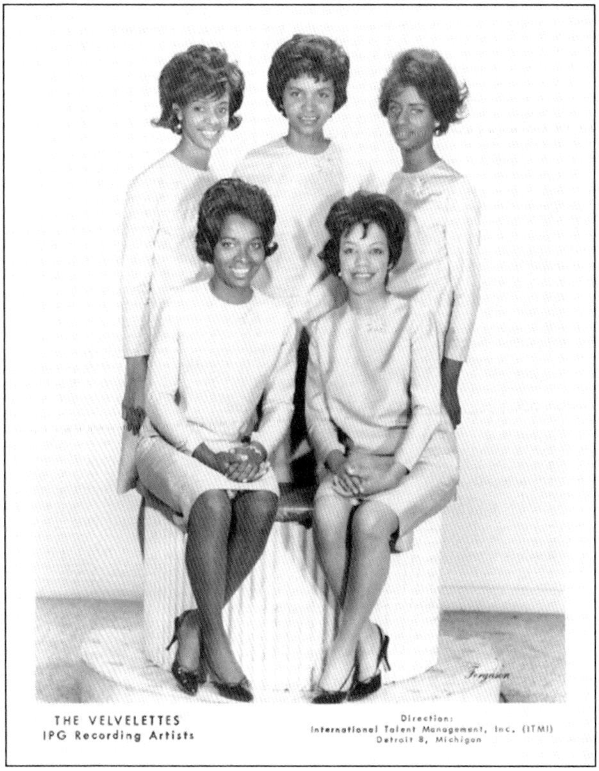

Founded at Western Michigan University in 1961, the Velvettes were Bertha Barbee McNeal, Mildred Gill Arbor, Carolyn Gill, Betty Kelley, and Norma Barbee. Their 1964 hit, "Needle in a Hay Stack," charted at No. 45 on the *Billboard* Hot 100.

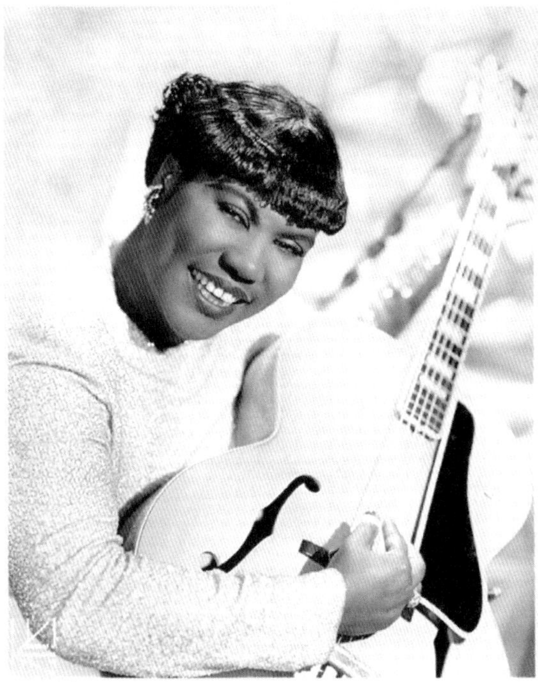

SISTER ROSETTA THARPE

"Original Soul Sister" and "God-Mother of Rock and Roll," Rosetta Tharp was an institution by herself. This vocalist, who sang both gospel and secular music, was criticized by many of her gospel music–lovers for "serving two masters." She influenced music greats like Little Richard, Chuck Berry, Elvin Presley, Johnny Cash, and Jerry Lee Lewis.

"Come on baby, let's do the twist" were the lyrics of an earth-shaking song recorded by Ernest Evans, known professionally as "Chubby Checker," in the 1960s. Hank Ballard and the Midnighters originally recorded the song in 1959, but Checker snatched it and took it to another level. The Twist was danced around the world! Late night comedians joked that Queen Elizabeth may have been secretly twisting in Windsor Castle. *The Twist* topped the *Billboard* Hot 100 twice and sold 15 million units. Checker appeared in the Twist Show at the Indiana State Fair Coliseum on May 1, 1967.

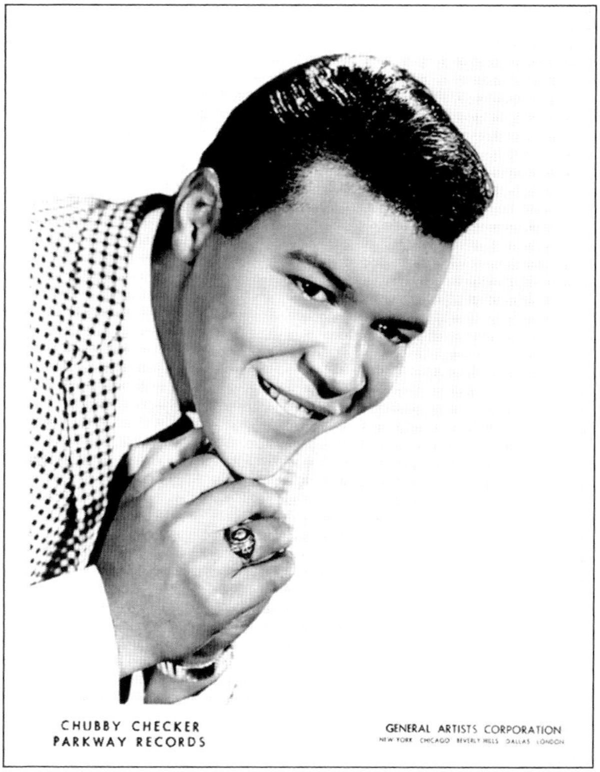

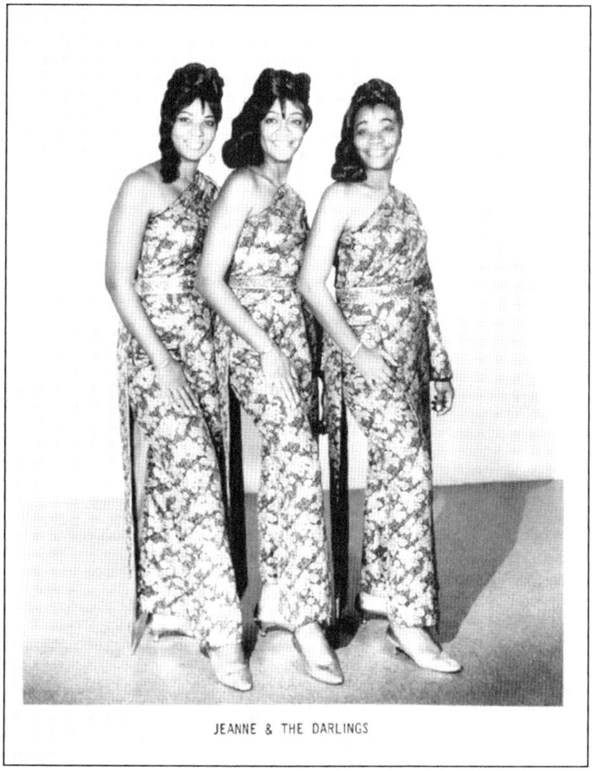

Jeanne Dolphus and daughter Paula with sister Dee Dolphus and family friend Phefe Harris made up Jeanne & the Darlings, an Arkansas-based gospel group that backed many of the recordings on the Stax label. They produced six 45s on the Volt label.

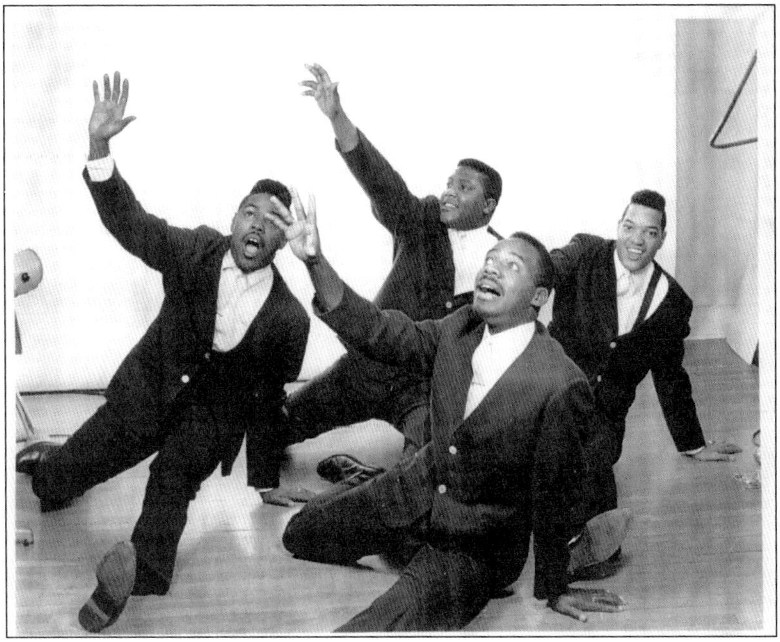

There were several editions of the Monograms. This group was comprised of, from left to right, Bobby Bernard, Bobby Penick, John Vardiman, and George Black.

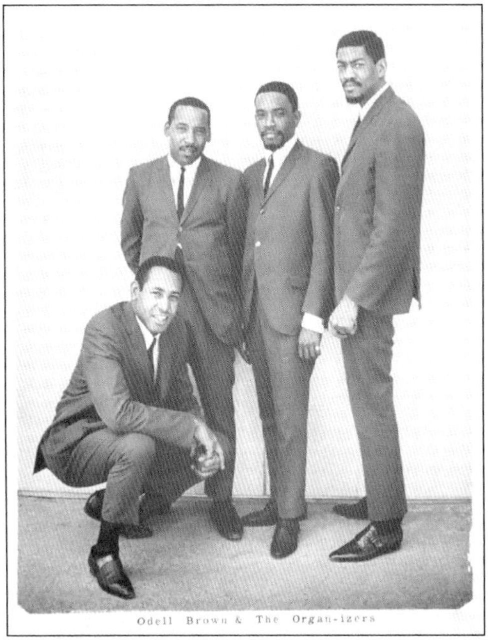

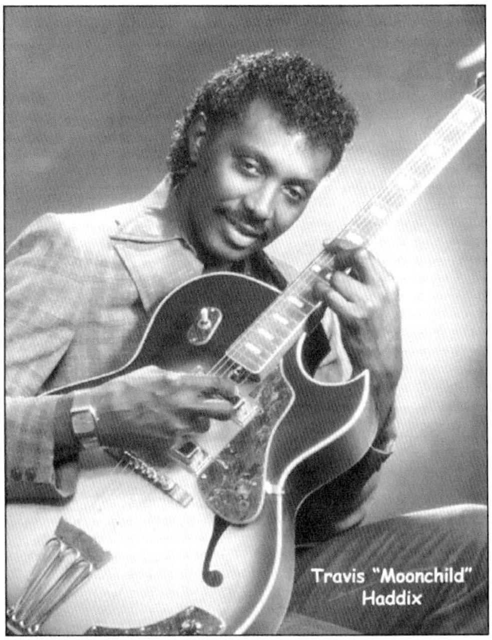

Odell Brown & the Organ-izers (left) consisted of Brown, Artee "Duke" Payne, Curtis Prince, Henry Gibson, and Tommy Purvis. In 1961, they formed their group on the campus of Tennessee State University in Nashville. Travis "Moonchild" Haddix (right) was born in Walnut, Mississippi, and learned to play the piano at the age of seven. His group consisted of Ray DeForest, Ed Lemmens, Brian Hager, Gil Zachary, Don Williams, Jeremy Sullivan, Bob Frank, and Mike Calhound.

One of the legendary rhythm-and-blues groups from Philadelphia's stable of stars, Harold Melvin and the Blue Notes were popular during the 1970s with their hits "If You Don't Know Me by Now," "The Love I Lost," "Wake-Up Everybody," "Bad Luck," and "I Miss You."

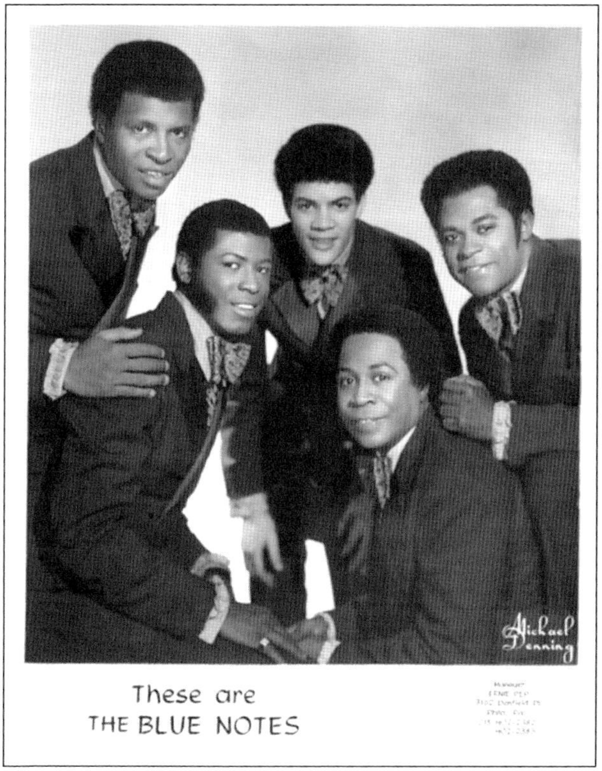

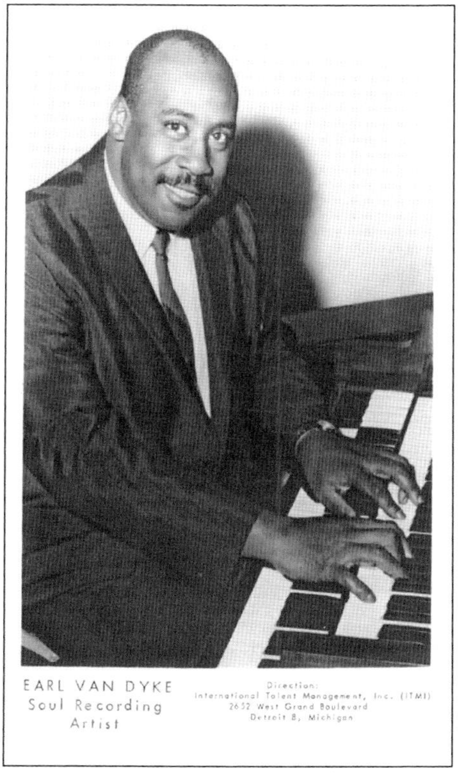

Keyboardist of Motown orchestra the Funk Brothers, Earl Van Dyke played with them in the 1960s and early 1970s. He also recorded as a jazz organist with saxophonists Fred Jackson and Ike Quebec on the Blue Note label.

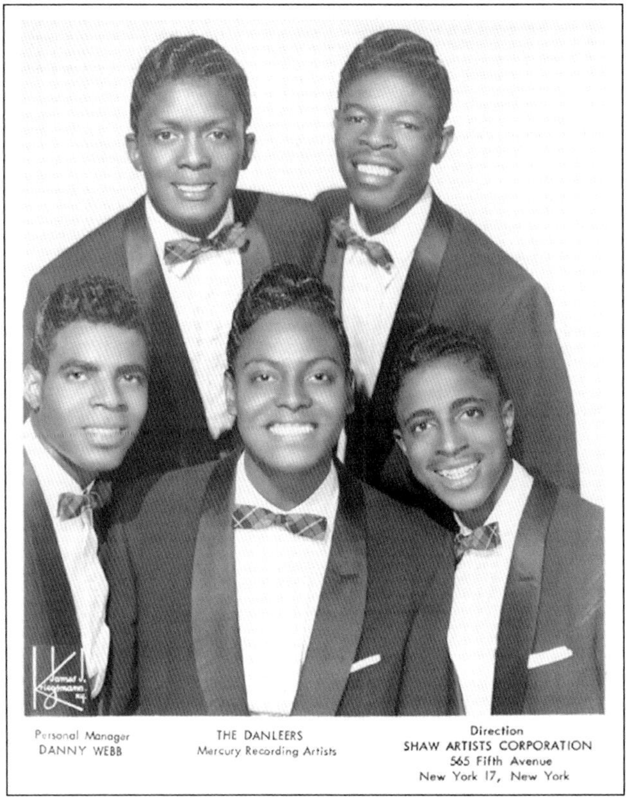

The Danleers formed in Brooklyn in 1958. The members were Jimmy Weston, Johnny Lee, Willie Ephraim, Nat McClune, and Roosevelt Mays, and their hit was "One Summer Night."

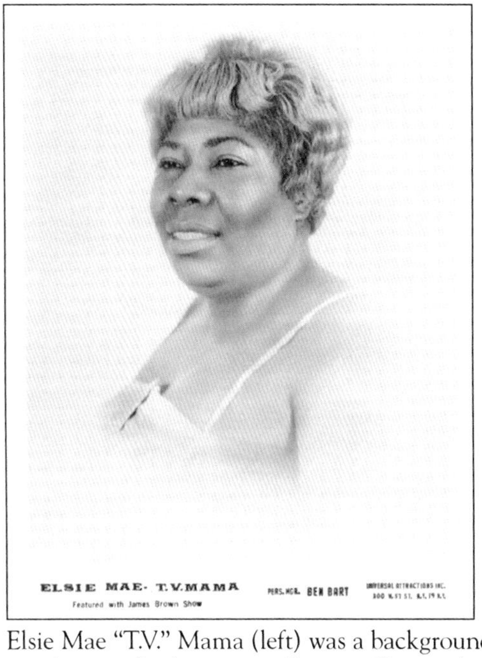

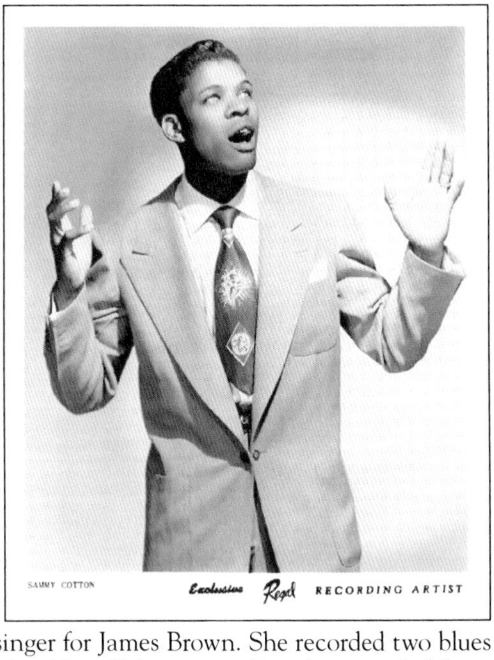

Elsie Mae "T.V." Mama (left) was a background singer for James Brown. She recorded two blues numbers under her name. Sammy Cotton (right), a New Orleans vocalist who recorded from 1949 to 1952, was widely overshadowed by more popular vocalists. His hit song, "Give Me One More Drink," is a New Orleans classic.

The Mighty Vanguards of Indianapolis were a singing group during the 1960s and 1970s. Their lineup included James Davis, Richard Pierson, Wilbert Winston, Vonzell Wheeler, and Elaine Livingston. Their signature hits were "It's Too Late for Love" and "Somebody Please."

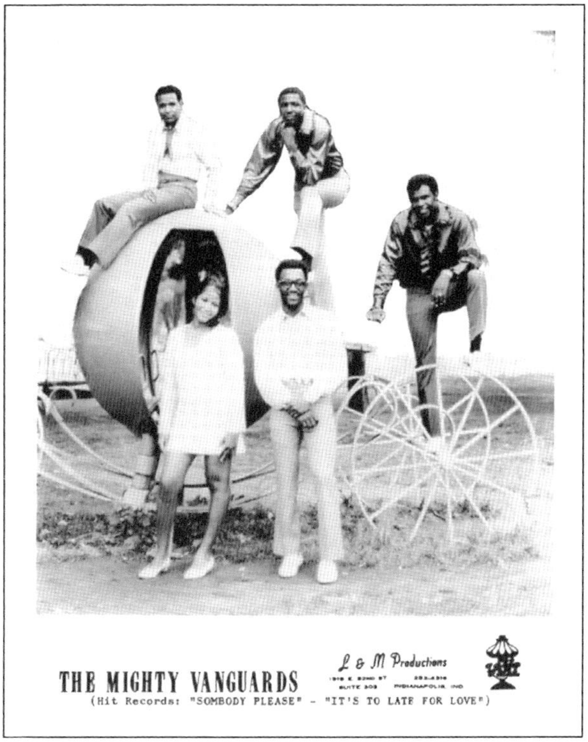

Although considered primarily a jazz drummer, Ray Cumberland performed with many of the top rhythm-and-blues aggregations in the 1960s. After stints with the Lavon Kemp Orchestra, he performed with Rudy (Craig) & the House Rockers at the Udell and 40th Street Taverns. (Ray Cumberland.)

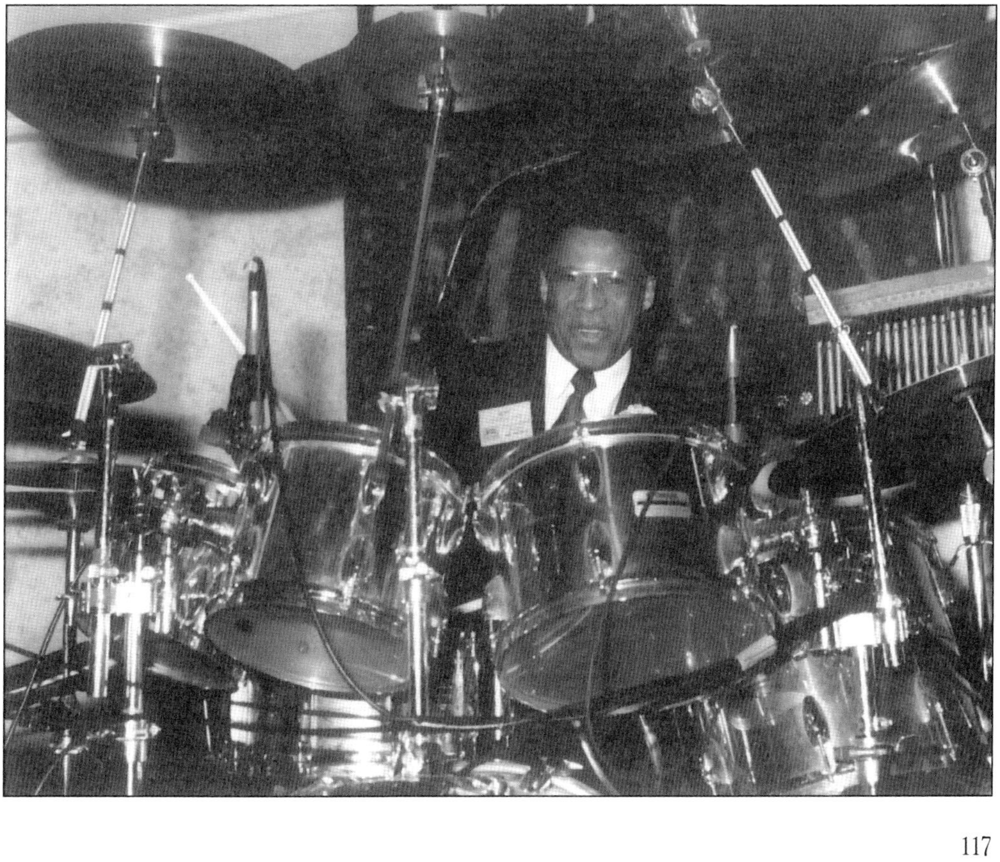

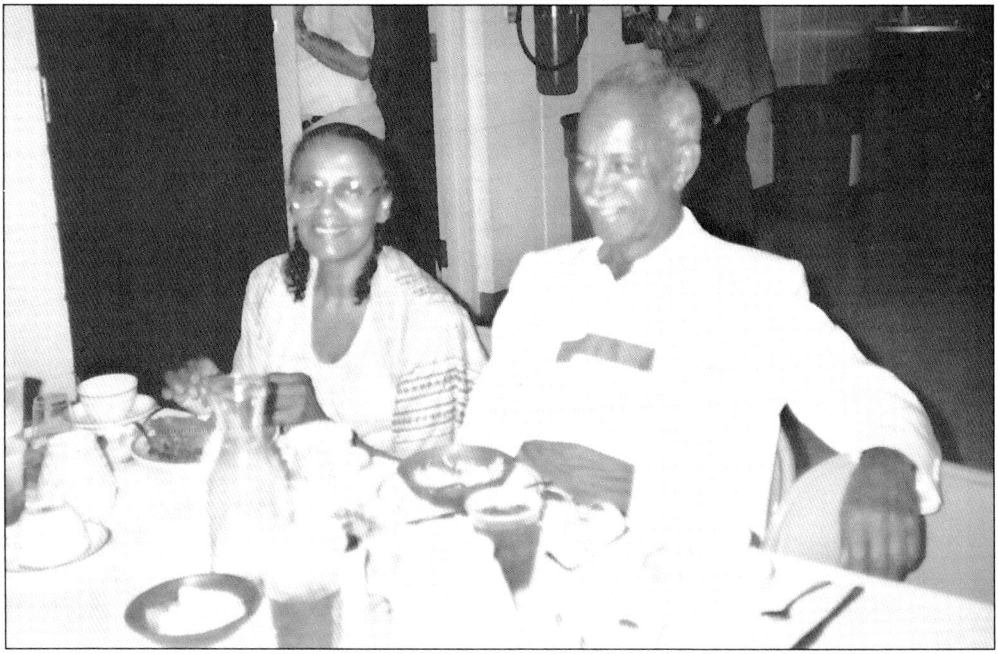

Norma Lewis was a fantastic pianist/organist who performed on and off Indiana Avenue. She performed with Bertha and Donnie Eubanks at the Brass Rail and also displayed her mastery on the keyboards at the Cotton Club and Trianon Ballroom, owned and operated by Sea Ferguson. She is pictured with orchestra leader Lavon Kemp. (Indianapolis Musicians Union.)

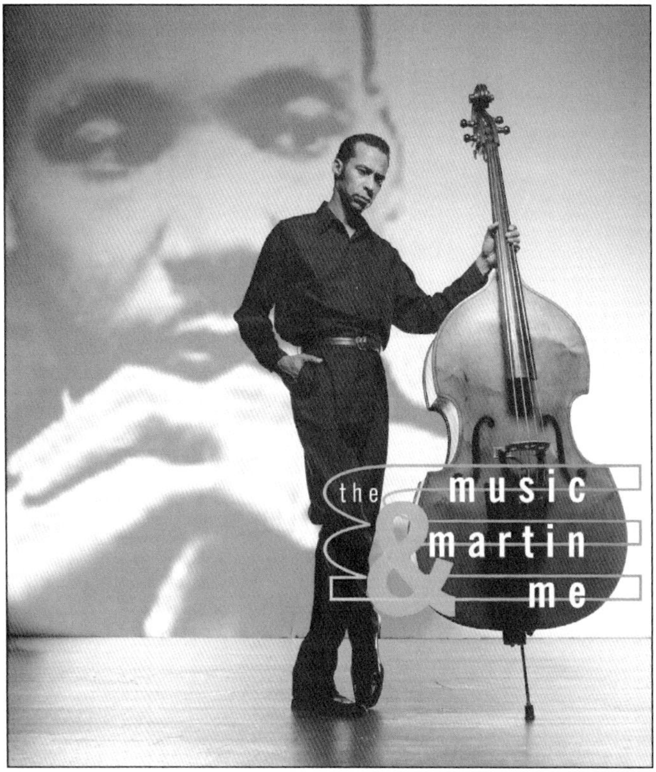

Billy Myers performed with many of the rhythm-and-blues and jazz groups around the city. In 2009, he produced "Martin and Me," a historical, musical journey through the civil rights era just days before the inauguration of Pres. Barack Obama. *NUVO* magazine reporter Rita Kohn's review spoke volumes: "I've never before witnessed anything as immediate, seamless, and indelible as this two-hour performance of music, spoken word and video documentary and it will set the standard for what can happen." (Billy Myers.)

Rhythm-and-blues vocalist James Bell performed with the Highlighters Band and recorded "Trying to Get Chosen" while he was on break from his job. He has traveled to Europe to entertain many fans of Indianapolis rhythm-and-blues music who still hold the Highlighters records and his solo recordings in high esteem. (Indiana Historical Society.)

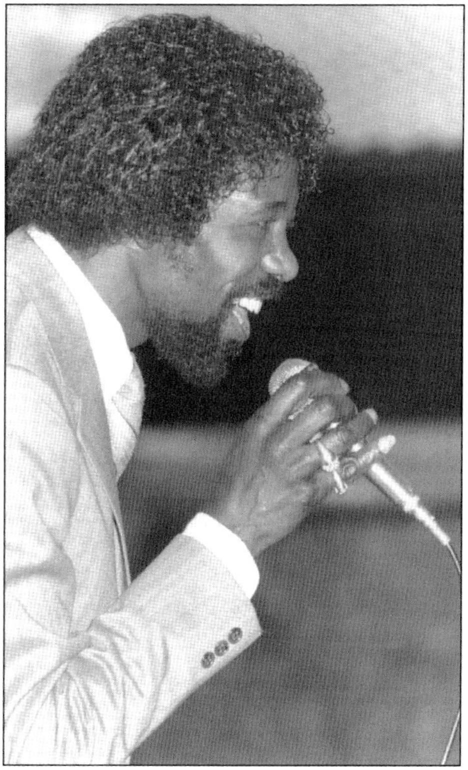

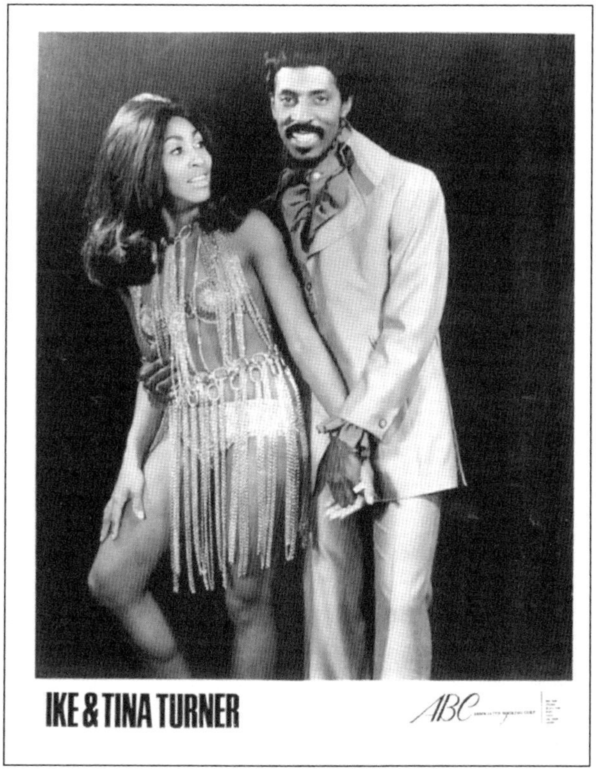

Ike and Tina Turner were the first rhythm-and-blues male/female duet to propel themselves to stardom in the 1960s. Ike, born Izear Luster Turner in Clarksdale, Mississippi, and Tina, born Anna Mae Bullock in Nut Brush, Tennessee, formed the Ike and Tina Turner Revue show, which swept the country with standing room–only audiences. Their signature tunes were "It's Gonna Work Out Fine," "I Idolize You," "Poor Fool," and "Tra La La La La." In 1978, they divorced, and Tina Turner reinvented herself and launched an extraordinarily successful career that received worldwide acclaim. In 1984, her album *Private Dancer* sold five million units, and *Foreign Affair* topped the previous album by a couple of million. The Ike and Tina Revue rolled up into Indianapolis at the Southside Armory on Saturday, June 23, 1962.

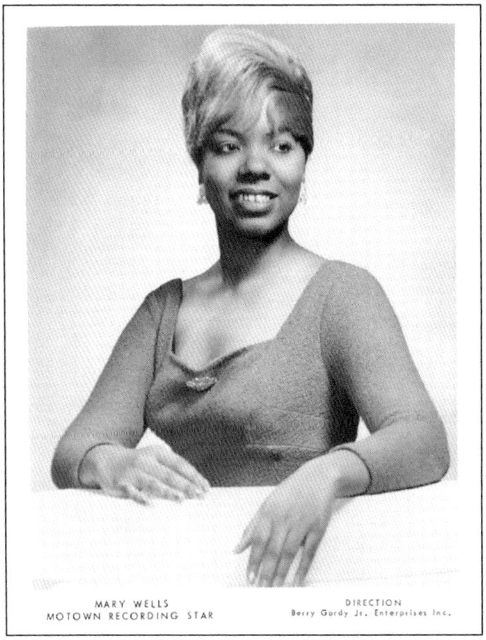

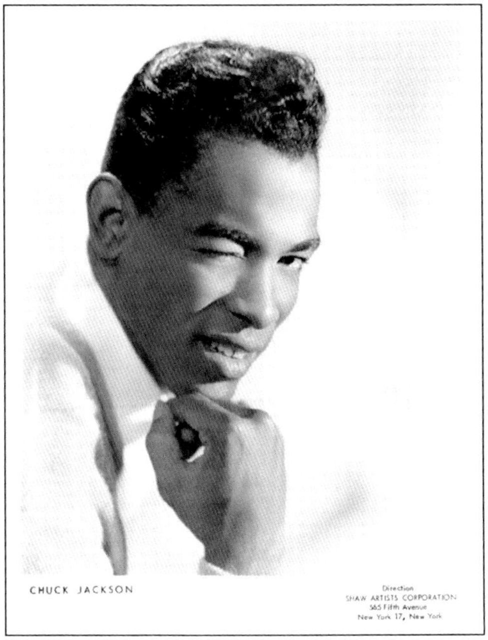

The earliest star to introduce the fledging Motown Record Company to the world was Mary Wells (left). Crowned the "Queen of Motown," Wells recorded a series of top-10 hits that charted in the United States and Europe. Composers Burt Bacharach and Hal David were responsible for the rise to stardom of Chuck Jackson (right). In 1962, "Any Day Now" topped the rhythm and blues charts and became his signature song.

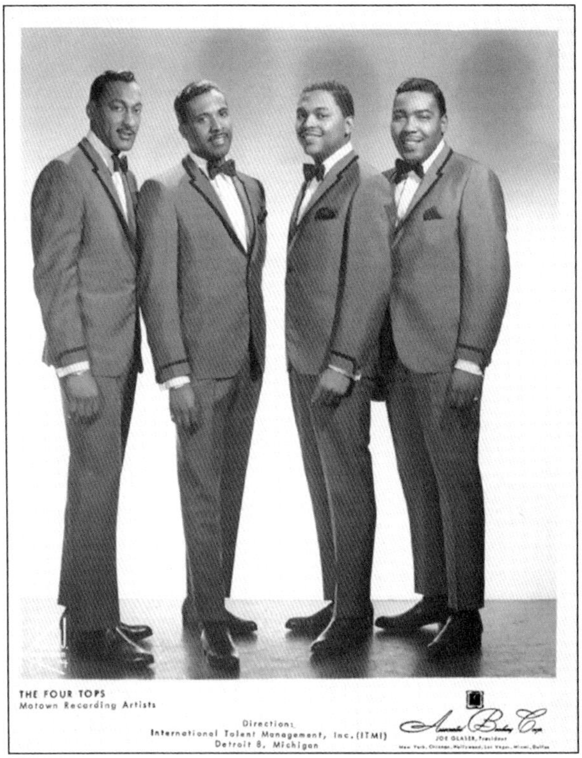

The Four Tops of Motown Records were lead Levi Stubbs, Abdul "Duke" Fakir, Renaldo "Obie" Benson, and Lawrence Payton. They were among the leading stars of Berry Gordy Jr.'s stable of entertainment greats during the 1960s. Their signature hits "I Can't Help Myself" (1965) and "Reach Out I'll Be There" (1966) were soundtracks for college students throughout America. Leaving Motown in the early 1970s, the Four Tops joined ABC Records and recorded another mega-hit, "Just Ask the Lonely." The Motown Revue and the Four Tops appeared at Bush Stadium on May 30, 1968.

The Supremes were the headlining attraction and face of Motown Records in the 1960s. Originally named the Primettes, this group became the most commercially successful of all the stars in the Motown constellation. The original members were Florence Ballard, Mary Wilson, Diana Ross, and Betty McGlown. The success of the Supremes sky-rocketed in the 1960s, as they joined songwriting team Holland-Doxier-Holland and recorded many hits that topped the *Billboard* charts. The Supremes brought their revue to the Indiana State Fair on August 29, 1968.

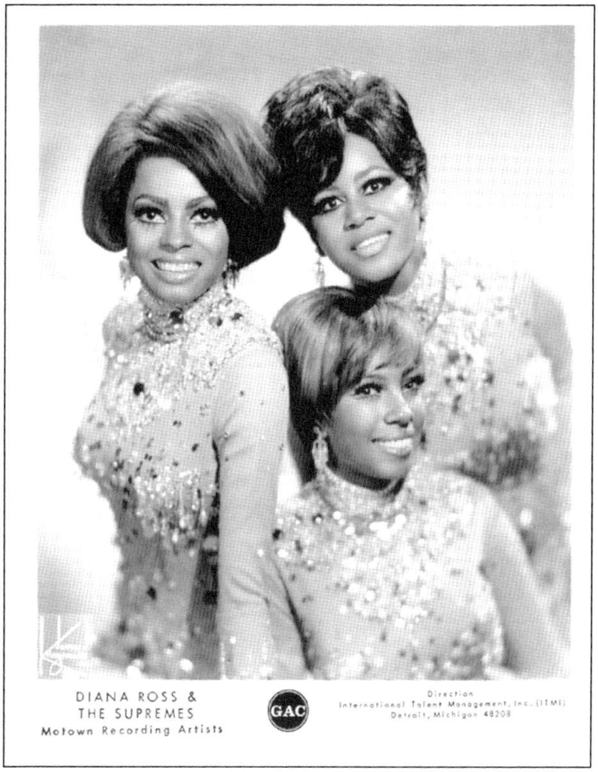

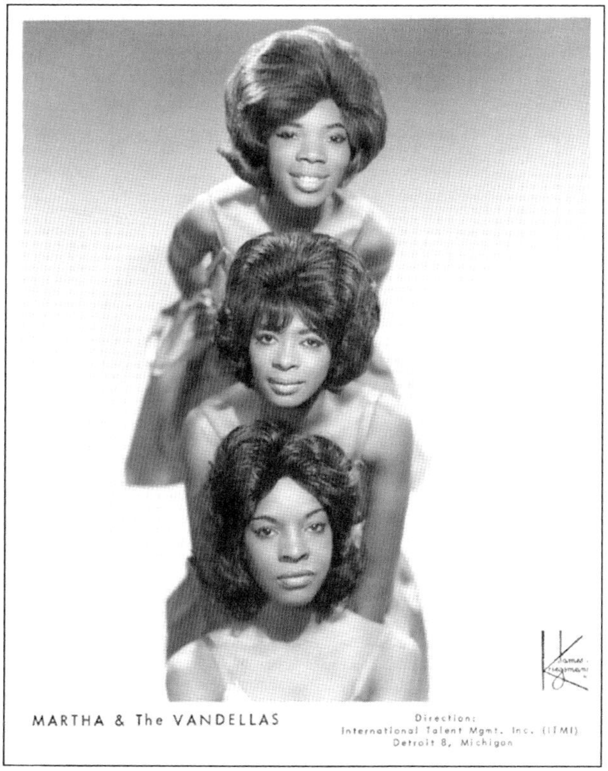

Among Motown's early stable of stars, Martha and the Vandellas were among the most electrifying. The group consisted of Annette Beard, Rosalind Ashford, Gloria Williams, and Martha Reeves. Reeves took the lead when Williams left the group in 1962. Their 26 hits that appeared on the *Billboard* charts included "Come and Get These Memories," "Heat Wave," "Quicksand," "No Where to Run," and "Jimmy Mack." The Motown Revue appeared at the Circle Theater on April 7, 1964.

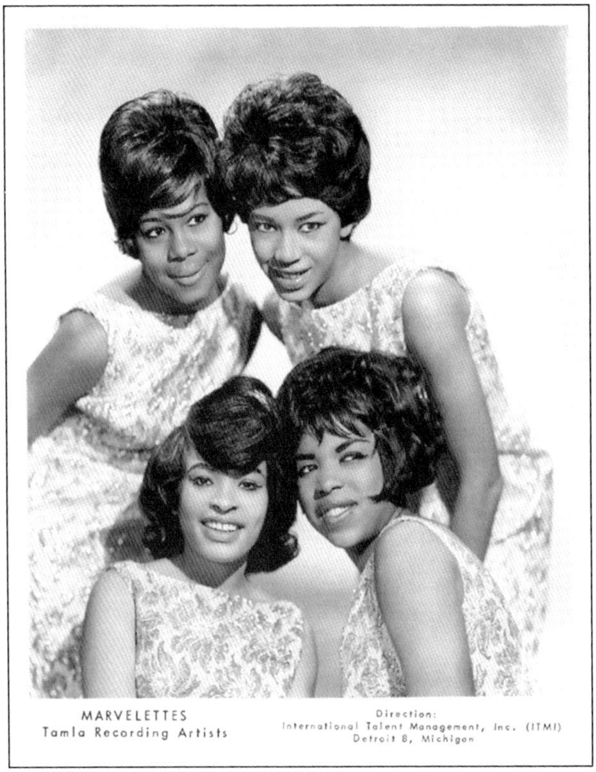

The Marvelettes were one of Motown's pioneering female groups who were unfortunately overshadowed by the Supremes and Martha and the Vandellas. The members were Gladys Horton, Katherine Anderson, Georgeanna Tilman, Juanita Cowart, and Georgia Dobbins. Their 1961 hit "Please Mr. Postman" topped the rhythm-and-blues charts. "Don't Mess with Bill," their hit of 1966, managed to return them to the radar screen, but they ceased performing in 1969.

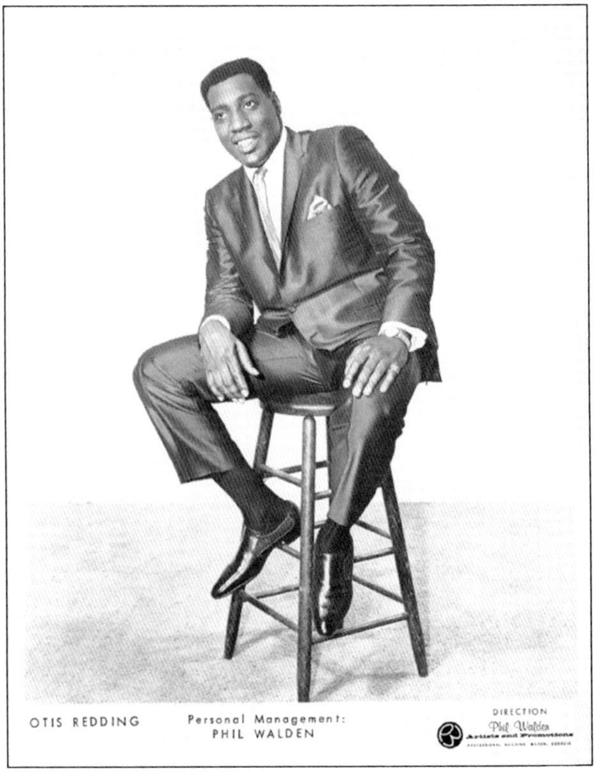

In 1967, *Melody Maker* magazine of Great Britain determined that Otis Redding surpassed Elvis Presley as the No. 1 male vocalist in the world. Sadly, on December 10, 1967, en route to an engagement at the Factory Night Club in Madison, Wisconsin, Redding died in a plane crash with several members of his band. His debut album with Stax Records, *Pain in My Heart*, was a million-seller, and subsequent hits topped the rhythm-and-blues charts. The song "Dock of the Bay" was the most memorable to many of his fans because it was his last record before his untimely demise.

Early television viewers in the 1950s fondly remember a small, brown-skinned, cherubic Gladys Knight winning first place in Ted Mack's popular *Original Amateur Hour.* Decades later, she teamed with her brother Merald "Bubba" Knight, sister Brenda, and their cousins William and Eleanor Guest and chose the moniker "the Pips." In 1961, they recorded their first hit record, "Every Beat of My Heart," which topped the rhythm-and-blues charts along with Van McCoy's "Giving Up," recorded in 1964. Other monumental hits were "I Heard It Through the Grape Vine," "Neither One of Us Wants to Be the First to Say Goodbye," and "Midnight Train to Georgia." Gladys Knight & the Pips won numerous Grammy and American Music Awards and were inducted into the Rock and Roll Hall of Fame in 1996.

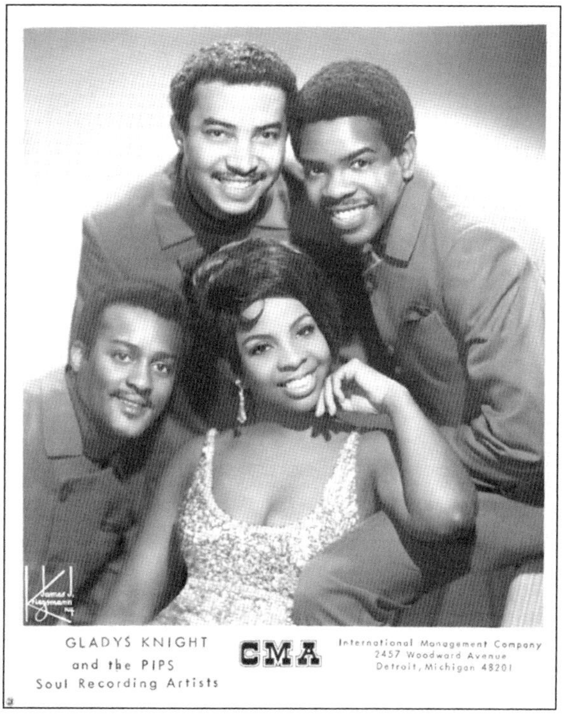

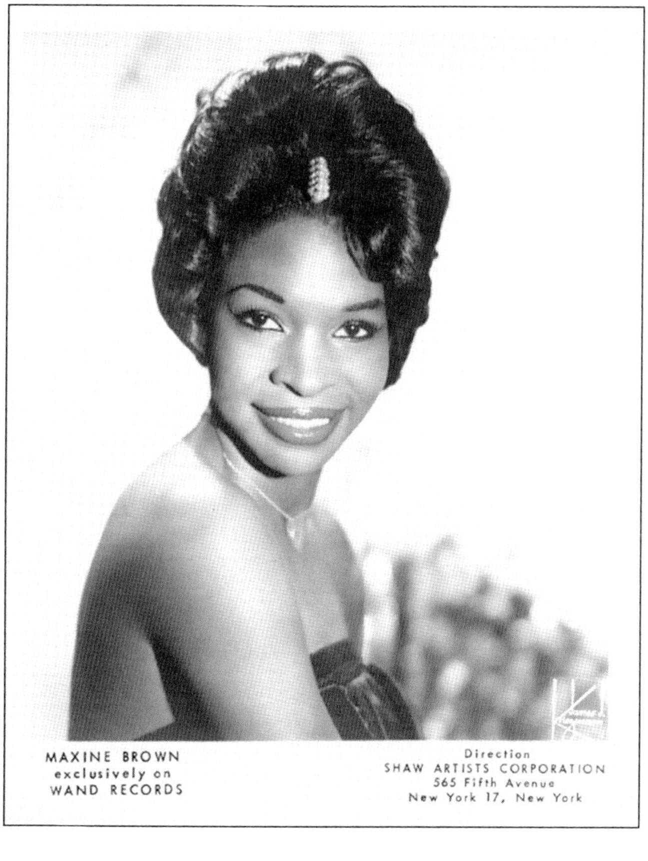

Maxine Brown, the sultry vocalist who gained fame with her recordings "All in My Mind," "Oh No Not My Baby," and "Funny," began her music career with gospel groups the Angelairs and the Royaltones. She took her gospel-music training to the rhythm-and-blues recording studios, and her songs charted highly on the *Billboard* polls. Her background singers were Cissy Houston, mother of Whitney Houston, and her group the Sweet Inspirations. She was one of the headliners at the Shower of Stars show at Victory Field on June 15, 1967.

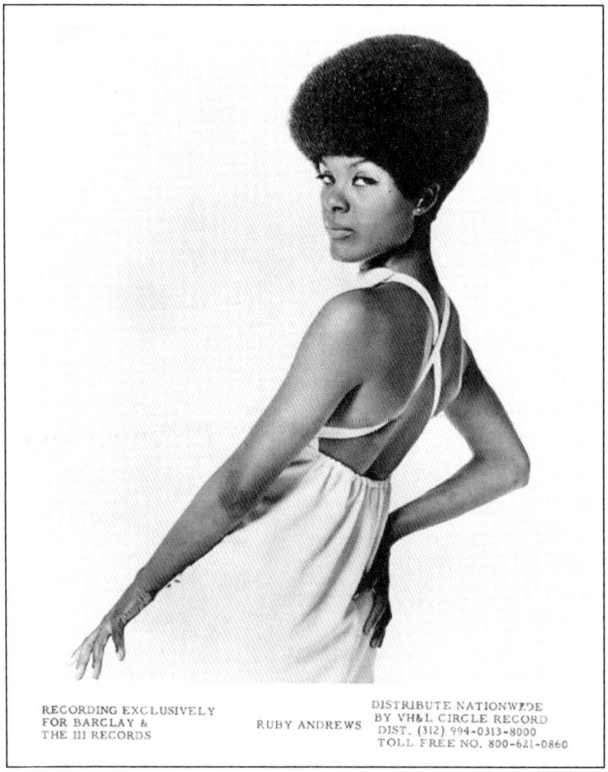

Ruby Andrews was a Mississippi-born Chicago transplant who brought the soul power of the Mississippi Delta to the Windy City. In 1967, she recorded her signature song, "Casanova Your Playing Days are Over," which reached the No. 9 spot on the *Billboard* Hot 100 and No. 51 on the popular music chart. She appeared at the Twenty Grand Club with the Mar-Kays on Friday and Saturday, March 5 and 6, 1971.

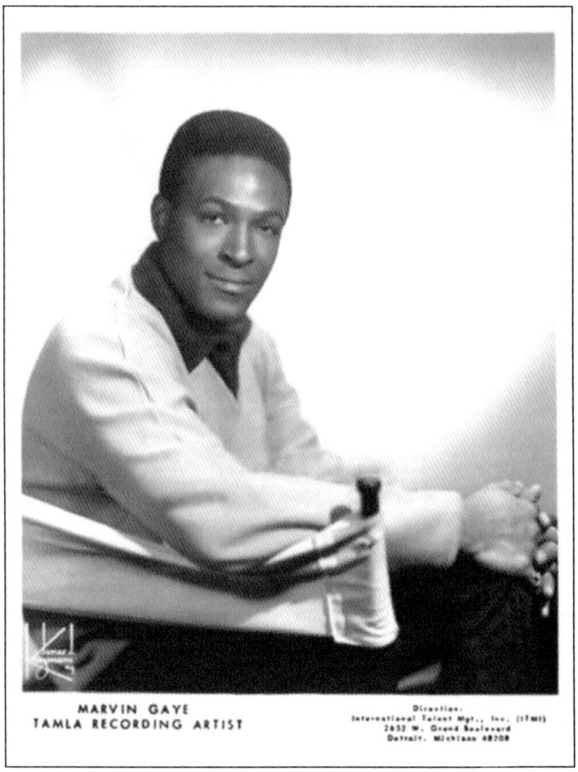

"Mother, mother, There's too many of you crying, Brother, brother, brother, There's far too many of you dying." These were the politically electrifying lyrics sung by Marvin Gaye on his anti–Vietnam War hit "What's Going On?" Gaye began his career with Motown Records as a session drummer and developed into one of the most brilliant stars in Berry Gordy's stable of great entertainers. With hits like "Hitch Hike," "Stubborn Kind of Fella," "Can I Get a Witness," and many other chart-topping songs, Gaye cemented his name in the Motown Hall of Fame. Sadly, on April 1, 1984, he was shot and killed by his father during a domestic dispute. Gaye appeared at the Indiana Convention Center on August 9, 1974.

Wilson Pickett began his musical career singing gospel numbers with the Violinaires and transitioned to secular music and joined the Falcons. His first recording singing lead was "I Found a Love," which featured his smooth, silky voice backed by future rhythm-and-blues stars Eddie Floyd and Sir Mack Rice. In the 1960s, he joined Stax Records and recorded his first mega-hit "In the Midnight Hour," which soared to the top of the rhythm-and-blues charts and sold a million copies. Other hits were "Mustang Sally" and "Funky Broadway."

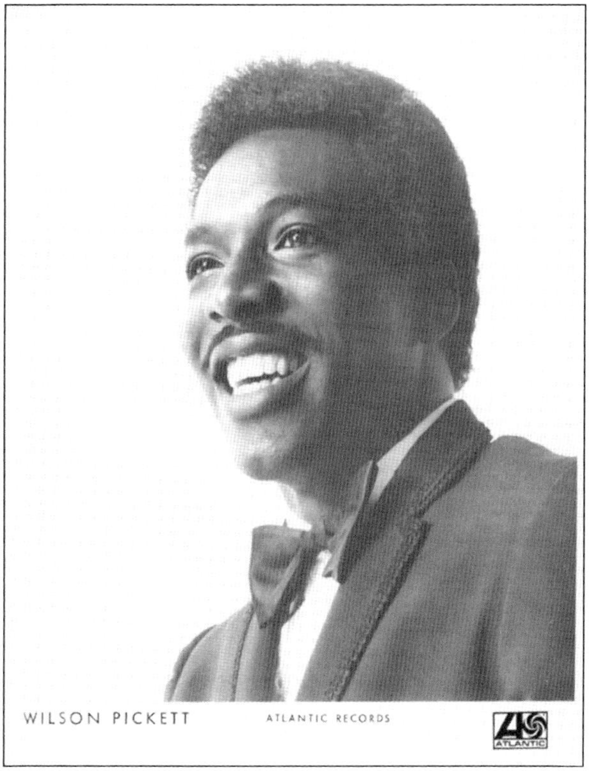

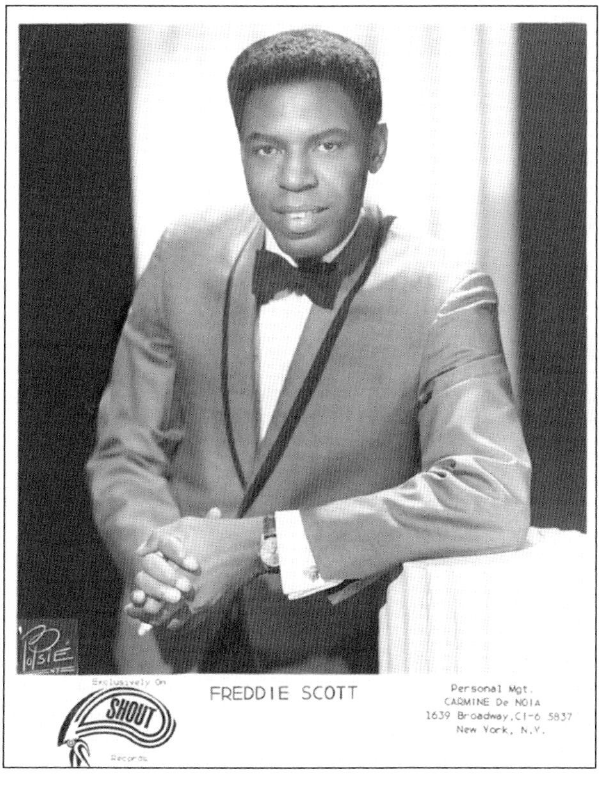

Freddie Scott may have the distinction of being the only African American rhythm-and-blues recording star from Rhode Island. As a child, he sang in his grandmother's gospel group Sally Jones and the Gospel Keys and toured England. His breakout hits were "Hey Girl," which was a top-10 hit in 1963, and "Are You Lonely For Me," a No. 1 rhythm-and-blues chart hit in 1967. Scott thrilled the audience with his hit song "Are You Lonely for Me?" at the Murat Theater on April 22, 1967.

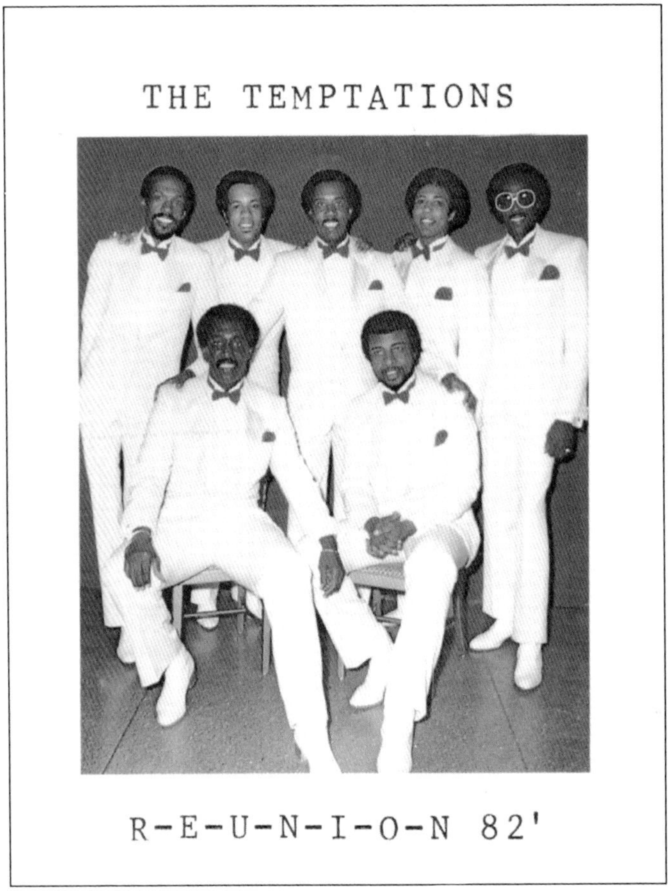

The Temptations defined the grandeur and popularity of Motown in the 1960s and 1970s. The original members were Otis Williams, Elbridge "Al" Bryant, Melvin Franklin, Eddie Kendricks, and Paul Williams. In 1964, Bryant was replaced by David Ruffin. Known for their smooth, seamless harmony, flashy wardrobe, and ultra-precision dance steps, these rhythm-and-blues giants wrote a new and exciting chapter in the annals of American music. Their early hits "The Way You Do the Things You Do," "My Girl," and "Ain't Too Proud to Beg" and later hits "Just My Imagination" and "Papa was a Rollin' Stone" made them the premiere rhythm-and-blues group during this period. They appeared during the Temptation Ball at the Indiana State Fairgrounds on May 28, 1966.

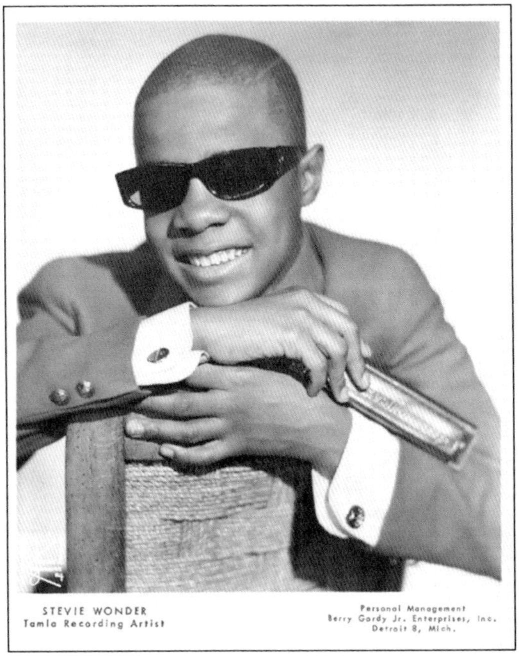

Undoubtedly, the greatest entertainer to walk the halls of the Motown Record Corporation was Little Stevie Wonder, who later was renamed Stevie Wonder. His 1963 masterpiece "Fingertips," from the album *Recorded Live: The 12 Year Old Genius*, was recorded during a live concert at the Regal Theater in Chicago. It was a No. 1 hit on the *Billboard* Hot 100 and made him the youngest artist to ever top the charts. Considered by music historians as one of the greatest entertainers, composers, and lyricists of the 20th century, Wonder recorded more than 30 top-10 hits and won a whopping 25 Grammy Awards. He recorded 10 No. 1 popular hits as well as 20 No. 1 rhythm-and-blues hits and has sold more than 100 million records. Little Stevie Wonder, along with Mary Wells and Marvin Gaye, headlined the Motortown Revue concert at the Circle Theater on Thursday, November 7, 1963.

About the Author

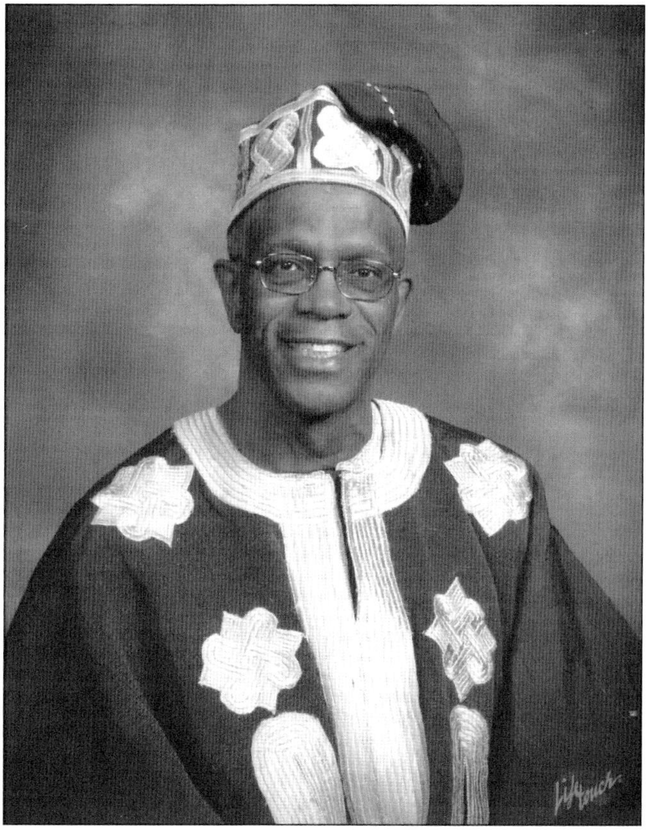

David Leander Williams was born and raised in the Lockefield Gardens public housing project, which borders Indiana Avenue. He is a collector of historical artifacts and information on African American history, specifically slavery and African American music, and authored *Indianapolis Jazz: The Masters, Legends and Legacy of Indiana Avenue*, which chronicled the evolution of jazz on Indiana Avenue from 1900 to 2000. He has undertaken the monumental task of chronicling and documenting the history of rhythm-and-blues music that developed on Indiana Avenue beginning in the late 1940s until its demise in the 1980s. He holds bachelor's and master's degrees from Colorado State University and Fairleigh Dickinson University, but is especially proud of being a graduate of Crispus Attucks High School. Williams is a researcher and historian of many talents and interests, including African/Middle Eastern political history, Brazilian slavery history, and foreign languages (his collegiate undergraduate major was Spanish and Portuguese literature, and he had to be proficient in Arabic for his graduate school program).

Williams takes a spiritual and nostalgic walk down Indiana Avenue and paints a literary portrait of many of the personalities, sights, sounds, and events that give this thoroughfare such a mystifying and fascinating appeal.